# WE MAKE
# MAGAZINES
## INSIDE THE INDEPENDENTS

# WE MAKE
# MAGAZINES

EDITED BY ANDREW LOSOWSKY
DESIGNED BY JEREMY LESLIE

741.
65
WEM

First published in Luxembourg
© Editions Mike Koedinger SA 2009
All rights reserved. No part of this book
may be reproduced without the prior
written permission of the publisher

Published by
Editions Mike Koedinger SA
10 rue de Gaulois, L-1618 Luxembourg
Grand-Duchy of Luxembourg
www.mikekoedinger.com

Produced by John Brown
136-142 Bramley Road
London W10 6SR
United Kingdom
www.johnbrownmedia.com

Exclusive worldwide distribution:
Gestalten, Berlin
www.gestalten.com
sales@die-gestalten.de

Publisher: Mike Koedinger
Editor: Andrew Losowsky
Art director: Jeremy Leslie
Designers: Alex Hunting, Lars Laemmerzahl
Photography: Guido Kröger
Illustrations: Jean Jullien/YCN

Typeface: Verlag by Hoefler & Frere-Jones
Printed in Luxembourg by Imprimerie Centrale
ISBN 978-3-89955-246-1

Mike Koedinger

# CONTENTS

# INTRODUCTION

You'd think with the digital age and everything that magazines would be dying out like the dinosaurs. But many of us are still here, busting our nuts to create a magazine that makes kids wanna spend ten bucks to own. You'd think with so many titles, there'd never be room for a new mag, but new ideas are hard to repress and even harder to instigate, so if there are innovators out there, good luck to you, whoever you are.
–
Woody W
Sneaker Freaker

Our magazine is built on blood, sweat and tears. If we weren't totally committed and prepared to make sacrifices, it wouldn't exist.
–
Matthew Bochenski
Little White Lies

A magazine happens because someone, somewhere needs it to exist. They need the medium of a magazine to help them capture a feeling, distill a sensation, bottle an attitude. They want to reach out and touch it, to explore its texture, its taste, they want to turn it upside down and inside out, they want to see it close up and from far away, and to let it fan the flames of their passions ever higher. And they want more than anything to share this experience with as many people as possible, both people who already think like they do and others who may be ready to make the switch. Someone, somewhere is reaching out to you through their magazine, and they keep doing it, again and again and again, every time a new issue comes out.

Is it a form of madness, this act of trying to hold the snowflake, to swallow the rainbow, to force lightening onto paper? Is it a pointless activity, to strive to make the perfect magazine, and then have to keep doing it from the beginning each and every issue, however close they got the last time?

Madness, genius or both, there is something about magazines that has

people like me hooked. At its height, it is the perfect marriage of an old medium (text) and a more modern one (graphic design), a truly popular and often populist way of sharing images, ideas and information. In its most successful forms, a magazine is both ephemeral and long lasting, invoking both familiarity and surprise in every edition. A magazine is a never-ending story. For millions of people, reading them is a pleasure; for the people mentioned inside these pages, making them is a drug.

Putting together this book has been an incredible journey around the world, surrounded by the creative energy of hundreds of people who put their passion and talent into publishing outside their country's mainstream (while doubtless informing and inspiring it). We – that is, designer Jeremy Leslie, publisher Mike Koedinger and myself – started out by making a personal selection, one that we felt reflected some of the essentials of the independent magazine world as it stands in 2009. Some of those magazines that we chose asked not to be included, and we respected their wishes. Others didn't get back to us in time, and we reluctantly removed them too. Still more magazines, doubtless thousands more, haven't yet crossed our path, which may explain their omission. This is not a complete list of anything, not even of our favourite magazines.

What it is, however, is a representation of why and how independent magazines continue to lead the way, showing the mainstream media how to innovate and excite through their variety, originality, tenacity, thoughtfulness, creativity, inspiration, individuality, defiance. Beauty. Truth. Ugliness. Fiction.

We couldn't have made this book without the incredible generosity and patience of all of the magazines found within. In most cases, we only included small excerpts from their answers to the questionnaires we sent out; the full interviews can be found online at www. colophon2009.com/archive

This book is, admittedly, a frustrating read – you instantly want to dive into the pages and pick these magazines up, to flick through their pages, feel their weight, smell their ink, to read them page by page.

Instead, read this book as a travel guide, filled with dizzying tales

of beautiful sunsets, adrenalin-filled climbs, dense forests and endless beaches. Make note of the places you want to visit. Then track them down.

Or read this book for inspiration. Enjoy the stories, listen to the advice, revel in the brief glimpses of the wizards behind the curtain.

Or read this book as a souvenir brought back from the creative underground at the beginning of 2009, a hinterland beyond the reach of the mainstream, where dragons lurk and ingenuity blooms.

Read this book. And keep reading magazines.
–
Andrew Losowsky,
Rhode Island, USA

**What is the secret of our success? Humanity and community, trust in ideals, absence of fear to break rules and even laws, love of life and people, curiosity, an eager desire for non-stop revolution, a strict intention to change the world, a forever-young feeling of flying, a flexibility to circumstances combined with stable principles, a readiness to be open and to accept everything, to lose, to fail, to recover, to be happy.**
–
**Alena Boika
Umelec**

# COLOPHON2009

This book has been published in conjunction with Colophon2009, the second edition of the biennial Colophon international magazine symposium.

During the weekend of 13th-15th March 2009, people from around the world travelled to Luxembourg to celebrate excellence and innovation in the independent magazine industry.

With fifteen exhibitions spread across Luxembourg City, and approximately forty hours of conferences, creative roundtables, presentations and workshops, it was an essential event for everyone connected with, or interested in, the independent magazine world.

This book is a collaboration between the three curators of Colophon – Mike Koedinger, Jeremy Leslie and Andrew Losowsky – with the invaluable support of Didier Damiani and Rudy Lafontaine.

To find out more, and to be a part of Colophon2011, visit www.colophon2009.com

# HOW DID IT ALL BEGIN?

# 125

UNITED KINGDOM

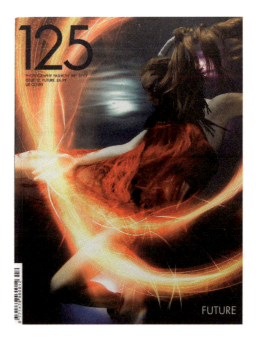

A showcase for new work and ideas across all genres of photography. It's a gallery space in print that anyone around the world can contribute to and anyone can buy from – if you see an image in the magazine that you like, you can order it as a limited-edition print.

How did it all begin?
The four founding partners are photographers Perry Curties and Jason Joyce and art directors Rob Crane and Martin Yates. We had all worked together in various ways over the years and talked about joint projects. 125 grew out of a fairly selfish desire to get more of our own photography out into the public domain, but very quickly became something much bigger, with many photographers, illustrators and stylists contributing.

Apart from the strain on the credit cards, issue 1 was fairly easy to produce because we didn't really know what we were doing and at that time there was no infrastructure to support. We just made a few phone calls and suddenly we had a magazine.

Making the step from the first to the second issue is probably the hardest thing to do, because you still have the costs of the first one and you are about to start work on another. Once you get on that treadmill, you are committing yourself.
—
Answered by Perry Curties
Editor in chief
*www.125magazine.com*

# ACIDO SURTIDO

ARGENTINA

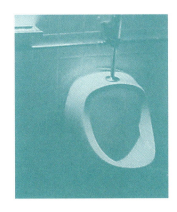

An art and design magazine distributed for free across Argentina. Acido Surtido edited Acido Surtido|Acid Experience, a book that compiled representative work from its first ten issues.

How did it all begin?
The first issue of Acido Surtido was published in 2001, as an answer to the inaction and depression that threatened Argentine creativity during the country's economic crisis. Its format is a 65cm x 95cm sheet of paper, with a single theme acting as a conceptual framework for different collaborators. Each contributor gets the same 16cm x 23.5cm space to fill with whatever they choose.

Since issue one, Acido Surtido has received collaborations from Mexico, Colombia, Brazil, Venezuela, Israel, Spain, Germany, South Africa and more. And, of course, from Argentina.
—
Answered by Lucas López
Editor / Art director
www.acidosurtido.com.ar

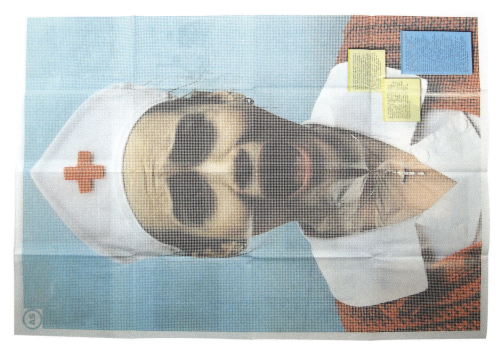

# ADDICT

DOMINICAN REPUBLIC NA

Innovation, creativeness and modern culture.

How did it all begin?
It began with the idea of producing a creative magazine for the Dominican market, where at least 98% of the magazine market is about social events. Carlos Alonso and myself decided to create a magazine that was truly different and innovative, where people could learn new things about objects, people, places, etc…

Now when I look at issue 1, I wonder, what were we thinking! It looks boring, filled with lost design opportunities… but it will always be the first, where it all began. Like your first kiss, no matter how bad it was, you can never forget it.
—
Answered by
Wendolyn Rodríguez de Alonso
VP/Editor
www.addict.com.do

# B EAST

ESTONIA

B EAST Magazine is a triannual fashion/attitude glossy for the New Europe. It promotes the vibrant zeitgeist of Eastern Europe, while also critiquing and de-hyping the west.

How did it all begin?
The founder and guiding editor of B EAST is Vijai Maheshwari, an Indian-American who was probably a Slavic rake in his former life. Brought up in India and educated in New York, he moved to Russia in the early 1990s to pursue a career in journalism and live the high life denied him in the US of A. He was, for a short time, editor-in-chief of Russian Playboy. Moving to Berlin and Amsterdam in 2002-3, he was shocked by the culture of 'guilt' in the west, and the lack of excitement in the local nightlife. Western Europe seemed over-hyped and lacking in any real direction, except for recycling the highlights of past decades. He was also stung by the arrogance in the west towards Eastern Europe. He thus moved to Prague to set up B EAST, on May 1st, 2004 – the day many of these countries joined the European Union.
—
Answered by Vijai Maheshwari
Founder/ Editor in chief
www.beastnation.com

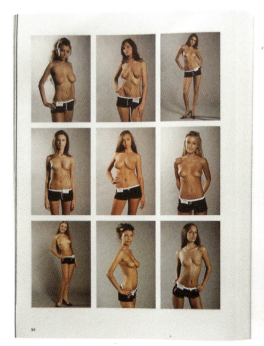

The untouched images show the girls' provincial naiveté. Without the aid of Photoshop, the reality of Russians' love of fame is unmasked through bra-strap marks, off-guard poses and desperate sultry smiles.

# BEAUTIFUL/ DECAY

UNITED STATES

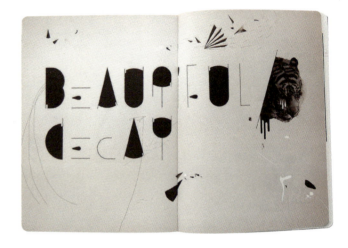

Documents the convergence of art, design, music, and fashion with a focus on emerging talent.

### How did it all begin?
Beautiful/Decay started in 1996 when my friend Jay and I decided to make a small zine. I have always been a huge magazine junkie, and I would buy a few every week, mostly high-end art magazines or graffiti zines. I never could find a magazine that filled in the gap between fine art and pop culture, and wanted to make a zine about my interests, which at the time included: punk/hardcore music, fine art, graffiti, hip-hop. We did three monochrome issues and gave them out and sold a few in stores. We soon got bored with the idea and at some point Jay and I stopped doing it.

Four years passed and I was living in NYC, doing a exchange program in college. At the end of my stay I had a small art show and sold five paintings. I made $5,000, and, after thinking for a few weeks about what I should do with the cash, I decided to bring back Beautiful/Decay as a real magazine with professional printing and proper distribution. There were no US publications at the time documenting the convergence of art, design, street culture and fashion.

Having no formal training in design and barely being able to use a computer, I asked two college friends to design the first issue. I had no idea what I was getting myself into. Even purchasing a barcode took days of research at the school library. Somehow we got the first full-colour issue done and I went and sold it to 40 stores around the country.

I slowly learned how to use a computer and began doing the layout of the magazine. It's funny because if you place the issues in chronological order, you can literally see when I learn certain design and layout techniques and rules. Shortly after the second full-colour issue came out, I met my current business partners Ben Osher and Fubz.

Once the three of us came together, B/D began to pick up a lot of steam. In just a few years, we have gone from being a small side project to an internationally distributed art & design publication that has branched off to curate art shows, start a clothing label and run a website that remains a daily destination for millions of people around the globe.

—
Answered by Amir H Fallah
Founder/Creative director
*www.beautifuldecay.com*

# DIK
# FAGAZINE

POLAND

For everyone interested in arts and men.

How did it all begin?
I have always wanted to run my own magazine. One day, I decided to do it. I called my friend Monika Zawadzka, who is a graphic designer, and asked if she was interested in helping me. When she said yes, I knew it would work out.

I created a general idea of the magazine and Monika designed a logo and a fantastic layout. And so DIK Fagazine was born. Step by step, some quite cool people started to create a specific small DIK community.

At the beginning we had some problems with homophobia in Poland – some printing houses were even rejecting the job. It is much better now.
—
Answered by Karol Radziszewski
Publisher/Editor in chief
www.dikfagazine.com

# DUF
## NETHERLANDS

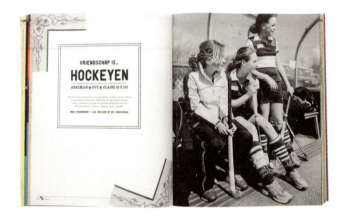

An annual bookmagazine for teenagers. Its name means "dull".

How did it all begin?
When I was twelve, I made my first magazine, Het Roddelblad (The Gossip Mag). It was about the gossips at school, and the idea was that teachers had to pay 25 cents to borrow the magazine for two hours. The fine I received from the school was much higher than that though! While studying graphic design, I bought many different magazines to learn more about them, to nourish my designer's mind. No single magazine had it all. Although teen magazines can be interesting, they are all short-lived and very light. A mag that would draw you into another world like a novel didn't exist. And so I decided to realise my ideas and see if it would work out.

—

Answered by Suzanne Hertogs
Founder/Publisher/Art director
*www.duf.nl*

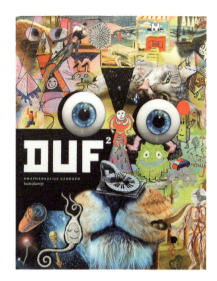

# DUMBO FEATHER, PASS IT ON

AUSTRALIA

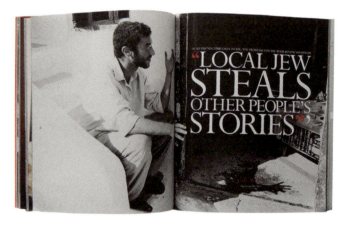

A 'mook' – half mag, half book. In each quarterly issue, five remarkable individuals tell you their stories.

### How did it all begin?
Once upon a time, on a wintery, stormy night in Sydney, Australia (yes, we do have winters), Kate Bezar walked into a newsagent wanting to buy a magazine to read. She walked round the shop picking mags up and putting them down again. She didn't want to devour gossip, nor perve at pictures of fashion shoots or amazing homes, nor be depressed by the news.

Kate realised that she wanted to read about the designer rather than the object, the artist rather than the artwork, the entrepreneur rather than the business. She wanted to know how people who were passionate about what they did had figured out what that was and pursued it.

She was a little bit lost. She'd quit her high-flying corporate career a couple of years earlier because she knew it wasn't what she wanted her life to be about it, and dabbled in everything from architecture to painting to yacht design… but nothing felt quite right.

In the newsagent that night, she decided that there must be other people out there like her, people who wanted a different kind of magazine, and that she'd make one for them. It would feature in-depth interviews with fascinating individuals, people who'd taken the road less trampled, with creativity, guts and integrity. She wanted it to be beautifully designed and to feature stunning photography. It would be authentic (with no hair and makeup stylists, no artificial lighting, and no Photoshopping) and feel intimate (with verbatim interviews and a smaller size than usual).

She hoped that it would become a treasured part of its readers' lives. Dumbo feather, pass it on is the result, with a mission to foster a community of creative, courageous individuals.
—
Answered by Kate Bezar
Founder/Accidental publisher
*www.dumbofeather.com*

# FOAM

NETHERLANDS

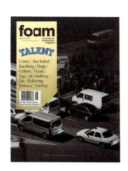

A quarterly photography magazine featuring six portfolios per issue, each printed on its own paper stock.

### How did it all begin?

The magazine was initiated by Foam, the photography museum founded in Amsterdam in 2001, and Vandejong, a communications agency based in Amsterdam. Or more specifically by Marloes Krijnen, director of Foam and Pjotr de Jong, director of Vandejong.

The motivation behind Foam magazine was to create an additional high-quality platform for photography, almost like an extra exhibition space for the museum, in a magazine format. The Foam Museum has always tried to look beyond its own walls and organises many projects outside the building. A magazine fits very well within that philosophy; it can travel to faraway places and to people who may never be able to visit the museum, and stimulate discussion on photography.

The first issue was published in December 2001, on the occasion of the opening exhibition at the museum, and served as a catalogue to the exhibition, as did the second issue. Foam #3 was the first independent issue based on the six portfolios format. While the relation to the museum is obvious, given the title, the selection of themes and portfolios is now unrelated to the exhibition programme of the museum. There may be an overlap occasionally, but that's entirely coincidental.

Printed matter has always been an important medium for the presentation of photographers' work, perhaps even more important than exhibitions – look at the current boom in photobook publishing and collecting. So a magazine, especially in the way Foam is published, remains an excellent medium for the presentation of photography to a worldwide audience.
—
Answered by Tanja Wallroth
Managing editor
*www.foammagazine.nl*

# FRAME

NETHERLANDS

Interiors.

How did it all begin?
The magazine was founded in 1997 by Peter Huiberts (publisher) and myself (editor in chief). We met while working at a Dutch trade magazine about interior design, and discovered we had the same interests and ambitions.

Since we couldn't achieve our goals working on that magazine, we decided to launch a magazine ourselves. Sounds easy, but it took us a year to find a publisher who believed in our plans.

Since then, our mission has been to create a global platform for interior designers, to inspire them and to make them proud of their job – which, at the time we started, they usually were not. They felt like second-rate artists.
—
Answered by Robert Thiemann
Editor in chief
www.framemag.com

# HERE
# AND THERE

## MY FATHER'S GARDEN
## Anne Daems

When I go visit my father the first thing I do is to go into the garden. Even in the middle of winter when there is nothing to harvest I put on some rubber boots, take a big red bowl and scissors and open the sliding doors. You can always find something: a half frozen red beets, sprouted turnip leaves, rosemary and rue. With the shovel I dig up burdock roots. Then I cut off some cherry blossoms and forsythia branches which start blooming a few days later in a vase in my apartment in Brussels. White, pink, yellow.

When the garden transfers from winter into spring, I like to look at my father when he turns the moist soil, sometimes he finds a daikon that survived winter or a Jerusalem artichoke.

I remember when we were young, after he'd worked in the garden on a beautiful summer day, he cooked up a delicious and festive supper with only the weeds he pulled out.

With a saw he cuts off dead branches of an old apple tree and afterwards puts cement in the holes to prevent it from rotting. Cementing is probably the thing he likes second best after making green tea.

In his garden he has built two Japanese tea pavilions. Although he's Flemish he practices tea ceremony very seriously and tenchos Japanese women dressed up in beautiful seasonal kimonos. The smallest pavilion (2 3/4 tatami) is my favorite. It's based on TEIGYOKUKEN, designed by Kanamori Sowa in the 16th century. There is a little window in the ceiling where the full moon shines through on cloudless nights, lightning up the teapot on the charcoal fire or my pillow, when I stay overnight.

(Tomorrow I have to seed clover in my garden.)

Photo: Anne Daems

父の庭　アン・ダムス

父の家を訪ねる、私はまず庭に足を運ぶ。真冬で何も収穫するものがない季節でも、長靴を履き、大きな赤いボウルと鋏を手に、引き戸を開ける。いつでも何か見つかる。半ば凍りついた赤いビーツ、芽が出たカブの葉、ローズマリー、ヘンルーダ。スコップで牛蒡の根っこを掘る。それから桜と連翹の枝を切る。数日後にブリュッセルのアパートに帰ってから、花瓶で花が開き始める。白、ピンク、黄色。

私は庭が冬から春に移り変わるときに、父が湿った土を掘り返す姿を目で追うのが好きだ。生き越した大根やキクイモを発見することもある。

幼い日を思い出す、父が楽しい夏の一日を庭仕事で終えたあと、おいしくて楽しい夕食を、抜いた雑草だけで作ってくれたものだ。

父は倒れ、老いた林檎の木の枯れた枝を切り落とし、腐らないように、穴にセメントを詰めてくれたりする。セメントを塗ることは、父が茶を点てることの次に好きなことだろう。

庭の中、父は二つの日本式の茶室を設えている。フランダース人だが、真剣に茶道と向き合っていて、美しい季節の着物姿の日本人女性たちに教えている。小さい方の庵（約2畳半）が私のお気に入りだ。16世紀に金森宗和が設計した、大徳寺真珠庵庭主軒をもとにしている。天井には小さな窓があり、雲のない夜には満月の光が差し込み、炭火の上の茶釜や私の枕を照らし出す。

（明日は私の庭でクローバーの種を蒔く予定だ）

MY FAVORITE CLOTHES

Fruits of the founder's life from
the previous year.

How did it all begin?
After woking for more than ten
years in the magazine industry,
I felt an urge to express my emotions
through editing.
—
Answered by Nakako Hayashi
Founder/Author
www.nakakobooks.com

NAKAKO HAYASHI

here    and    there

The Loneliness Issue

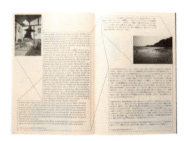

# MARK

NETHERLANDS

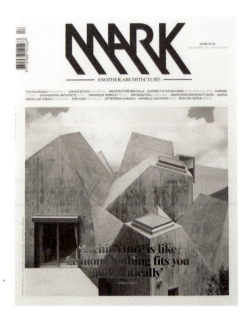

Architecture; stories about beautiful things.

How did it all begin?
The first issue of Mark was published in September 2005. It was thick, large, expensive and contained a visual explosion of photographs, illustrations, graphic effects and text. The editors received big applause from graphic designers, illustrators and other creatives, but not from architects. Moreover, the first issue didn't sell well. The second issue sold even worse. While making issue three, publisher and editors decided to radically overhaul the magazine. Size, weight, price and graphics were changed. From issue four onwards, the magazine finally began to be recognised by architects. Even better: they started to buy it.
—
Answered by Robert Thiemann
Editor in chief
*www.mark-magazine.com*

# MEATPAPER

UNITED STATES

### Head Games
*An intrepid home chef braves the brain.*

The fleischgeist: the art and culture of meat.

## How did it all begin?
It began with meat-related artwork that Sasha Wizansky, an artist and designer based in San Francisco, was engaged in several years ago. In speaking to people across the USA about her project, she began to see evidence of the fleischgeist. People were never neutral about the topic of meat, and that made it a compelling conversation starter.

Amy Standen, a writer, editor and public radio reporter based in San Francisco, joined Sasha to add journalistic expertise and cultural curiosity to the project.

When we started Meatpaper, instead of fundraising, we spent a year creating a sample issue and printed a small run in full-colour. The idea was so different from any other magazine, we felt we needed to create a physical magazine to explain our concept. Based on our prospectus, Issue Zero, we were able to secure national distribution in the U.S. and advance subscribers for Issue One.

—

Answered by Sasha Wizansky
Editor in chief/Art director
*www.meatpaper.com*

# PLAZM

UNITED STATES

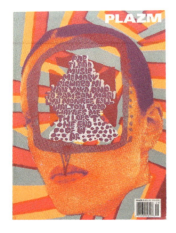

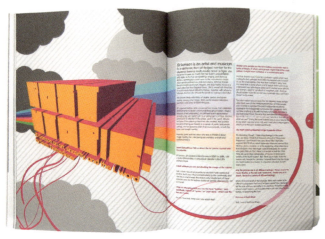

Art and culture with an emphasis on design.

## How did it all begin?

In 1991, a group of Portland artists, dissatisfied with avenues of expression available to them, started a series of weekly gatherings called Plazm. There were writers, photographers, illustrators, and designers all coming to these weekly gatherings. We were talking about things like media control and how we'd like to see artists representing artists. We decided to start a magazine.

For 17 years, we have tried to figure out how to make a living from making the magazine, which has never made any money. In the beginning, we all had other jobs and worked on the magazine on the side. Starting in 1993, we tried to subsidise it with Plazm Fonts, now a separate company owned by former partner Pete McCracken.

In 1995, we decided to take the form, content and ideas we had been exploring in Plazm magazine and apply them to commercial design work. This is what has sustained us. The irony is that the magazine is still something we do on the side and Plazm Design has become the day job.

—

Answered by Joshua Berger
Art director
*www.plazm.com*

# RUBBISH
UNITED KINGDOM

JACKET
POTATOES

Photography Jenny Van Sommers / Fashion Jenny Dyson

Saxon wears jacket by DIESEL.

The silly side of style.

How did it all begin?
Our motivation was frustration.
Why does fashion have to take
itself so seriously?!
—
Answered by Jenny Dyson
Editor in chief
*www.rubbishmag.com*

# SCARLET CHEEK

UNITED KINGDOM

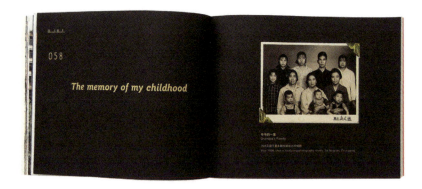

Recommended dawang locations: Jiefang Momentum, Beicheng Tianjie, Nanping Commercial district, Shabaping Commercial district

A personal perspective on local Chinese culture.

How did it all begin?
I'm studying lens and digital media in the UK, and first got the idea for a magazine while doing a documentary project as part of my studies. I made three documentary segments about Changsha, my hometown. As I filmed, I realised the city had experienced a profound transformation, and I really missed what I remembered from the past.

I'm a magazine lover and had always dreamed about having a magazine of my own. I also had the title "Scarlet Cheek" in mind for a long time – my friend Richard and I came up with it. I love the idea behind the word 'scarlet', more intense and evocative than just 'red'; it conveys the colour and emotion in violence and sex, reflecting strong, provocative views of a city.

"Scarlet Cheek" describes a range of expressions: happy, angry, embarrassing... Strong feelings are physically evident on the face. The title reflects the focus of my magazine – ideas of the city and of the individual in society.
—
Answered by Cindy Chen
Founder/Editor
www.scarletcheek.com

# SLANTED
GERMANY

Design and typography; illustration
and photography.

How did it all begin?
Everything started 2004 with a
weblog about typography. Since the
founding of the design company
MAGMA in 1996, we have designed
more than one hundred typefaces,
distributed by our own foundry; the
Slanted Blog was the perfect medium
to talk with other designers about
typography and design. In a very
short time the number of readers
increased enormously.

The magazine was kind of an answer
to the daily speed of blogging,
slowing things down and giving
type its perfect medium: paper.
—
Answered by Lars Harmsen
Publisher
*www.slanted.de*

# SNEAKER FREAKER

AUSTRALIA

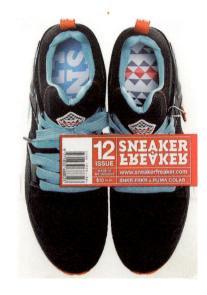

Sneakers, sneakers and more sneakers. And sneakers.

How did it all begin?
I started it in 2002, largely as a way to get free sneakers and introduce myself. There was no business plan, no grand scheme, no idea that I could see into the future or imagine that I'd still be doing it years later on a global scale. I've done a lot of projects and jobs over the years and the mag was a good idea at the right time. But you never know how true that is until you've already done it.
—
Answered by Woody W
Editor/Founder
www.sneakerfreaker.com

# SUPER SUPER
UNITED KINGDOM

Fun, colour, positivity, expression, individuality, inclusivity, inspiration, creativity, community, accessibility.

How did it all begin?
Founded by Supersteve and Namalee, to make the world a better, brighter, more fun place! When we put out the first issue some people loved it immediately and some said 'uuurggh'! Our fave diss was "it looks like a clown's been sick"! Then, not long after, partly due to the whole 'nu rave' phenomenon, our style & aesthetic was eeeeverywhere across Europe, from high fashion to the high street. We've also been influential in terms of design, with the underage scene in the UK, and more...
—
Answered by Super Steve
Founder/Creative director
www.myspace.com/thesupersuper

# TANK

UNITED KINGDOM

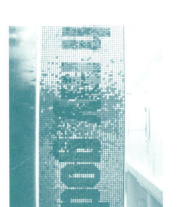

Elitism for all.

How did it all begin?
Iranian-born Masoud Golsorkhi studied photography at the University of Westminster in London before working as a fashion photographer for such publications as Interview, Jalouse, Vogue Gioello and Harpers & Queen. German-born Andreas Laeufer studied communication design in Constanz, Germany. He worked as an art director for advertising agencies in Germany and Switzerland before becoming a freelance art director for such fashion companies as Hugo Boss and Joop!.

After moving to London he met Masoud, and together they launched Tank magazine in 1998, sparking the "bookzine" trend.
—
Answered by Caroline Issa
Publisher
www.tankmagazine.com

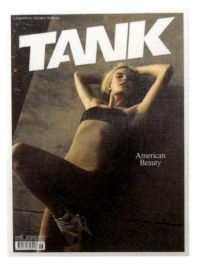

# UMELEC

CZECH REPUBLIC

Visual culture in Central and Eastern Europe. Umelec means 'artist' in Czech.

How did it all begin?
The magazine was founded in a commune in the early 1990s, and having experienced anarchy, autocracy, democracy and dictatorship, we are finally coming back to a social human model of slightly organised chaotic democracy that is pretty close to the first one. But its communist spirit is now enriched with the past experience of collisions with a growing commercial marketplace, consumerism and lost ideals.
—

Answered by Alena Boika
Editor in chief
www.divus.cz/umelec

# TELL US EVERYTHING:

## BABYBABYBABY
MEXICO

Photography : Roberta Rudolfi
Styling : Nao Koyabu
Model : Anna Konzen

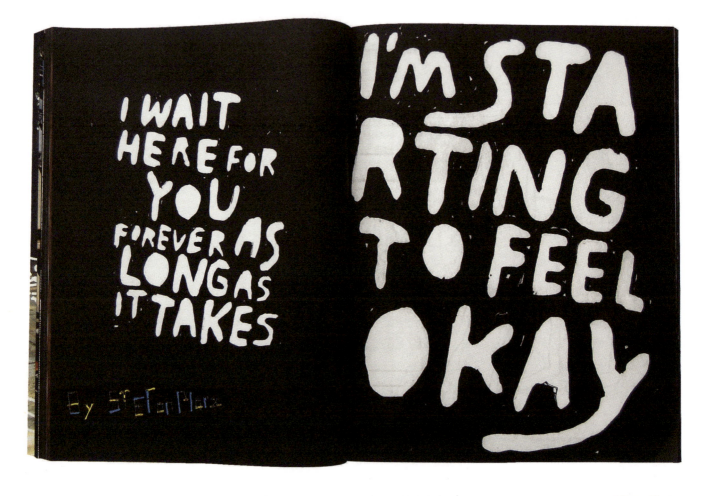

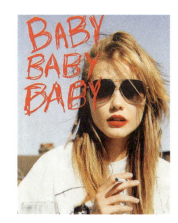

Contemporary culture.

How did it all begin?
After successfully launching Celeste magazine in Mexico in 2001, Vanesa Fernández and Aldo Chaparro realised there was an audience craving something even more fun, contemporary, edgy and bold. Vanesa has a background in contemporary art as curator and critic; Aldo is a conceptual artist.

It was, and still is, a time of profound change in Mexico; there is a new generation of young people with really good ideas, and the idea was for BabyBabyBaby both to inspire them, and become their outlet. So, together with the then-editor in chief José García Torres, Vanesa and Aldo decided to launch BabyBabyBaby as a new biannual project.

How do you make each issue?
It's a very organic, natural process; we go around collecting things that strike our fancy, things we really like, and then just decide what to include.

We invite all our friends from around the world, both old acquaintances and new ones that we meet along the way, to collaborate; they are hugely talented, but not necessarily professional artists, and we're always eager to meet new friends. We want to create a space in which to put a bunch of things that on the surface are unrelated, but once on the page, a dialogue begins among them that can gain a new significance or meaning.

There's very little planning for every issue, in the sense that we don't make a storyboard or layout of the magazine. We kind of think that that would kill the nonchalant spirit of it.
We like to think that it's the kind of magazine that happens when a group of friends get together after school and put together pages from their diaries, poems and friends photos and drawings in a sort of scrapbook, pasted up with everything that inspires them, reflecting their personality, their innocence, their way of seeing life.

What have been the most important stages in the life of your magazine?
There have been many, from collaborators believing in the project in its early stages, to having international distribution through American Apparel. This gave the magazine a more international scope, and it sparked the interest of other distributors in places such as Japan and Europe. In order for us to reach kids around the world, we changed the language of the magazine from Spanish to English.

What is the secret of your success?
I think it has to do with how naïve and simple it is. We show a lifestyle our readers can really relate to; I mean, our models are real, and not overdone with makeup and lighting. We don't Photoshop anything. We like to think of the magazine as an open space that doesn't really censor anybody's work; though obviously there is a very critical selection process.

What would be the one thing that would help the magazine to improve?
Money, LOL. We always seem to be short of cash.

Who are your readers?
It's difficult to describe the audience. It touches a cord in apparently unrelated people from all walks of life, ages, and interests. That being said, we focus on young, urban, a-little-bit-outsider kids in their late teens and early twenties who see the world in the same way we do. People who don't settle for whatever mass culture is feeding them, and who aren't afraid to be themselves.

Where do you want the magazine to be in five years?
Still alive. It's easy for an independent magazine to disappear, mainly because it starts losing its edge, hence losing its readers to new, fresher magazines. So it's really up to us to evolve in the same direction as our readers. In an ever-changing world, in five years we would like to be positioned in the exact same spot we are now.

What is your relationship with advertising?
Being independent translates into a complicated situation with most advertisers out there, which is understandable. They have to really trust the project in order for them to invest their money in a magazine that doesn't have a big media conglomerate to back it up.

We love our current advertisers. We have few, but very loyal ones, companies and brands that like the project for what it is; they understand it, and want to be attached to it. So, in a way they are more partners than simple sponsors. They don't really influence the content in any way, because they like it just the way it is.

At the beginning we did some advertising-driven editorials, some we actually weren't very comfortable with, but we had them just to keep the advertiser. We stopped doing them because it affected the relationship with our readers. We've only done one or two since – when we're all really happy with the outcome.

How many magazines do you read?
I'm such a magazine addict; I buy about 15-20 magazines a month that vary from the very independent fashion magazines to literary reviews; and I keep them all.
—
Answered by Carlos Carbajal
PR Manager
www.babybabybaby.com.mx

# TELL US EVERYTHING:

## GOOD

UNITED STATES

## One Big Crisis

**ALEX STEFFEN** says solving our current planetary crisis could lead to an unimaginably good future. Here's how we get there.

### as told to GOOD

**We are at a moment** unique in human history, when we are using the planet's bio-capacity so quickly that we risk a catastrophic collision with ecological reality. Every creature and every biological system on Earth is now dependent, intentionally or unintentionally, on our management. We've never been in the position of managing the planet before and we have no idea how to do it.

It's really serious. What's at stake here is not just the ability of civilization to function in a way that we have come to take for granted, but possibly even the survival of human beings. And, unfortunately, the causes of the crisis are complex and everyone on Earth is involved. There's a tendency for people to think that there's an environmental crisis and a poverty crisis and a war and terrorism crisis, and so forth. But in reality they're all the same big crisis. Right now we are coming to realize the magnitude of that big crisis.

The future toward which we are moving quickly is unthinkably bad. However, the kinds of things we need to do to solve these problems could lead to a future that is unimaginably good.

In 2009, we're going to have what may well be the most important international summit of our lifetimes:

the Cop15, the United Nations Climate Change Conference, in Copenhagen, where we will decide what the successor to the Kyoto treaty will be. It is the last opportunity we're going to have as a species to decide the degree to which we're going to tackle climate change before it's too late. And the United States will play a critical role, because we've been the ones holding up progress.

**In the last** five years the politically expedient form of environmental activism became privatizing responsibility, encouraging us to think that the future of the planet depends on us making small choices in our daily lives: recycling, buying organic shampoo, whatever. But most of the damage that we cause in our lives is caused by big systems we have very little control over as isolated individuals. We have this idea that changing the world ought to be reducible to simple steps, but it just doesn't work that way; this isn't that kind of a world. Even if we all followed every last eco-tip and simple step, we'd still be hurtling towards catastrophe.

If we want to avoid that catastrophe, we need to not just do fewer bad things: we need to do different things altogether. We need to reinvent the way our whole society works. We need bright green upgrades to our cities, our energy systems, industrial design and technology, farming and forestry—everything. It all needs to change, essentially immediately. That will take millions of people transforming their lives to pursue new solutions, to become more effective and innovative citizens, business people, investors, community leaders, and so on. We need people to actually step up and do big things. We need people who change their thinking and not just their light bulbs.

**I don't think** that we have ever experienced, at least in American history, a transformation of political opinion like the one we've seen in the past several years on the environment and climate. Young people understand that the world we're talking about is the world they're going to raise their kids in, that this isn't distant reality, that the ice caps are melting now. While that gives me hope, the gap of understanding between those people and the 70-year-olds who are in the U.S. Senate is staggering. It's a generation gap that makes everything the boomers talked about in the 1960s look like a disagreement at a tea party.

> We need people who change their thinking and not just their light bulbs.

**I really think** that the biggest political difference on the planet right now is what time frame you define moral responsibility in. Most politics is really all about hoping the good times last until the rich old people die. There's even a denial that we can do anything about the problems. It's all about delay, fake debates, and encouraging cynicism, inducing apathy.

**But there's another** political force growing fast, and that's the politics of optimism. It's a politics that says transformation is not just a duty, it's an amazing opportunity. We might, instead of doing nothing and leaving our kids a ruined planet, decide to build them an awesome future and spend the rest of our lives enjoying it. That's the choice we wake up to every day now: cynicism or change.

GOOD

### WHATEVER HAPPENED TO...
## The Rainforests?

**Remember back in** the early 1990s when everyone was freaking out about the rain forests? So much so, in fact, that activists were chaining themselves to trees and Ben & Jerry's launched an ice cream to raise awareness? Guess what? It's still a problem. And according to a recent study by the World Wildlife Federation, we may be just 15 years away from the point of no return. An area the size of a football field is lost to deforestation every 10 seconds, and when that happens, the destroyed rain forests belch massive amounts of carbon dioxide into the atmosphere, setting off a domino effect of global warming, disrupted ocean currents, and drought. Logging, urbanization, hunting, and tourism have also contributed to the extinction of thousands of animal species a year. Time for a new ice-cream flavor.

### Goodbye, Cruel World
#### The Animals on the Edge of Extinction

**Extinctions can** be a natural part of evolving ecosystems, but right now we are pushing many species of animals and plants to the brink by polluting and occupying their habitats and interrupting the food chain. Here are the number of threatened species in 2008, as determined by International Union for Conservation of Nature:

8,448 PLANTS

1,808 AMPHIBIANS

1,217 BIRDS

1,201 FISH

1,094 MAMMALS

978 MOLLUSKS

623 INSECTS

160 CRUSTACEANS

422 REPTILES

11 ARACHNIDS

CASPIAN SEAL

SLENDER-BILLED VULTURE

BLACK-EARED MANTELL

EUROPEAN EEL

RADIATED TORTOISE

**? NOW WHAT**
For an interactive guide to making your own home rainforest-friendly, visit ARCHIVE. GREENPEACE.ORG/ FORESTHOUSE

56
GOOD Jan/Feb 09
Environment

**BIO** Alex Steffen is the executive editor of Worldchanging.com and editor of the book, *Worldchanging: A User's Guide for the 21st Century*

**MORE INFO** rainforestalliance.org
**PHOTO** Flickr user andresfib

**BLOW ME DOWN** Denmark generates 20 percent of its electricity from wind power, making it the world leader.

57
good.is/ planet

In the crude futures pit, brokers at the New York Mercantile Exchange react to soaring gas prices.

Things that matter for people who give a damn.

How did it all begin?
Ben Goldhirsh founded the company in 2005 (he was 26) with a group of friends who were as committed as he was to filling the gap between publications about significant world events and publications that are fun to read and inspire people.

How do you make each issue?
Our small staff – about five people, give or take –works steadily on each issue for about two months at a time, with longer-term planning happening a couple times a year.

What have been the important stages in the life of your magazine?
Being nominated for two National Magazine Awards in our first year of eligibility was a nice validation that our concept was viable, and that people were ready for it.

What is the secret of your success?
Passion for potential mixed with fierce pragmatism. Also, this global moment in which we find ourselves, where people are collectively ready to affect change in the world, but aren't quite sure how to do it. We're trying to help.

Where do you want the magazine to be in five years?
We want to be thought of as analogous to this moment in culture, something essential for this generation in this moment.

Who are your readers?
Good's readers have been raised by the benefits of capitalism and now they're interested in making the market work better for more people and the environment. They like money, but want to put it to good use. They are hungry for news, but suspicious of their sources of information. They are discriminating, conscious consumers who actively seek out quality, invention, and responsibility in the products they purchase and the companies behind them. They are social metropolitans who are not defined by what they do, but by how and why they do it.

What is your relationship with advertising?
There's a high wall between the editorial and business sides of our operations, but we're interested in exploring ways to take advantage of the resources advertisers have at their disposal, in service of products that have actual value for our readers. We don't really know what that means yet.

How many magazines do ou read?
I subscribe to around 20, so I think I'm close to maniac status.
—
Answered by Zach Frechette
Editor in chief
www.good.is

# HOW DO YOU
# MAKE EACH ISSUE ?

A
ACHTUNG
AD!DICT
DIF
H
I-JUSI
MAGAZINE
ME
ROJO®
S/N°
SHIFT!
STIRATO
VAROOM

FRANCE

A cultural statement, a statement against homogenisation and for individuality. Each issue gives a new fashion designer total freedom to present their atmosphere and vision of the world. Every magazine is a new story.

How do you make each issue?
It depends on the dynamic of the guest curator. We always start by meeting with them, so basically we always start from zero.

Each issue takes at least six months to produce, and is created by a very small team. There are two chief editors, each of whom works on one issue a year; plus the art director, advertising director, editor-at-large and the publisher. The team of the guest curator is also very much involved in the entire process.
—
Answered by Nathalie Ours
Chief Editor
*www.modenatie.com/amagazine*

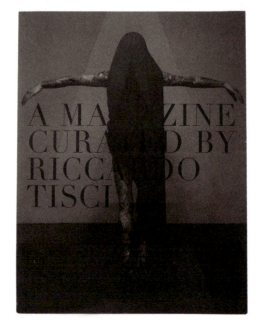

# ACHTUNG

GERMANY

A magazine about fashion. Unlike some fashion magazines, it does not cover any other lifestyle areas.

How do you make each issue?
We are very meticulous about it. First, we attend the international designer collections for men and women in New York, Paris and Milan every season – quite a costly undertaking for a small magazine, but it gives us a competitive edge in our market. Then we formulate our fashion

selections – which naturally change from season to season – matching our broader German vision of fashion culture. Thus we shape our shoots, which are large collaborations where meetings with our photographers are key. With them we shape a story to the tiniest detail. This generally takes several weeks.

We do not accept unsolicited contributions, as we see it as our responsibility to craft the international

fashion access we have into a tangible print product for the German-speaking market.
—
Answered by Markus Ebner
Editor in chief /Founder
www.achtung-mode.com

# AD!DICT

BELGIUM

The printed tool of the addictlab.com 'global creative think tank'. Talent, people, concepts.

**How do you make each issue?**
We are not a magazine but a lab. A research theme is selected. Labmembers (about 4000 people from 150 countries) upload ideas. Labresearchers select content for the book/magazine/exhibition and start the process of creating the publication.

When a book/magazine comes out, this also becomes the catalogue of an exhibition. We create two themes a year.
—
Answered by Jan Van Mol
Founder
*www.addictlab.com*

# DIF
PORTUGAL

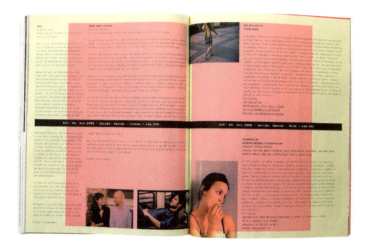

Fashion, music, cinema, art.

How do you make each issue?
With a great deal of effort! We have a
very small team and rely a great deal
on collaborators donating their time
and skill. The magazine is produced in
everyone's spare time, which usually
means a lot of late nights and large
amounts of coffee.

—
Answered by
Trevenen Morris-Grantham
Editor in chief
www.difmag.com

# H

SPAIN

# I-JUSI

SOUTH AFRICA

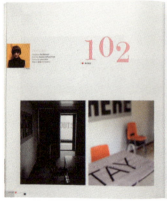

Fashion, trends and culture.

How do you make each issue?
The process of making each new issue

is quite different from the last, and is always challenging.

First, Carlota (fashion editor) and I generate the contents and the spirit of the issue – each issue is special and almost themed. Then we start working with our team of journalists. Then we start on the design of the pages with Jose (editor) and Oscar (art director), treating each page as an individual event: we don't work with templates, so the magazine has a ever-mutating (yet always appealing) form.
—
Answered by Raül De Tena
Chief editor
www.hmagazine.com

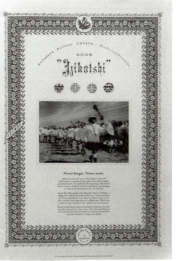

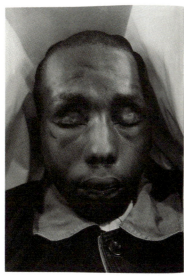

FREE!
"SOUTH AFRICA NOW" Poster

An opportunity for South African designers, writers, illustrators, comic artists, photographers to explore their personal thoughts or views on "what makes me African". The name is Zulu for "juice".

How do you make each issue?
Each issue is themed, generally around issues that at are current to the South African way of life (AIDS, death, identity etc). A brief is sent out to anyone who shows interest, and the submitted work is then selected for publication. Each issue may publish anything from one designer's work to as many as can be fitted inside. Generally size A3 (or A4 if there are many contributors) and 16 - 36 pages. Each issue takes about a week of designing. The entire publishing team is one person (Garth Walker) with occasional assistance from others as required.
—

Answered by Garth Walker
Publisher/Editor/Designer
*www.ijusi.co.za*

# MAGAZINE

FRANCE

Magazine culture and art, fashion
and graphic design.

How do you make each issue?
I choose a new Art Director and... go!
The ten contributors to Magazine are
always the same from one issue to the
next. I work for one month on each
issue, and rest for one month.
—
Answered by Angelo Cirimele
Editorial director

ME

UNITED STATES

All about one person, the "guest editor", who commissions the photographer and chooses the friends, family, colleagues they want to be in the issue.

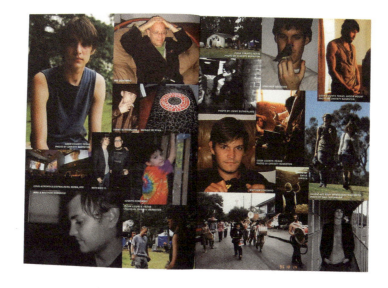

How do you make each issue?
The guest editor and guest photographer have a lot of responsibilities in terms of pulling together all the content for the magazine. We rely on them to be in contact with their friends to get everything in. All the design and layouts are done by me, and I'm working on getting some more people to help in terms of ad sales and other things. It all takes about three months.
—
Answered by Claudia Wu
Founder/ Editor in chief/
Creative director
www.memagazinenyc.com

# ROJO®

SPAIN

A place where everybody can have their artwork published.

**How do you make each issue?**
We have four people working full time in Barcelona, with 40 associate directors worldwide and more than 800 active contributors.

ROJO® is an ongoing production factory for all kinds of content. We have no submission deadlines as we work on an atemporal timescale. We have no theme, no censorship. The artist is free to submit, and ROJO® is free to choose.

Issues are created one week before going to print, and contents are selected from all the submissions sent in since ROJO® began in 2001. This means an issue can include works received one week before going to print, or from months or years ago.

When the magazine appears, we enjoy looking at it for hours and finding all the little mistakes that make us human.

—

Answered by David Quiles Guilló
Founder/Director
*www.rojo-magazine.com*

S/N°

BRAZIL

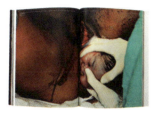

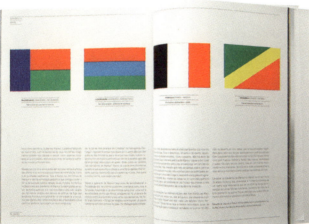

Brazil's art, culture, fashion.

How do you make each issue?
We usually spend about four months producing each issue of s/n°. The entire team is myself and journalist Helio Hara, plus a guest art director, a producer, and the help and support of assistants.

We first choose a subject and then invite creators from different fields to express themselves around that

subject through as many ideas/approaches as possible. This can be done through photography, collage, text, design – for example, for an issue about "Salt", a team of designers created a salt shaker which was impossible to handle; they wanted to suggest the idea of risks. Salt protects organic matter from rotting, but it can also be a risk if ingested in excess. It was used as currency, it helped create empires, it preserves food, but prevents life from growing

(think of salt deserts). There is also a popular saying in Brazil that says the world is divided between people who are salty (sparkling, interesting) and those who lack salt (boring, flat). The artists OsGemeos used this idea for an original graffito, used this idea in an original grafitti produced for this issue.

—

Answered by Roberto Wolfenson
Editor in chief/Creative director

# SHIFT!
GERMANY

Shift! is about a different subject
every time.

How do you make each issue?
The initiator and editor of each issue
is Anja Lutz, a graphic designer based
in Berlin with a particular interest in
print and experimental publishing.
Each project is entirely developed
in collaboration with a number of
people, ranging from one person
to one hundred or more. This ever-
changing team of collaborators and
co-art directors allow shift! to totally
change and reinvent itself with each
publication. Depending on the nature
and scope of the project, we spend
between six months and two years
on each project.
—
Answered by Anja Lutz
Editor and Art director
*www.shift.de*

# STIRATO
ITALY

A free poster magazine dedicated to the visual arts.

How do you make each issue?
The first step is to decide on a theme. We've had themes such as Violence, Girls, Animals, Fear, Dreams, Human Body and Fairy Tales. The second step is contacting the artists we hope to guest in the issue – for example, we asked seven international artists to choose a recipe and do an illustration about it, for the Foodissue. Our favourite image is then chosen to be printed on the giant poster and featured in the long interview. The others will receive smaller spaces in the magazine.

After having done all the interviews and after having received all the images, we start to create the design. We always try to have a similar impact but different structure from previous issues, creating new graphics close to the theme of the issue. We change fonts and small details. We design articles flipped at 90° or 180°, and we often write in really tiny-sized letters, because we don't want to create a sensation of calm in the readers, we love to demand their attention and concentration. Stirato takes a maximum 8-10 minutes to read, and we want the full attention of the reader

during that time!

Stirato is like a map of the big sea of the Internet. Every interview or suggestion on Stirato can be a first step for a personal trip that will carry the reader someplace and sometime far away.
—
Answered by
Sebastiano Barcaroli
and Siriana Flavia Valenti
Founders
www.stirato.net

# VAROOM

UNITED KINGDOM

Illustration and made images.

How do you make each issue?
We have a small committed team,
producing the magazine from the
Association of Illustrators office,
while editor Adrian Shaughnessy,
and designers Non Format work
remotely. We come together for
meetings. Lots of time is spent on
Varoom – more time than we have.
—
Answered by Derek Brazell
Production manager
*www.varoom-mag.com*

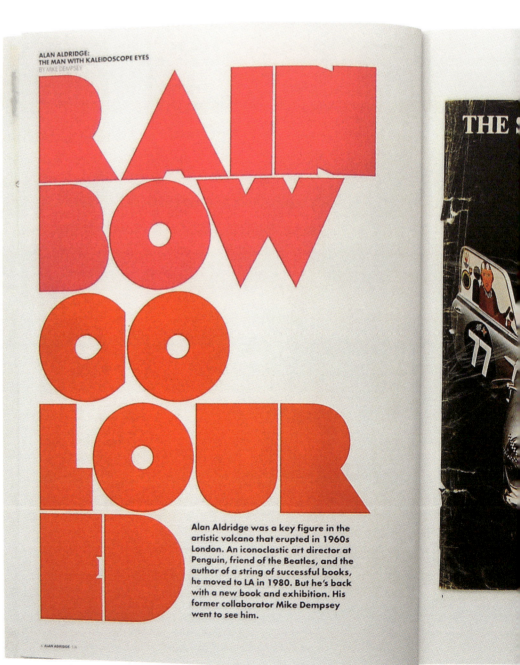

ALAN ALDRIDGE:
THE MAN WITH KALEIDOSCOPE EYES
BY MIKE DEMPSEY

RAIN BOW OO LOUR ED

Alan Aldridge was a key figure in the
artistic volcano that erupted in 1960s
London. An iconoclastic art director at
Penguin, friend of the Beatles, and the
author of a string of successful books,
he moved to LA in 1980. But he's back
with a new book and exhibition. His
former collaborator Mike Dempsey
went to see him.

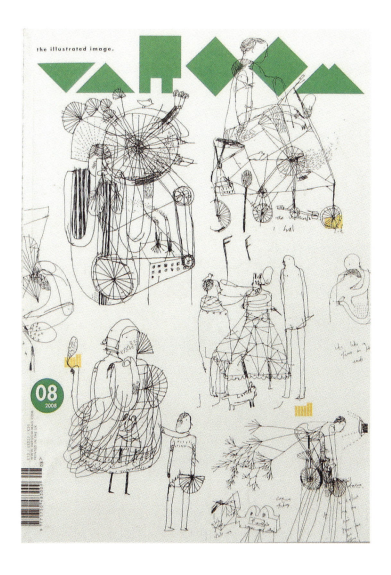

the illustrated image.

08
2008

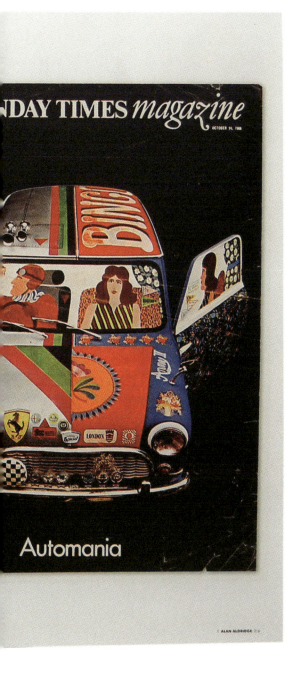

NDAY TIMES *magazine*

OCTOBER 14, 1966

Automania

NOT
STAT
IO

Four artists reveal how new accessible digital tools, and new hybrid working methodologies, have allowed them to take image-making beyond the static and into the realm of motion. In the past they might have been traditional illustrators, but in the new era of computer-aided creativity, anything is possible. As Nando Costa says: 'I like to think of animations as moving illustrations and illustrations as static animations.'

# TELL US EVERYTHING:

## IDN
CHINA

Thus, when the curator of the Mu Gallery in Eindhoven, The Netherlands, invited Gauckler to host an exhibition there, the avant-garde French artist had no hesitation in deciding to build it around the theme of the 'Food Chain'. It may take a Master's degree to analyze in depth the complex relationship between us and food, but Gauckler has tackled it in a light-hearted, almost child-like way. This approach is a reflection of her unique design style, which often involves vaguely human, potato-shaped forms. Despite, or probably because of their simplicity, her characters are extremely appealing.

Filling the 500sqm area with these cute, primary-coloured characters, and utilising graphics, installation and motion works, Gauckler takes us on a journey that illustrates how the food chain grows and is altered along the way by how, and what we consume – and how we, in turn, are changed by our experiences.

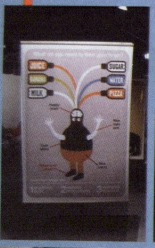

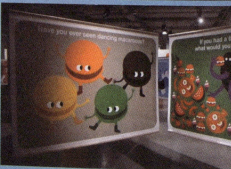

IdN: Could you give us some background about the 'Food Chain' show and how this collaboration came about?

GG: It was actually very simple. I was contacted by Angelique Spaninks, who runs the Mu Gallery in Eindhoven (The Netherlands). She was interested in my work and specifically the artworks I made for the Someday Gallery in Melbourne a year ago. She asked me to come up with an idea, so I went to Eindhoven to the opening of the previous show, featuring Geoff McFetridge. I thought it was great – I'm a big fan of his – and I got to know the space, which is quite big. At first, I thought I wouldn't be able to fill it. But after a while I came up with the idea of working with the food theme. I've always been fascinated by food images, and, as a vegetarian, by food in general – from the very sophisticated to the very basic, but also all the issues related to food such as bulimia and

obesity. Food is also strongly connected to the whole question of consumption and I'm very interested in this theme because I believe that in Western societies we are now reaching the limits of the system because of ecological and psychological pressures. In this culture of 'too much', food makes a good metaphor to explore these limits. I wanted to adopt a funny, even absurd approach to all this, so I decided to make some 'educational plates' that would explain all these serious topics in an apparently childish way.

### Did you know that when you're dead you actually become food?

# IdN

International
designers
Network

Volume 15 Number 3
THE EXHIBITION ISSUE

## SHOW/ DESIGN

What it takes to put
on a memorable
exhibition.

> Featuring:

1. Helmo
2. Small
3. Bleed
4. Serial Cut™
5. Burneverything
6. Twopoints.net
7. Studio Round
8. Project Projects

**+ Why Chile's HOT**
Design in this neglected South American
country is coming out of its cocoon.

**Do it yourself notebooks**
What happens when you leave 1,000
sketch books just lying around?

**Jumping to it**
Vibe + Energy – Jump Studio
re-models Red Bull's London HQ

**Art for foodies**
Geneviève Gauckler's latest exhibition
demonstrate that "we are what we eat"

**PLUS the fully loaded
non-stop motion in
this issue's DVD**
Including Robert Seidel's graphic
projection on ancient walls, Processes:
Living Paints; 30 short titlings for EA
Music by Andy Martin; live demos of the
videogames No More Heroes and Omega
Five; opening title for the B&A new
media conference by Manhattan-based
design studio Karlssonwilker; all the
latest TV commercials, music videos ...
and much, much more.

International edition
€15 / £10 / C$17 / US$15

Volume 15 Number 3
2008, Three

The Exhibition
Issue

www.idnworld.com

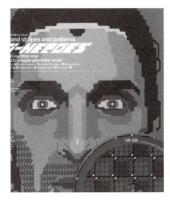

Visual aesthetics and creative cultures.

How did it all begin?
Laurence created IdN in 1992, after many passionate years in the magazine industry. He's still very much involved in the day-to-day running of IdN as its publisher.

How do you make each issue?
We have a team of around ten people, consisting of people who are really good at doing what they're not supposed to, giving us flexibility, sustainability and an ability to adapt. We start each issue from scratch, and it takes us more than half a year to move from the ideas stage to the published magazine.

What have been the important stages in the life of your magazine?
A major step for us was the decision to host design conferences, back in the early 2000s.

What is the secret of your success?
Our key success relies on you, the creative people out there that keep on truckin' and staying fresh. Our job here at IdN is merely to serve as a catalyst.

Who are your readers?
Most of them are designers or people working in creative industries.

Where do you want the magazine to be in five years?
Hopefully the magazine's influence and reach will have further extended among creative people everywhere.

What is your relationship with advertising?
Advertisements are an essential part of many magazines, however they play a minor role in IdN and have little, if any influence on our editorial decisions. IdN is for the people, by the people.

How many magazines do you read?
Somewhere between 10 and 20. We have people in the office who sniff the ink from newly printed IdNs or any other magazines for that matter.
—
Answered by the IdN team
www.idnworld.com

# TELL US EVERYTHING:

## KAREN
UNITED KINGDOM

Tina's Top Ten Breads

1. Soda (brown or white)
2. French Stick
3. Granary
4. Ciabatta
5. Olive
6. Split tin
7. Twisty loaf with poppy seeds
8. Rye
9. Thick sliced white
10. Cottage loaf

Go to position 5 please.
Go to position 5 please.
Go to position 5 please.

**2 for 99p**

"Two pineapples for 99p. Buy one get one free. Extraordinarily cheap considering where they have come from."
"I don't know where they have come from. There's no labels on them."
"Look at them bristling away, I bet they taste gorgeous."
"Is this an example of fair trade?"
"I don't know, somehow I think some trade is never fair."

"I went to town today and saw a group of people sitting next to the olive stall in the market, drinking strong cider they were. I felt sorry for one of them."
"Why?"
"I just did. You can tell when someone's had a bad time. Town's not a bad place or a dangerous place. It's no different from any other town. People still say hello, but it is depressing. Would it make me happy if I lived in town? No. But I can buy two pineapples for 99p there."

Karen
a magazine made out of the ordinary

ISSN 1754-033X

> had to bid for and the prize was a Sunday dinner that Sandy and I would come and cook. One bloke bid £190 for one voucher. There was a table of six people there that had not really tasted proper gravy like my mum and my gran used to make. We turned up and cooked it and had a good time and they tried proper roast beef and organic vegetables from the shop. Sandy cooked traditional crumble and a fruit pie, none of this fancy stuff, just traditional food. People asked us, 'how did you get the Yorkshire pudding to rise? How did you get the roast potatoes so nice and crispy?' Well it's ever so easy.

People come in here, especially on a Saturday, and they could be in here for an hour just chatting, chatting to everyone else. Everyone calls me by my first name, tell me stories about themselves, I get to ask them how their family is. You go to the supermarket on a Saturday, talk to nobody and go home and it's really boring. I talk to all the kids that come in here, some of them call me Mr Thomas. One little girl and her mum sent us all a Christmas card. They also sent a personal card to Dean as well, 'cos at the moment all the little girl can say is 'dad' and 'Dean' and nothing else.

My favourite meat is roast brisket, slowly cooked with traditional vegetables and gravy.

**Sophie**

I came to work here because Michael's my uncle and he just needed help stacking up the shelves and everything. I was working a lot of hours cleaning in another job, 50 to 60 hours a week, and he said, 'well come and work for me, it will be a lot better for you.' I've been here four years on and off now. I'm sort of full-time part-time, if it gets a bit quiet then Michael will say go. I am flexible, if it gets to two o'clock and he asks me to stay, I will.

I am a qualified hairdresser, but hairdressing was a lot more hours and the pay wasn't very good. The cleaning was hard work, I cleaned offices, schools, libraries. I'd get up at four o'clock in the morning and not get home till seven o'clock at night. It was a long day.

Here I can get to know about food and meet people. You get to learn different things each day, everyone's different. Sometimes customers want to know how to cook something or they tell me how they are going to cook it and I say, 'oh, that's a good idea.'

A lot of people, all ages, even middle-aged people and some vegetarians, if they're cooking for the family, come in and ask how do you >

"Who does the deliveries?"
"The grandads, mine and Michael's."

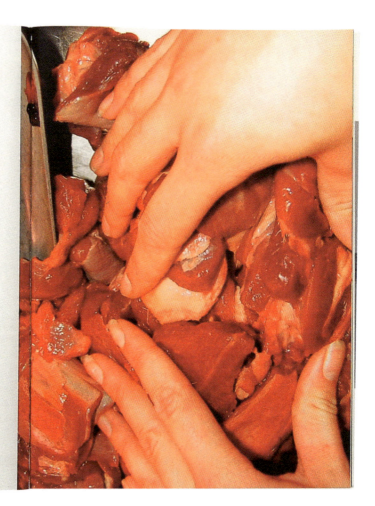

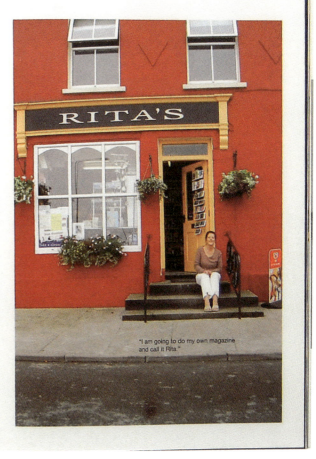

"I am going to do my own magazine and call it Rita."

Made out of the ordinary.

How did it all begin?
I wanted to make work that features the 'ordinary' people, places, conversation – life as I experience it.

Issue 01 came out at the end of a period of study and research I had undertaken. I was (and am) particularly interested in celebrity culture and how celebrity and ordinary people are mediated. I contacted mainly gallery bookshops and asked them if they would stock it and then personally distributed. I did no promotion, it quietly went into a few bookshops and people bought it and I remember, I was so happy because I absolutely believed in the concept. This was the first time I had thoughts that there would be an issue 02.

How do you make each issue?
My first response was to say my 'team' is me + 1. But then my friends and family talk with me about my work and inspire me so maybe they are part of the 'team'; also people who feature in the work inspire me so are they part of the 'team'? And where do my readers fit in, some are in dialogue with me. Maybe my team is bigger than I think.

The time taken on any one issue varies, as I do not pre-determine the narrative, therefore I really don't have any idea what will be in the content of each issue, the process reflects the unknown that is within day-to-day life. I collect material and when I have enough, I edit it down until it's ready.

What have been the important stages in the life of your magazine?
Birth. Growing up. Crying. Laughing. Studying. The respect and love of many people, and a big thanks to David Shrigley, Russell Herron and Jeremy Leslie.

What is the secret of your success?
Nice people reading and enjoying the content.

Where do you want the magazine to be in five years?
Brushing its teeth, washing the bits that show, combing its hair and getting ready for another day.

Who are your readers?
Anyone. International readership not age, gender, culture specific. From the feedback I receive, I usually like them – and I like that.

What is your relationship with advertising?
Karen doesn't carry any adverts.

How many magazines do you read?
I struggle with magazines as I find that they don't relate to my life, and I am not that unusual.
—
Answered by Karen Lubbock
Publisher
www.karenmagazine.com

# WHO ARE YOUR READERS?

AFRO
BRAND EINS
CABINET
CANADIAN ART
COUPE
DUMMY
GIRLS LIKE US
KAISERIN
LULA
NICO
NUSIGN
RUSSIA!
S MAGAZINE
TRUCE
VANIDAD
VORN
+81

# AFRO

SOUTH AFRICA

New Africa.

<u>Who are your readers?</u>
Very young Africans who want to
believe that Africa is better than the
West. And also some Europeans who
love anything from Africa because
they find it entertaining.
—

Answered by Peet Pienaar
Designer/Editor

# BRAND EINS
GERMANY

A magazine about the economy.
Its main theme is change.

Who are your readers?
People who are open to change
and the future and not afraid of it.
This means entrepeneurs as well as
freelancers in every area of business,
and also public servants, teachers,
managers. Our readers are aged
16 - 85, though most of them are
25-40 years old. And almost 40
percent of them are women.
—
Answered by Gabriele Fischer
Editor in chief
*www.brandeins.de*

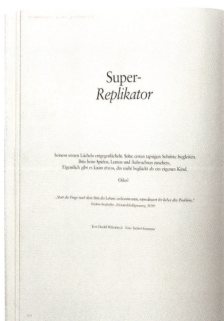

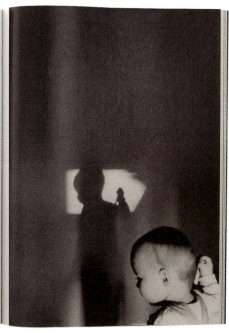

# CABINET
## UNITED STATES

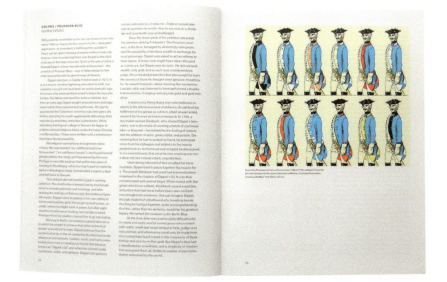

Producing a culture of curiosity about the world at large, and dismantling the divide that separates the various branches of human knowledge and activity.

Who are your readers?
We never survey our audience so we do not know. We think that roughly half of our readers are artists but we also have many historians, writers, scientists, college students (and even a few prisoners) among our readers.
—

Answered by Sina Najafi
Editor in chief/Co-founder
*www.cabinetmagazine.org*

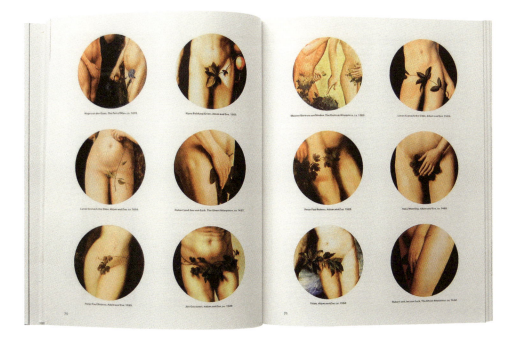

# CANADIAN ART

CANADA

# COUPE

CANADA

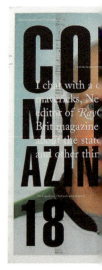

**Who are your readers?**
Our readers are spread across
Canada: one-third in large urban
centres, one-third in small and
medium-size cities, and another
third in smaller towns and rural areas.
Half of these readers have a non-
professional interest in art while 31%
are artists and 18% are involved
in visual arts professionally. 96% visit
art galleries, 75% more than four
times a year.
—
Answered by Richard Rhodes
Editor
*www.canadianart.ca*

A chronicle of the contemporary
Canadian art scene.

A magazine about visual culture.

<u>Who are your readers?</u>
Designers, creatives,
magazine whores.
—
Answered by Bill Douglas
Founder/Publisher
*www.coupe-mag.com*

# DUMMY

GERMANY

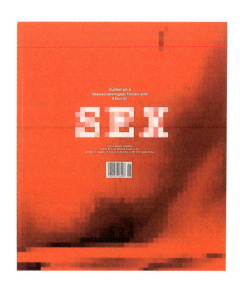

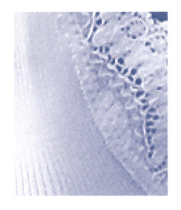

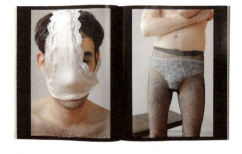

Themed around non-trendy topics.

**Who are your readers?**
Our readers live in big and bigger cities, urban centres. They hate the mainstream and they search for intelligent life out there in the mediaspace. They are politically left, which means that they have a sense of morality and integrity, but also a sense of good living, which means being surrounded by good things that make sense.
—
Answered by Oliver Gehrs
Publisher
*www.dummy-magazin.de*

# GIRLS LIKE US

NETHERLANDS

A magazine for women who are seeking a contemporary representation of lesbian identity.

<u>Who are your readers?</u>
A progressive, international audience comprised of lesbians in the 18-45 age range, looking for a fresh message and style. GLU readers are interested in design and cultural phenomena. Crossover audiences include artists and gallerists, stylists and fashion designers, and people working in media and communication.
—
Answered by
Jessica Gysel and Kathrin Hero
Editors
*www.glumagazine.com*

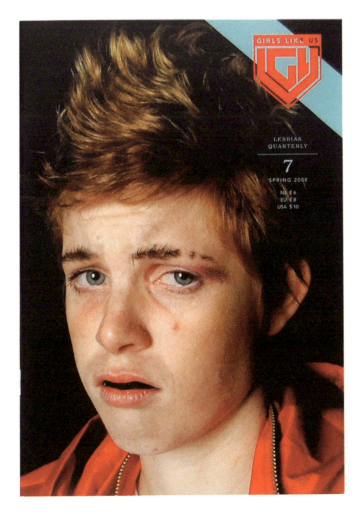

# KAISERIN

GERMANY

KAISERIN 05

a magazine for boys with problems

outside

PREMIER SEMESTRE 2009
FRANCE 6 EU €11.00   UK €8.50   USA $27.00

L'OUTSIDE

WORK No.11

# TIMBER WOLF_

| Photographies: | Lieu: | Date: |
| Grant Willing | Colorado & Massachusetts | 2005-2007 |

Avec la série "Grand County" de Grant Willing, marcher dans les traces documentaires d'un exil vagabond c'est faire l'expérience d'un *road movie* photographique au cœur de la nature sauvage. L'image transporte au gré des déplacements du photographe qui isole les clichés de son errance. Mais si cette image nomade use des instruments du réalisme, elle ne restitue jamais le réel dans son objective platitude. Alors la déroute : le document ne "donne" pas de réel mais le construit, le déplace, le met en scène. Au fond, les territoires dans lesquels il s'engage se libèrent de toute contrainte en même temps que les conditions de réception de l'œuvre se déterritorialisent. On est frappé par la caducité du traitement du paysage, et séduit par l'expérience d'un regard dé-rangé, déplacé hors du cadre naturaliste et plongé dans une mise en scène improvisée. L'économie générale du motif, minimalité (parfois à l'excès), ne se compense que par l'introduction d'éléments perturbant ce théâtre de l'extérieur : un panneau signalétique, un animal hybride, un défilé de tronçons d'arbre. Compositeur, Willing joue aussi subtilement avec les couleurs et les luminosités. Si des points roses réveillent un paysage enneigé, d'autres photos en "grisaille" introduisent un rapport distancié tant sur plan émotionnel que sur le mode du rationnel. En jouant des gros plans et des plans d'ensemble, Willing cherche autant à créer une intimité qu'à offrir une perspective contemplative. La nature vécue, pleinement pénétrée, telle est la fin de cet acte

With Grant Willing's Grand Country series, a roaming exile becomes a photographic road movie in the heart of the wilderness. The images take us in the footsteps of the photographer, freezing moments of his wanderings. But even though these nomadic images use the instruments of realism, they never reproduce reality in its objective platitude. Hence the upheaval: the document does not "give" a reality but constructs it, moves it, sets the stage for it. Deep down, the territories in which Willing moves are freed from all constraints, while the conditions in which his work is received lose their territoriality. We are struck by the obsoleteness of the landscape's treatment and seduced by the experience of a de-ranged perspective, taken out of the naturalist context and placed in an improvised setting. The general economy of the (sometimes excessively) minimalist object is only compensated by the introduction of elements that disrupt the scene from the outside: a signpost, a hybrid animal, a line of tree stump. A true composer, Willing plays subtly with colours and light. Pink dots can stimulate a snow-clad landscape, while other pictures of greyness introduce an emotional and rational distance. By the interplay of close-ups and broad perspectives, Willing aims to produce both intimacy and contemplative perspective. Experienced, entirely penetrated nature is the final purpose of this solitary, fulfilled act. So as much as he clamours, as he hitchhikes

I'D RATHER BE MASTURBATING, COLORADO, USA, 2005

solitaire pleinement réalisé. Il a alors beau clamer en partant en auto-stop *I'd rather be masturbating*, on a peine à croire que le périple ne soit pas jouissif. Le terme d'exil est ici bien approprié, s'extérioriser se conjugue avec conquérir sa liberté. Liberté de ton certes, mais encore celle de l'arrachement à l'ère du post-industriel : les maisons sont en bois, la forêt quadrille avec ses troncs la totalité de l'espace. La nature, ici rendue à sa dynamique intrinsèque, est affaire de lignes : lignes de force végétales, lignes directrices de routes esquissées, lignes de fuite enfin d'un horizon qui confond ciel et terre, plaine et sol, les dimensions même. C'est finalement moins le paysage que la dénature à laquelle nous invite Grant : un voyage en dehors, une raison de prendre l'extérieur pour lui-même. (Texte : Florian Gallé)

away, that *I'd rather be masturbating*, it is hard to believe that this exile is not sensual. The word "exile" is appropriate here, as exteriorising himself is paramount to conquering his freedom. Freedom of tone, of course, but also freedom to break away from the post-industrial era: the houses are made of wood, the forest's tree trunks fill space. Nature, returned to its intrinsic dynamic, is a matter of lines: axes of greenery, outlined roads, lines of escape, and a horizon that blends sky and earth, plank and soil, dimensions themselves. In the end, Grant invites us less to see the landscape than the denature of things: a trip outdoors, a reason to take the exterior for what it is. (Text: Florian Gallé)

www.grantwilling.com

KAISERIN MAGAZINE
- 74 -

KAISERIN MAGAZINE
- 75 -

Boys with problems and contemporary art.

Who are your readers?
Cute boys.
—

Answered by Arnaud-Pierre Fourtane and Didier Fitan Publisher/Editors
www.kaiserin-magazine.com

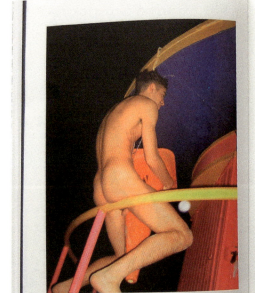

KAISERIN MAGAZINE
- 60 -

KAISERIN MAGAZINE
- 61 -

UNITED KINGDOM

Fashion and lifestyle with a difference.

Who are your readers?
It's a big mix from the very young to
the very old – and people like me!
—
Answered by Becky Smith
Creative director
*www.lulamag.com*

# NICO

LUXEMBOURG

Fashion and interviews.

Who are your readers?
The magazine is published entirely
bilingual, French/English, and we've
many readers in Paris, but we also
distribute in NY, LA, Tokyo, Australia
and all over Europe including
Amsterdam, Barcelona, Berlin,
Brussels... Wherever they are in the
world, our readers work in the creative
industries, have a strong education
and some money to spend.
—
Answered by Mike Koedinger
Publisher/Editor in chief/
Creative director
www.nicomagazine.com

# NUSIGN

FRANCE

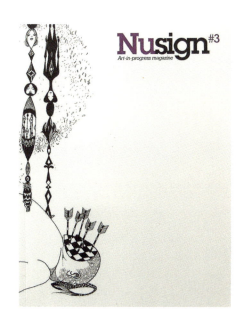

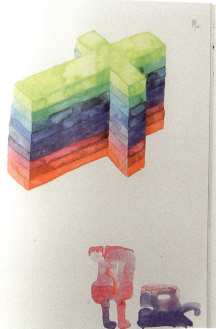

Where writing, graffiti, street art
and contemporary art collide.

Who are your readers?
From writers to museum curators.
From art students to their
teachers. Even your mum could
read Nusign magazine.
—
Answered by Piero Preitano
zFounder/Editor/Creative director
*www.myspace.com/nusign*

# RUSSIA!

UNITED STATES

Russia.

Who are your readers?
People who like well-made magazines
– and who would like to learn about
Russia from an independent,
authoritative, and entertaining source.
—

Answered by Michael Idov
Editor in Chief
*www.readrussia.com*

# S MAGAZINE

DENMARK

At the crossroads of contemporary art and culture.

Who are your readers?
Everybody who has a love for magazines, art and fashion – but also has a mind of their own and has grown tired of the conformity of traditional magazines.
—
Answered by
Martin Tradsborg Christophersen
Publisher
*www.spublication.com* .

082

# TRUCE
SWITZERLAND

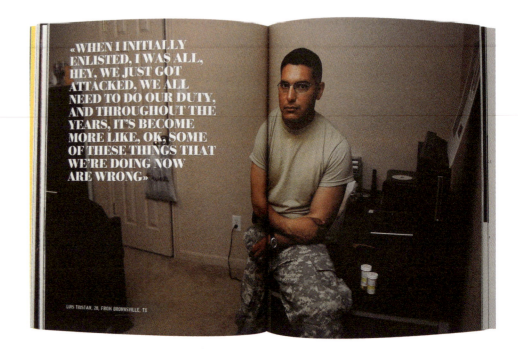

Culture, art and life.

Who are your readers?
25- to 48-year-old urban creatives
with an extraordinary sense of taste.
—
Answered by Stefan Jermann
Founder/Creative director
*www.truce.ch*

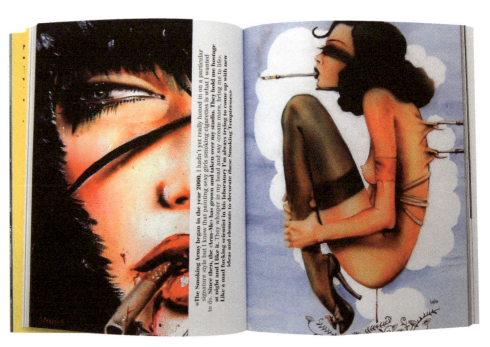

# VANIDAD

SPAIN

The original Spanish trendsetter magazine.

Who are your readers?
Our readers are aged between 18 and 35, with the majority female. They are very receptive people, concerned about local and international trends. They are creative opinion leaders in art, cinema and culture.
—

Answered by Olga Liggeri
Managing director
*www.vanidad.es*

# VORN

GERMANY

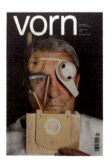

Art, design and life.

Who are your readers?
No idea… we hope intelligent people.
—
Answered by Joachim Baldauf
Co-publisher
www.vornmagazine.com

# +81

JAPAN

A Japanese design/culture magazine, introducing readers to varied and exciting creative scenes.

Who are your readers?
53% Design-related work. 22% Students. 17% Company workers.
—
Answered by Satoru Yamashita
Founder / Creative director
*www.plus81.com*

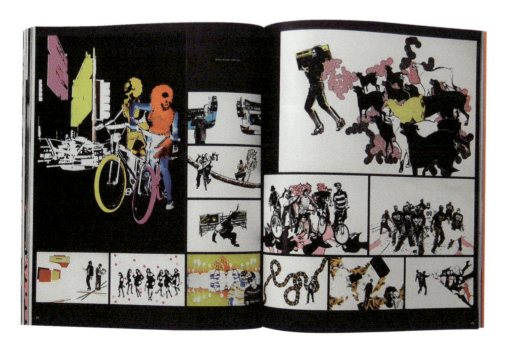

# TELL US EVERYTHING:

## KASINO A4

FINLAND

# KASINO

KASINO A4 MAGAZINE   ISSUE #8   AUTUMN/WINTER 2008–09

A4

THE BEST SEX ISSUE

THE MOST MELANCHOLY MAGAZINE

EU €7   GB £5.20   US $12.50

9 771796 061407

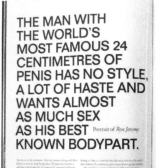

THE MAN WITH
THE WORLD'S
MOST FAMOUS 24
CENTIMETRES OF
PENIS HAS NO STYLE,
A LOT OF HASTE AND
WANTS ALMOST
AS MUCH SEX
AS HIS BEST
KNOWN BODYPART.  Portrait of *Ron Jeremy*

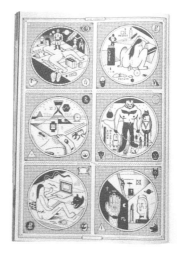

SELF SERVICE

You are your own best lover.
By Elina Pirinen, Illustration Rämi Niemi

# LIP SYNC

FEAT. OLIVIA &
NAUGHTY JAMES

FOR THOSE ABOUT TO SPAM

Every day we receive email from complete strangers,
who want to improve our sex lives. Who are they?
By Anttu Tolonen, Illustration Overture

Timeless themes with its feet in the
now.

## How did it all begin?
We wanted to create a magazine in
which we could express our vision
of magazinemaking without being
forced to compromise. The four of
us are magazine professionals with
years of experience in art directing,
photographing and writing/editing.
The founding threesome (director
of photography Jussi Puikkonen, art
director Pekka Toivonen and editor
Jonathan Mander) were already
collaborating on other projects, and
realised that this was a perfect trio for
making a fantastic magazine.
Soon we realised "perfect" was a slight
overstatement, but we were lucky to
get Antti Routto as part of the team
to assist us on all things Kasino A4
outside the magazine's pages.

## How do you make each issue?
Our core team is four people, a few
other people help us out at the busiest
times. then there's a talent pool of
around 30 writers, photographers,
illustrators, models and stylists who
contribute. We set a theme, which is
like a magnifying glass through which
we look at the world around us. We
continue discussing ideas among
ourselves and with our talent pool.
Then we fine tune the ideas and go
ahead with them. Finally, in a blinding
rush, it all comes together.

## What have been the important stages
in the life of your magazine?
Stage 1) The decision to make the
first (#0) magazine. And getting
it done within a month. Stage 2)
Getting international distribution
for the second issue (#1-2) through
ExportPress. Stage 3) I predict several
important steps for 2009.

## What is the secret of your success?
We never compromise our vision.

## Who are your readers?
Open-minded creatives around
the world.

## What is your relationship with
advertising?
We look for brands that are a natural
fit with our vision. In that sense, the
content dictates the advertising not
vice versa.

## Where do you want the magazine
to be in five years?
Quality bookshelves.
—
Answered by Jonathan Mander
Editor
*www.wearekasino.com*

# TELL US
# EVERYTHING:

# LA MÁS BELLA

SPAIN

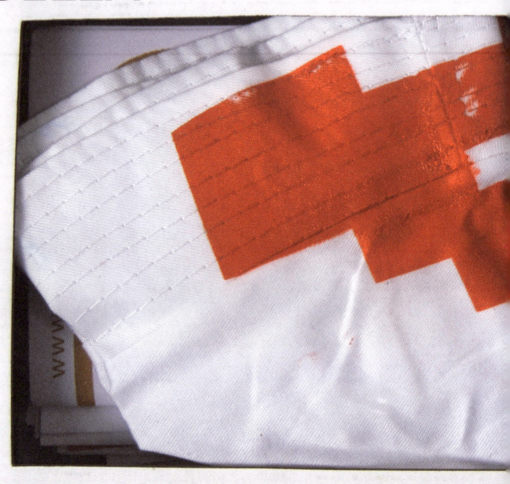

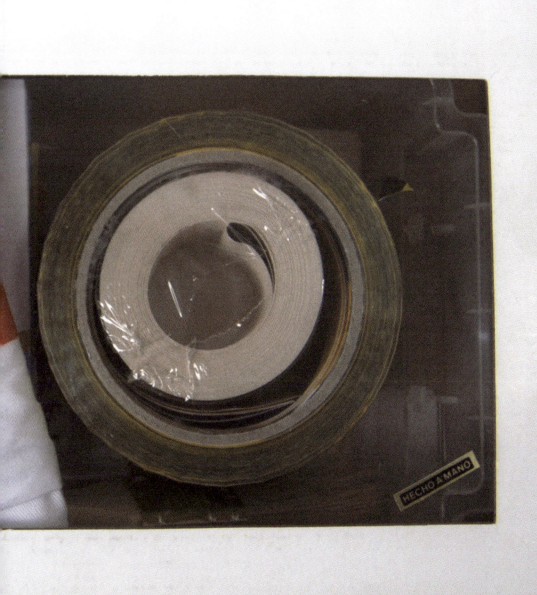
HECHO A MANO

# la más bella

# de pega

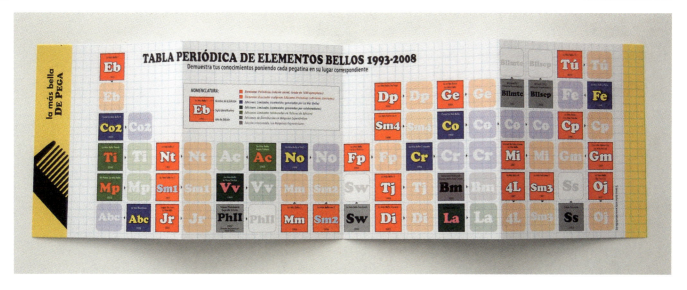

Contemporary art; La Más Bella is Spanish for "the most beautiful".

How did it all begin?
La Más Bella was born in 1993, published by Diego Ortiz and Pepe Murciego in Madrid. All the contents of the magazine were and are contributions by artists made specially for La Más Bella, according to our proposals. We make La Más Bella as a personal artistic project, we don't have any commercial aims.

How do you make each issue?
La Más Bella publishes one big edition per year. Our team is just two people, Pepe and Diego. We ask for contributions, almost one hundred artists in every new edition, and we do everything with our own money and effort.

What have been the important stages in the life of your magazine?
The most important step was fifteen years ago, when we decided to make "a fanzine or something like that". Nowadays La Más Bella is almost our main personal and professional activity, so every new day is an important step for the project.

What is the secret of your success?
To make something personal, different and fun. And of course, the work of the contributors, really the most important ingredient of La Más Bella.

Where do you want the magazine to be in five years?
Our plan is just to survive.

Who are your readers?
La Más Bella is interesting for anyone involved in the worlds of contemporary art, experimental poetry, sound and video art, visual poetry, performance art. We publish art, so our audience is also people involved in that world, either as an artist or collector.

What is your relationship with advertising?

We have not any relationship with this world. Our only relationship with advertising is when an advertising agency copies our ideas to make their work, which has happened a couple of times.

How many magazines do you read?
One of us is a hardcore collector of magazines, the other doesn't read any. These are two different types of foolish.
—
Answered by Diego Ortiz
Co-publisher
*www.lamasbella.org*

# WHAT IS YOUR RELATIONSHIP WITH ADVERTISING?

ATYPICA
B-GUIDED
CELESTE
CODE
DESIGN INDABA
DOT DOT DOT
FAIRY TALE
MK BRUCE/LEE
MONUMENT
MOUVEMENT
NEO2
NEUE MODE
PARKETT
REVOLVER
YUMMY

# ATYPICA
ARGENTINA

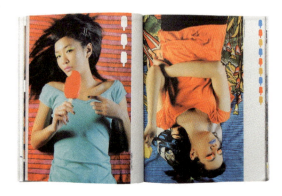

Life, death, urban and rural culture, fashion, watermelons and music.

What is your relationship
with advertising?
Probably one of the best things we've achieved is to make our advertisers understand that is better for them to not have any influence over our editorial content. It's one of our key secrets (the other one is that we design our mag in CorelDRAW....
shhhhhhhhhh).
—

Answered by Ygelman Guillermina
Founder
www.atypica.com.ar

# B-GUIDED

SPAIN

Emergent ideas on contemporary culture that represent cultural evolution, the dynamism of the market, symbols of our times and a commitment to creativity.

What is your relationship with advertising?
We work with brands who make products we are interested in. Otherwise, they would not advertise in our magazine and we would not propose that they should.

If you aim to have a certain level of quality in your work, you will do that regardless of whether or not your work is influenced by your clients. For me, to be influenced by advertisers doesn't mean a loss of quality; if you're professional, your work doesn't have to be any less creative or less authentic for it.
—

Answered by Juan Montenegro
Editor in chief/Art director
www.b-guided.com

# CELESTE

MEXICO

A unique, quarterly editorial project that addresses and questions contemporary culture in its many disciplines.

<u>What is your relationship with advertising?</u>
Advertisers are our means of survival, so they deserve all of our appreciation and respect. They are brands and companies that believe in the project so much they are willing to invest on it. It would be untruthful to say they don't influence our content, because they do; but we don't see this fact as a negative thing.

One of our most emblematic issues, Manipulación (number 6, summer 2002) basically assumed, embraced and celebrated this fact and to prove our point we sold our cover to Absolut Vodka. And I don't mean it was a case of product placement; we literally sold the space, and ran a full page ad. Advertising affects and influences collective consciousness, so we decided to embrace this fact.

A magazine like ours can't pretend to talk about contemporary culture without addressing advertising, moreover because some of the people we admire and write about in the magazine are the same people that are designing and photographing the ads.
—
Answered by Carbajal Carlos
Commercial director
*www.celeste.com.mx*

NETHERLANDS

Explores the boundaries of documentary photography as a means to depict fashion.

### What is your relationship with advertising?

Advertising does influence our content in the sense that advertising brands (can) expect to be in the magazine. I have no problem at all with that. Pretty much all of the brands advertising in CODE match the world of the magazine, and a fashion magazine is not a news magazine. Advertising does not influence our content in the sense that we cannot feature things we would like to feature.

We also have paid-for editorials that we call 'collaborators'. They are exactly this: creative collaborations and recognisable as such for the reader, since they are titled 'collab'.

The idea of 'journalistic independence and objectivity' is a grossly overrated notion. Read Noam Chomsky and you're done with the idea of independent media. What a magazine has to strive for is to stay true to its identity. All a niche magazine has, in these times of fast information, is (creative) credibility. This is the reason for a reader to buy the magazine and for an marketeer to advertise.

Sacrificing that means sacrificing the long-term potential of a title and destroying the interests of the advertisers who bought into this identity.
—
Answered by Peter Van Rhoon
Editor in chief
www.code-mag.nl

# DESIGN INDABA

SOUTH AFRICA

# DOT DOT DOT

UNITED STATES

The design of language.

<u>What is your relationship with advertising?</u>
We have an eccentric advertising system involving standardised pages that look the same, with text inserted by anyone interested (with money); the contrast of the text increases according to the money paid. This was because: a) We didn't like ugly adverts, and b) It seemed and interesting way of exposing the economics without necessarily damaging those advertising.

Ultimately they appear to work as any other ad, so no one loses. I have a suspicion that all ads everywhere could just be the names of whatever the products or companies are, no images, no differentiation, and little would change.
—
Answered by Stuart Bailey
Editor
*www.dot-dot-dot.us*

An inclusive view of design.

<u>What is your relationship with advertising?</u>
Traditionally, the Design Indaba magazine has not been seen as an income-generator, so we have no advertising sales staff and very little advertising. Most of the advertising forms part of the sponsorship contract for the Design Indaba Conference and Expo. As such, we agree not to allow our sponsors' competitors to advertise. Any advertising-driven editorial or advertorial is marked as such – whether paid for or through trade exchange.
—
Answered by Nadine Botha
Editor
*www.designindabamag.com*

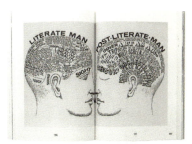

# FAIRY TALE
FRANCE

Fashion.

<u>What is your relationship
with advertising?</u>
We don't have advertising.
Sometimes we include something like
an ad for an institution we work with,
like the Cac Bretigny Gallery or the
Documenta 12 Festival. But in general
we don't have advertising, because
for us it is very important that we have
the freedom to create an independent
work, from the first page to the last,
without interruption.
—
Answered by
Achim Reichert and Marco Fiedler
Editors
*www.fairytale-magazine.com*

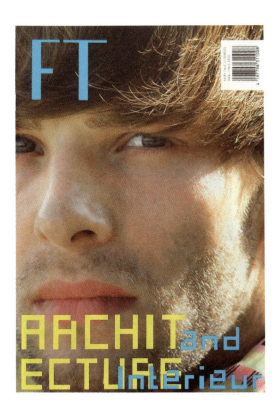

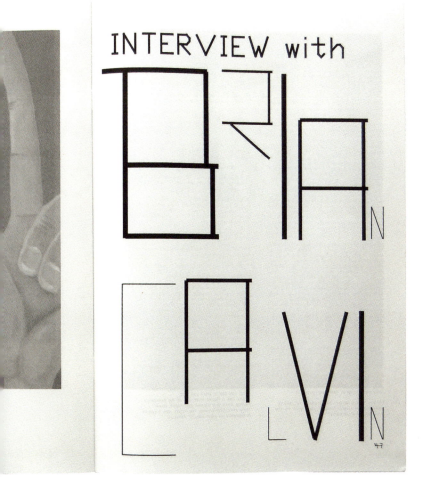

# MK BRUCE / LEE

SOUTH AFRICA

A loose-bound magazine for viewers of South African music channel, MK.

What is your relationship with advertising?
We have a unique advertising strategy in that we don't carry run-of-paper ads, only inserts. This creates a unique sampling opportunity for advertisers and added value for our readers.
—
Answered by Hannerie Visser
Business director
*www.mkbrucelee.co.za*

# MONUMENT
AUSTRALIA

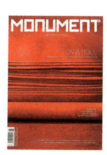

Architecture and design.

What is your relationship
with advertising?
We have a holistic approach
towards advertising and consider
it in every step of the process.
—
Answered by Leanne Amodeo
Editor
*www.monumentmagazine.com.au*

# MOUVEMENT

FRANCE

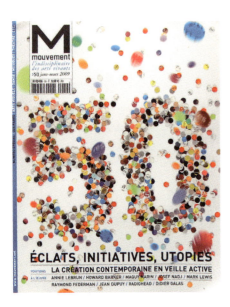

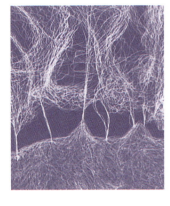

Contemporary artistic expression.

**What is your relationship with advertising?**

This is always an awkward topic. On one hand, Mouvement is highly dependent on advertisements, since more than 50% of our turnover stems from it. On the other hand, our independence protects us from the intrusion we are now used to noticing in the press every day (advertising-driven-editorials are one of the most serious diseases in today's press, and one of the reasons why journalism tends to merge with mere communication).

We do our best to keep the editorial part of the magazine as independent as possible from the advertisements, even with the "partnerships" we regularly organise; and I must say that it is very seldom that an editorial decision is linked to an advertisement.

I think this is precisely one of the things that advertisers may find attractive ("qualitative", as they say) in our magazine: the advertisements are not intrusive at all since they are divided in two blocks, 10 pages in the first half, 10 pages in the second half

of every issue. These are treated with the same attention paid to aesthetics and content as the rest of the magazine. In this way, I'd say that our advertisements are influenced by our content, rather than the other way around.

—

Answered by David Sanson
Editor in chief
*www.mouvement.net*

# NEO2

SPAIN

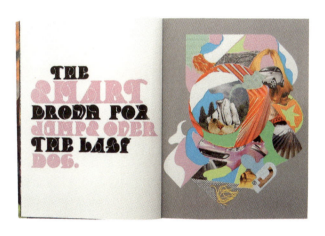

Creativity in all areas.

<u>What is your relationship
with advertising?</u>
We love advertisements, we come
from advertising backgrounds.
Everything in life influences our
content, including advertisements
– what is important is not losing our
soul. Readers are the ones who decide
which magazines still have one.

—

Answered by Ramón, Rubén,
Javier Fano, Manrique, Abio
Editors/Directors
*www.neo2.es*

# NEUE MODE

GERMANY

New platforms for personal communication.

What is your relationship
with advertising?
From the beginning, the aim was to
combine commercial commissions
with strong editorial content. Making
use of advertising-driven editorials is
a very good, subliminal way to focus
the reader's mind on a specific theme,
provided that the magazine remains
in total control of the representation.
—

Answered by Oliver Daxenbichler
Editor in chief/Publisher
*www.neuemodemagazine.com*

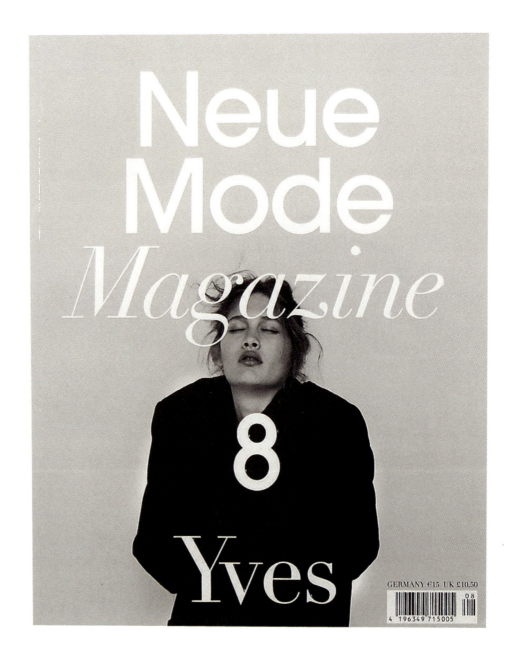

# PARKETT

SWITZERLAND

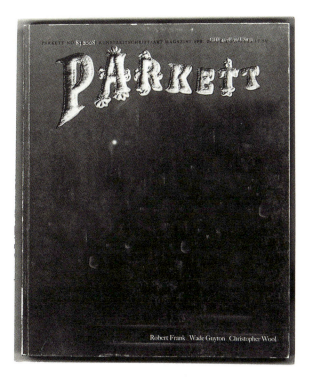

Collaborations with important contemporary artists.

What is your relationship
with advertising?
Advertising is placed at the back
of the magazine. Unlike some art
magazines, Parkett does not
publish exhibition reviews in
exchange for ads.
—

Answered by Dieter von Graffenried
Publisher
*www.parkettart.com*

# REVOLVER

FRANCE

How films are and will be made.

What is your relationship
with advertising?
We decided early on not to work with
advertisers, and there are no regrets.
—
*www.revolver-film.de*

# YUMMY

FRANCE

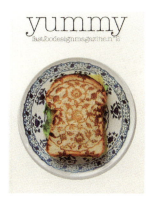

Junk food and more.

What is your relationship
with advertising?
I don't have any problem with the fact
that ads can drive editorials in fashion
mags. Those are the rules of a clever
business system.

We would love to sell more
advertisements but we don't have
time to work on it. Help!
—

Answered by Pascal Monfort
Editor in chief/Publisher
www.eat-fast.net

# TELL US EVERYTHING:

## LIEBLING

GERMANY

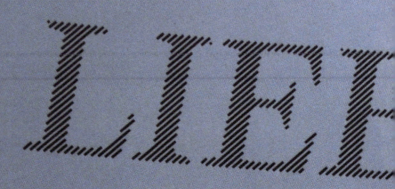

er / Dezember 2008

# LING

E, FILM, MUSIK UND KUNST

WEIZ SFR 5.90 | LUXEMBURG EUR 3.30

2,80 EUR

The glamour of empathy; Liebling is German for "darling".

How did it all begin?
Liebling was founded in 2005 by Götz Offergeld and Rahel Morgen. They published four issues in two years, then put Liebling on hiatus in 2006. In December 2007, the magazine was revived and reinvented. Markus Peichl, founder of the trailblazing 1980s magazines Tempo and Wiener, became the new publisher. A larger team of editors was assembled around editor-in-chief Anne Urbauer and art director Mario Lombardo, to guarantee a new bi-monthly publishing schedule.

How do you make each issue?
The team consists of two editors-in-chief, the art director, one graphic designer, three staff editors, one fashion director, two managers handling ads, printing and distribution, and a steady circle of freelance contributors of art, design, photography and writing. We spend six weeks making each issue, with roughly two weeks of intensive production time before going to print.

What have been the important stages in the life of your magazine?
When Alek Wek, Adam Kimmel and Terence Koh called at the same moment and said: "We have to be in this magazine."

What is the secret of your success?
Love and care for the people and things we embrace in the magazine. Finding the angle to a story that no one else has. And the ability to go 48 hours without sleep every two months.

Where do you want the magazine to be in five years?
Still here, of course, as fertile ground for new talent, new thoughts and visuals and in the hearts of its readers.

Who are your readers?
We want to reach everyone who's interested in what we are doing. Every age, every scene. Curiosity is the only criterion. Liebling readers possess a finely tuned radar for aesthetics, beauty and the vigor of life in all its shapes and sizes. A used piece of soap may appear as beautiful to them as the latest Gareth Pugh fashion collection.

What's your relationship with advertisements?
The support of advertisers who respect independent and credible voices in an otherwise-stalling magazine market is crucial. Our clients understand our concept and appreciate it. Just as we strive for collaborations with artists, we collaborate with advertisers who share our vision as well. However, advertisers have no influence on our editorial content. It might well be the other way round, since we are working with them on new concepts to communicate. Savvy readers are tired of fake editorial pages selling out to advertisers, and they are jaded by what we know as print advertising. It's time for something new and genuine.

How many magazines do you read?
We spend a lot of money on magazines from abroad. While we professionally scan almost every magazine, we only spend time with what is interesting. There are too many me-too products out there.
—
Answered by Markus Peichl
Publisher
*www.liebling-zeitung.com*

# TELL US EVERYTHING:

## NUKE

FRANCE

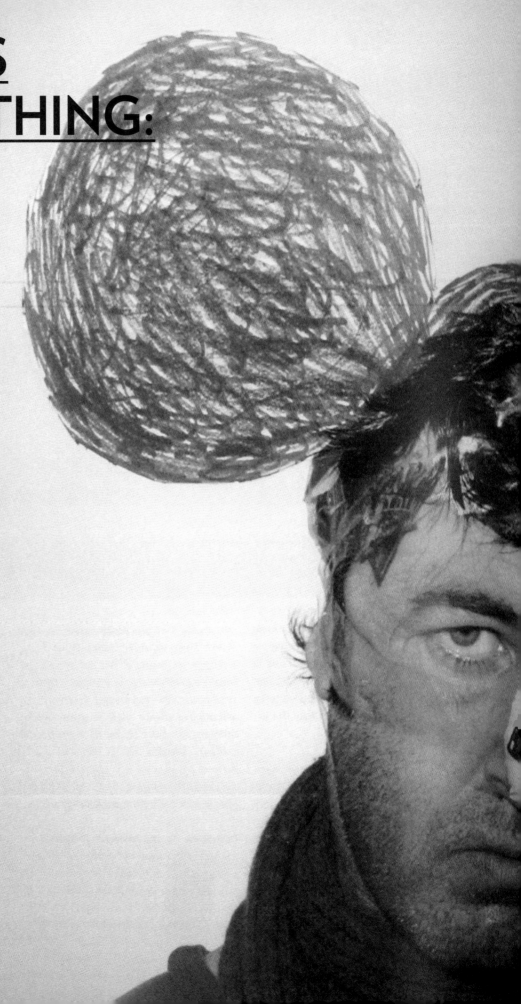

NUKE *Trouble* N°6

**WOMAN ISSUE**

France 10€   USA 19.99 U$   UK £7.80   Italy 11€   Belgium 11€   Austria 12€   Suisse 20€   Allemagne 12.50€

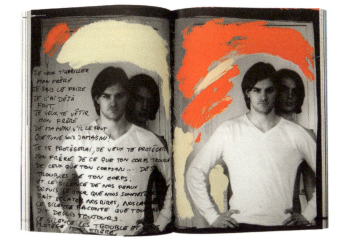

Female Trouble

Époque Troublée

L'art de l'éthique

The polluted generation, the
late arrivals.

How did it all begin?
In 2004, Swedish art director Jenny
Mannerheim launches Nuke
magazine and opens her own gallery
in Paris at the same time, Galerie
Nuke. During her years as art director
at major fashion magazines in Paris,
she feels the need to launch a product
that is not journalistic but rather a
platform for artists to express

themselves as freely as in their
art work.

Nuke 'Generation Polluée' is an art
magazine for artists, designers and
writers. It's not a journalistic magazine
and is not targeting critics, the market
etc. It aims to give space to issues like
global capitalism and political
despotism, with themes such as
historical change, economic forces,
death, guilt, destruction and beauty,
as opposed to being focused on the
internal concerns of artmaking.

Jenny continues to develop Nuke
magazine and gallery in parallel
with her career as art director for
Blast, Extra Small and Intersection
magazines as well as for the
contemporary art book series
"Madeby".

How do you make each issue?
We produce our magazine with
(a little) help from advertisers, sales
at Galerie Nuke and services that

we can provide such as consulting
or art directing.

What have been the important stages
in the life of your magazine?
Various encounters with artists.

What is the secret of your success?
Our straightforwardness and desire
to communicate deeper issues such
as death, guilt, destruction and
beauty, with no real economical
purpose. I believe Nuke and "Polluted
generation, the late arrivals" evoke a
philosophical purpose in the heads of
our readers and collaborators.

Where do you want the magazine to
be in five years?
In a world that is not divided into rich
and poor, a place where everyone has
the right to healthcare, education,
freedom of expression.

Who are your readers?
People interested in art, photography,
ideas and literature.

How is your relationship with
advertising?
Our relationship with advertising is
very good, I just wish that advertisers
understood our magazine better.
Sometimes, if we do special
operations with advertisers, we
propose editorial content, and we
are very happy to do this because
we collaborate with brands that
understand our editorial concept.

How many magazines do you read?
Maybe 10 a week, far too many.
I always buy commercial magazines
such as Elle, Vanity Fair, Vogue
because I like reading the news
sections.
—
Answered by Jenny Mannerheim
Publisher/Creative director
*www.nuke.fr*

# WHAT IS THE SECRET OF YOUR SUCCESS?

BON
CAPRICIOUS
CARL'S CARS
CHIMURENGA
DATUM
D[X]I
E&A
FRIEZE
HOTROD
LEMON
LING
LITTLE WHITE LIES
OMAGIU
QVEST
+ROSEBUD
SLEEK
THIS IS A MAGAZINE

# BON

SWEDEN

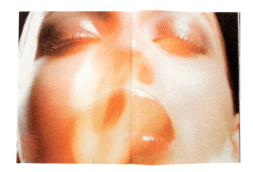

Fashion, art and innovative technology; the forces that drive popular culture.

What is the secret of your success?
I like to think that we are a fashion magazine with a brain. I also think we have the most sensitive antennae when it comes to picking up the important changes and innovations that affect society in general, and more specifically popular culture. I also think it helps that Bon is a great 10-minute visual experience but at the same time a publication that our audience, according to surveys, spends hours reading.

I also hope the fact that we stand for certain things, such as not using fur or anorexic models, is something our readers appreciate. And perhaps our final secret is that Bon is a nice magazine. We prefer to be passionate about things and tell people that we are, rather than waste our energy on being too cool for school.
—
Answered by Madelaine Levy
Editor in chief
*www.bonmagazine.com*

# CAPRICIOUS

UNITED STATES

A magazine for emerging fine
art photographers from all over
the world.

What is the secret of your success?
Never stop fighting for what you
believe in. I learned it from the
forest spirit.
—
Answered by Sophie Mörner
Founder
*www.becapricious.com*

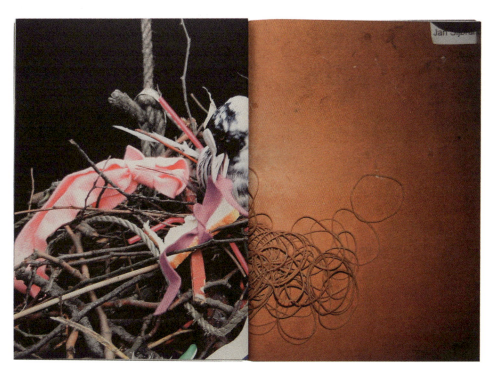

# CARL'S CARS

NORWAY

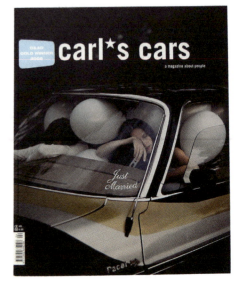

Carl's Cars is about people and cars in popular culture, design and art. It tries to capture that special mood when you drive without a purpose.

What is the secret of your success? It depends on how you measure success: Carl's Cars is a personal project that is not just another job. We wake up in the morning happy to know that we have a very loyal readership that appreciates what we are trying to create.
—
Answered by
Stéphanie Dumont-Haug
Creative director
www.carls-cars.com

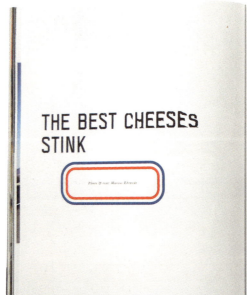 

# CHIMURENGA

SOUTH AFRICA

An advertising-free, non-profit platform from which Africans speak for themselves, to themselves, and to the world. The name Chimurenga is a Shona word loosely translated as 'struggle'.

What is the secret of your success?
Respect for authors/artists, the written word, the reader/viewer, our contributors, Africa and the human race.
—
Answered by Liepollo Rantekoa
Production/Distribution manager
*www.chimurenga.co.za*

# DATUM

AUSTRIA

# D[X]I

SPAIN

Politics, media and society as well as contemporary culture and science.

**What is the secret of your success?**
Until the beginning of 2006, everyone including the editor was working for free, so we more or less only had to take care of the printing bills. Since we've been successful in selling the magazine, most of the money that comes in through ads we put into marketing and promotion. Our business philosophy is very conservative: make small steps, keep a tight grip on the money and through this make small, but significant progress.
—
Answered by Klaus Stimeder
Chief editor
*www.datum.at*

A free, quarterly experimental platform devoted to creativity, visual culture and contemporary art.

What is the secret of your success ? We are not afraid. The magazine is open to experimentation, without prejudice. d[x]i is a mixture of artistic disciplines that are often separated. Design magazines are usually printed on good quality paper, and we want to demonstrate that we can make a good magazine using very cheap paper – what seems to be correct doesn't have to be a rule.
—
Answered by Alejandro Benavent González, Publisher
*www.dximagazine.com*

# E&A

UNITED STATES

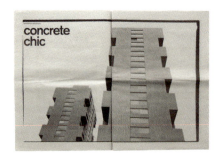

Fashion, pop & art.

What is the secret of your success?
Personality.

—

Answered by Katia Kuethe
Publisher/Creative director
*www.theglossyzine.com*

FRIEZE

UNITED KINGDOM

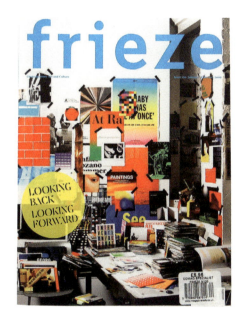

Contemporary art and culture.

What is the secret of your success?
Astute critical analysis, exquisite
design and the trust of our
audience through using informed,
dedicated writers.
—

Answered by Camilla Nicholls
Head of Communications
www.frieze.com

# HOTROD
NORWAY

Art and culture.

What is the secret of your success ?
Listen to your gut feeling, trust
yourself and have fun.
—

Answered by Jan Walaker
Founder

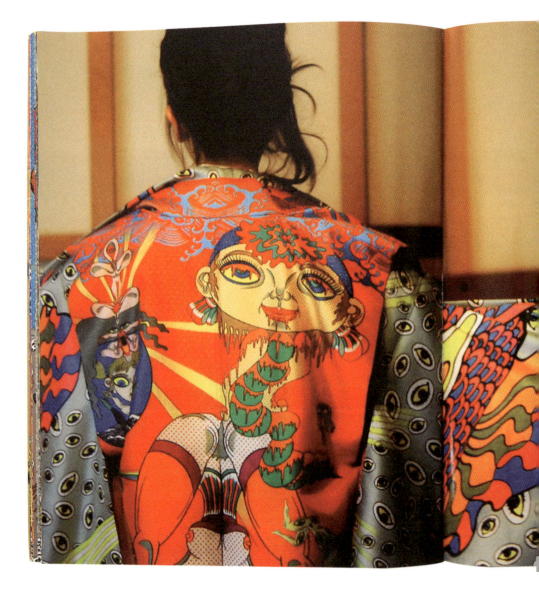

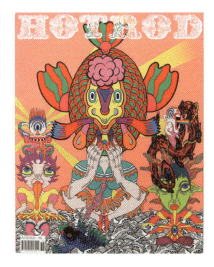

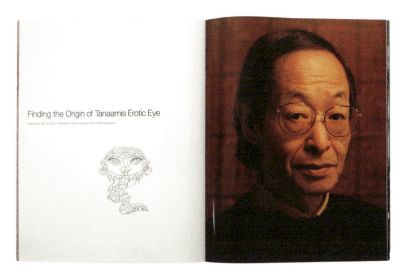

Finding the Origin of Tanaamis Erotic Eye

132

# LEMON

UNITED STATES

Pop culture with a twist.

What is the secret of your success?
The sheer time and effort that goes
into creating so much detail and
crafted continuity. It's prohibitive,
but it shows in the end.
—

Answered by
Kevin Grady and Colin Metcalf
Founders
www.lemonland.net

# LING

SPAIN

People and their cities, for passengers of the airline Vueling.

What is the secret of your success?
A conviction that you don't need much money to make a great publication (or to enjoy yourself, for that matter). A restlessness to constantly try out new things and to improve. We take our readers seriously. Our groundbreaking design. A lot of love.
—
Answered by Kati Krause
Editor
www.lingmagazine.com

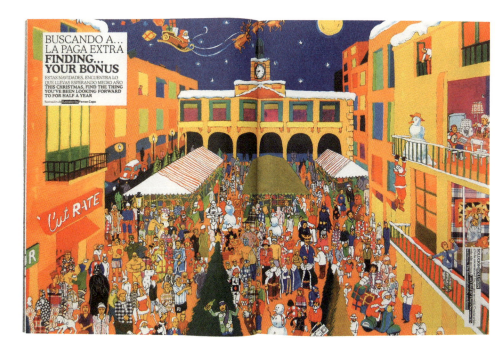

# LITTLE WHITE LIES

UNITED KINGDOM

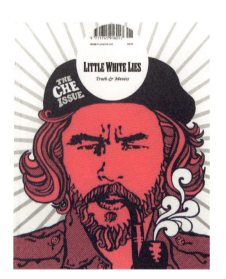

Life, truth and movies.

What is the secret of your success ?
Passion. The magazine is built on
blood, sweat and tears. If we weren't
totally committed and prepared to
make sacrifices, it wouldn't exist.
—

Answered by Matthew Bochenski
Editor
www.littlewhitelies.co.uk

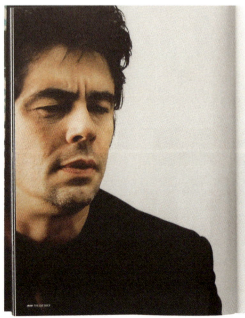

BENICIO DEL
TORO TALKS
EXCLUSIVELY TO
LWLIES ABOUT
CHE GUEVARA,
AMERICAN
TERRORISM
AND THE ALL-
IMPORTANT
DIFFERENCE
BETWEEN CRAZY
AND 'CRAZY'
CRAZY. WORDS
BY MIKE BRETT
PHOTOGRAPHY BY
SAM CHRISTMAS

# OMAGIU
ROMANIA

Remix culture; original voices from young Romanian creatives. Its name means 'homage'.

What is the secret of your success? Our ability to blend contrasting realities and borderline cultures. We follow, mostly, deviations from the norm.
—
Answered by Mihaela Popa
Art director
*www.omagiu.com*

# QVEST

GERMANY

Fashion, art, design, architecture
and lifestyle.

<u>What is the secret of your success?</u>
QVEST is a voluminous magazine
with a classic structure. In each
issue, we feature the most interesting
personalities from our areas of
interest, trace successful careers and
prepare the ground for promising
newcomers. Interest in fashion is
a global phenomenon; that's the
way we see it and present it. This
means our view of the fashion world
encompasses more than just Milan,
Paris, London and New York. Our
compass points north, south, east
and west. For us, a stylish design for
a new sports car is just as interesting
as the latest outdoorwear, a high-
tech trend in industrial design or an
interview with a long-silent star of
haute couture.
—
Answered by
Stefanie Troger and Line Jacobi
Marketing department
*www.qvest.de*

# +ROSEBUD

GERMANY

An ongoing experiment, exploring as-yet unused possibilities and potentials of paper and print

<u>What is the secret of your success?</u>
We invest a huge amount of time (sometimes months) to define the main theme and develop the creative brief for each issue. Then we invite our contributors, who range from designers and artists to writers, scientists, critics and more, to take part.

The key feature of the project is constant change: content, design, production and staff are always completely different from the previous issue. People know that they don't know what they will get.
—
Answered by Ralf Herms
Founder/Publisher
*www.rosebudmagazine.com*

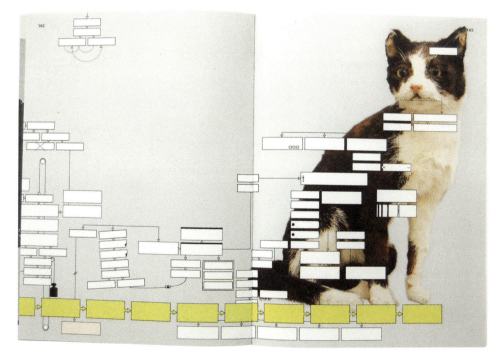

# SLEEK

GERMANY

The glamour of fashion combined with the intellect of contemporary art.

What is the secret of your success?
Being curious, stubborn and ignorant.
—

Answered by Lothar Eckstein
Publisher
*www.sleek-mag.com*

# THIS IS
# A MAGAZINE

ITALY

This is a magazine about nothing.

What is the secret of your success?
If by success you mean popularity,
freely available internet.
—
Answered by
Donnachie/Simionato
Futurologists
*www.thisisamagazine.com*
*www.thisisnotamagazine.com*

tight, on request, dress MULBERRY
neck choker J MASKREY
bra PHYLEA PARIS
leather hot pants STYLIST'S OWN
on ornahyra, dress VIVIENNE WESTWOOD
tights WOLFORD
*opposite page*
jumper GILES
belt ALAIA
leather hot pants STYLIST'S OWN
harness PHYLEA PARIS

# TELL US
# EVERYTHING:

## SANG BLEU

SWITZERLAND

SANG BLEU

→PAGE 7

→PAGE 273

ISSN 1752-1955

SANG BLEU ISSUE III/IV, 2009, EU 44 €, UK 33 £, CHF 66

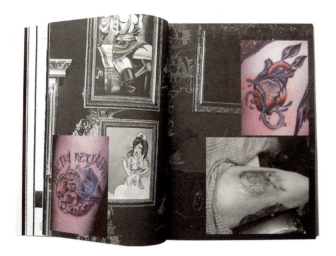

Pain and beauty.

How did it all begin?
Sang Bleu is a way for me to cook together all the things I love: Tattoo, Arts, fashion, literature, typography, photography, fetish, etc, and to have the opportunity to collaborate with people I love and look up to.

Sang Bleu was born in London in 2006, but had been an omnipresent idea for years before that. I had moved to London in 2005 after a short stay in Paris, where I worked for Self Service magazine. And before that I had worked in Zürich for NORM, but it just seemed neither Zürich nor Paris were the right places for me and my gestating baby. In London, I worked for a design studio

called North design, and for Arena Homme +. I am also, with Ian Party, the founder of B&P Typefoundry.

The idea of Sang Bleu had come naturally from a conjunction of events that occurred in my life since my early 20s and even before. I started studying graphic design, editorial design, typography and art at the ECAL (art school in Lausanne Switzerland) in 2000. From there, I grew a particular taste for printed matter and photography. Later, in 2002 (I think), I started getting tattooed.

My first tattoo was a back piece by Filip Leu. At the same time, I started to get more personally involved in the tattoo culture, which also allowed me to notice certain deficiencies in the panorama of tattoo-related publications.

So the idea of SB came naturally from a desire for a publication that would approach tattoo, and also other underground, cultures from another angle and would also address the way mainstream cultures such as Contemporary Art or fashion use, draw inspiration from or recycle them, and address this with a real critical sense and not with complacency or

anger. In a way, SB, takes things seen as vile and shows what's noble in them.

How do you make each issue?
Sang Bleu is an ongoing project and each issue simply represents a certain moment of my life and all the important people and things that it contains. Generally, I've tried to work with people I trust and who, I feel, share my values and visions, while still being complementary in some ways. My "team" is mainly composed of (besides me): Jeanne-Salomé Rochat (Arts Editor), Adrian Wilson (London Fashion Director), Lotta Skeletrix & Alban Adam (Fashion Editors), Craig Burton (Photographer).

What have been the important stages in the life of your magazine?
There is nothing I can point out really except some important proofs of trust and support I got from people I looked up to, and from friends who showed amazing love and some financial support as well.

What is the secret of your success?
Trust, love and hard work.

Where do you want the magazine to be in five years?
Hopefully, the magazine will be able to survive by itself financially and/or

will have given birth to other, more defined projects, such as art shows, books, films, etc.

Who are your readers?
They are split between people from the tattoo/fetish/body modification culture, people into fashion, people into the arts or into graphic design/typography/publishing. But generally, I think (hope) all these people share a passion for beauty and firewalking.

What's your relationship with advertising?
I have only had advertising from a few people who had a real understanding of the project and therefore didn't try to modify it. On the contrary, they were happy to blend in. I could compromise a bit if it allowed me to struggle less moneywise, but I am bad at doing what I'm asked to.

How many magazines do you read?
Most of the magazines I am after are biannual. I just got back from a shopping spree at RD Franks and Artwords bookshops, and bought £300 worth of magazines.
—
Answered by Maxime Buechi
Editor/Creative director/
Fashion editor/Editor in chief
www.sangbleu.com

# TELL US EVERYTHING:

# VOLUME

NETHERLANDS

Acre, Amazonia, 2006: An Ashaninka Indian paints patterns
as a social contract on her body. The patterns symbolize social
cohesion and local culture and serve as a protective shield
for culture in the new territories.

PATTERN PROTECTS !

"I PAINT PATTERNS ON A SCHOOL THE SAME
WAY I PAINT PATTERNS ON MY FACE,
TO PROTECT MYSELF AND MY CULTURE."
ASHANINKA INDIAN

~SCHOOL, ASHANINKA TERRITORY,
AMAZONIAN

Roof Marsh, 2008.

### The Post-Capitalist City Tagging Cloud
**Getting to grips with new ideas on unreal estate and urban sustainability**

This cloud of words forms the foundation of the many discourses, visions, imaginings, ambitions and agendas concerning the elusive notion of the 'Post-Capitalist City'. These terms can be conservative or revolutionary, practical or impractical, realistic or fairly utopian. We deliberately present them here without definition, since that would effectively prohibit something of their dynamism; and we subsequently propose a 'free association style' usage of this vocabulary in forming new ideas. We challenge you to pick and chose, stumble through the words and come to your own understanding of the possible futures of areas like Detroit, South Side Chicago, Rajasthan, Acre and Eindhoven, in a moment of global credit-crunch and political pessimism.

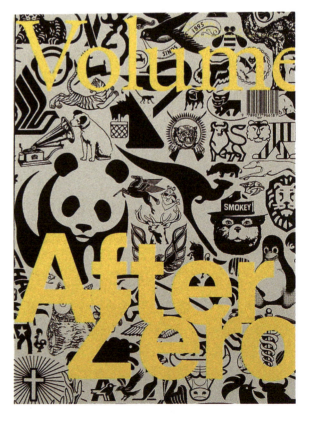

Photo Amy Davis, 2005

The preceding take place in dead zones not only with respect to free-market capitalism, but also to formal politics. Yet this is not to say that the occupations of unreal estate are apolitical. Rather it is to assert the difference between governmental politics and non-governmental politics and to locate the politics of unreal estate in the latter – a politics devoid of aspirations to govern. Like exits or expulsions from the market economy, rejections of formalized politics also comprise invitations: to neglect rather than resist, to mimic rather than replace, to supplant rather than reverse. These are invitations to consider political change and difference not even from the ground up, for the ground too is generally the province of the state, but on other grounds entirely, grounds that can usefully go by the name of 'unreal.'

The Detroit Unreal Estate Agency's disengagement from projects to save, solve or resolve Detroit does not comprise a denial or acceptance of the city's very real suffering and very real violence. On the contrary: for the agency it is the metaphysics of capitalism that provides the terms to marginalize and normalize suffering and violence. What is really necessary is to imagine and construct a world in which suffering and violence should have no place – a world beyond sustainability, at least as the term is framed in its usual contexts, and one that is in the present circumstances wholly unreal.

**Have We Got a Deal For You!**
Among the actions currently planned by the Detroit Unreal Estate Agency is the production of an *Unreal Estate Guide to Detroit*, a collective atlas of the city's alternative urbanisms currently undertaken by cultural entrepreneurs of all sorts; the formation of an activist land bank by means of which the agency will make

properties it has acquired or appropriated from among the 80,000 abandoned properties in Detroit available for year-long projects by artists, architects and community activists; the utilization of Detroit as a laboratory of alternative urbanisms in a series of workshops; and other programs that attempt to discover urban epistemologies adequate to the city's most veritable unrealities. The agency's 'agents' are envisioned as a loosely-organized experimental community with varied and unpredictable relations to one another and to the agency's only partly interconnected actions. These actions are envisioned as generative as well as reflective, with the definition, location, representation and exhibition of unreal estate opening up these estates both to each other and to a translocal array of other sites, other agents and other agencies.

Through these actions the Detroit Unreal Estate Agency does not propose to advance unreality as a new or counter-reality. It does not aim at a passage out from ideological aestheticizations of Detroit – whether the state-sponsored aesthetics of banality that structure representations of an 'ordinary' city or the slightly more provocative aesthetics of sublime urban ruins. It does not intend to hold a space open for supposedly non-aestheticized representations produced by the city's 'real' residents, stake-holders, avatars or shamans. It does not expect to extract profit from Detroit, introducing representations of a novel locality into a global circuit in which such representations are currently the object of intense speculation. Instead it poses unreal estate as merely a *different* mode of aestheticization, one whose current value lies in ignoring value, at least in its hegemonic formulation.

Image Koert van Mensvoort

## Next Nature

'Nature' is one of the most successful products around today.

---

medium. Traditionally, architecture adds buildings to society, whereas we were interested in how architecture could be applied to social, economic and cultural challenges.

This collaboration was initiated by Ole Bouman, Rem Koolhaas and Mark Wigley, our founding fathers. Each of the three organisations have other activities and projects, they have their own network and peer groups that all contribute to the magazine.

<u>How do you make each issue?</u>
The production of an issue takes 4 to 6 months. Each issue has one of the collaborators as initiator plus often a 'fourth party', so the team varies per issue. Constants are one editor in chief (Arjen Oosterman), two editors (Lilet Breddels and Christian Ernsten), a web editor (Edwin Gardner) and an office manager (Valerie Blom/Muike Leeuwenberg), who together

oversee, manage and facilitate the project, plus the designers (Irma Boom with Sonja Haller).

The teams in New York (director Jeffrey Inaba), and in Rotterdam (AMO, director Reinier de Graaf) vary in size. In New York, students take part in the 'C-lab certified' issues, and in Rotterdam and in Amsterdam, interns strengthen the work force.

<u>What is the secret of your success?</u>
A proactive approach combined with a global view that not only crosses borders but also domains (interdisciplinary). Volume sets an agenda for architectural practice.

<u>What have been the important stages in the life of your magazine?</u>
Launch in 2005, and presentation at Colophon2009.

<u>Where do you want the magazine to be in five years?</u>
At more newsstands worldwide.

<u>Who are your readers?</u>
Architects, designers, artists, decision makers, developers and policy makers with a keen interest in new tools, new approaches and new insights into spatial developments and how to influence them. In summary: curious people with creative and open minds.

<u>What is your relationship with advertising?</u>
We look for advertisers and sponsors who want to relate to the topics and themes we're engaged in; a shared interest.

<u>How many magazines do you read?</u>
Get: 25 a month. Buy: 1 - 4 a month.
—

Answered by Arjen / Lilet / Edwin/ Christian Oosterman / Breddels/ Gardner / Ernsten
Editor in chief / Publisher / Editor-director/ Web editor / Editor
*www.archis.org/volume*

---

Real-time spatial and cultural reflexivity. Some people call this architecture.

<u>How did it all begin?</u>
Volume is a project by Archis + AMO + C-Lab + .... As a collaboration between a magazine (Archis), an office (OMA/AMO) and a school (C-Lab/Columbia University New York) it wanted to research new futures for architecture and to go beyond the traditional

# WHERE DO YOU WANT YOUR MAGAZINE TO BE IN FIVE YEARS?

AFTERALL
CRASH
CREATIVE REVIEW
DANSK
DIRTY FOUND
ENCENS
EYEMAZING
FUTU
GRAFIK
KWANI?
LODOWN
METAL
REVOLUTIONART
SLASH
STERSO
SWINDLE
THE DRAWBRIDGE
TOKION

# AFTERALL

UNITED KINGDOM

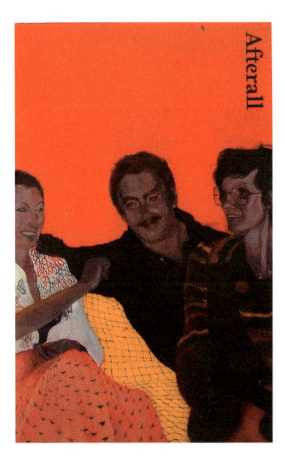

A journal that explores contemporary art practice in relation to a wider artistic, theoretical, social and zzpolitical context.

Where do you want your magazine to be in five years?
We would like it to be the international publication of reference for those interested in a critical consideration of contemporary art.
—
Answered by Pablo Lafuente
Managing editor
*www.afterall.org*

# CRASH

FRANCE

A magazine about today.

Where do you want your magazine
to be in five years?
Everywhere
—
Answered by Armelle Leturcq
Co-founder/Editor in chief
www.crash.fr

123

**MEETING MARKY RAMONE**
NEW YORK, 1974. THE PUNK MOVEMENT AWAKENS
WITH A SHRIEK IN A JAM-PACKED MANHATTAN CLUB
CALLED CBGB. MARKY RAMONE IS THE DRUMMER
OF TWO OF THE MOVEMENT'S FOUNDING BANDS:
RICHARD HELL AND THE VODOID AND THE MYTHICAL
RAMONES. TODAY, HE AND TOMMY HILFIGER REVIVE
THE ERA'S AGELESS STYLE WITH A NEW RAMONES-
INSPIRED CAPSULE COLLECTION.

HOW DID YOU MEET TOMMY HILFIGER? I've known Tommy for about 20 years and I am friends with his brothers. He used to come to our rehearsal studio at the beginning of The Ramones. He was always into rock and into music. Recently, people from Tommy Hilfiger approached me with the idea of doing jeans, jackets and t-shirts. So that's what I did. I made a capsule collection that is based around Marky Ramone and The Ramones style... It's nice and soft, it won't take ten years to break in... A lot of the jackets we wore in the seventies were too stiff, they were made for motorcycle riding and they were called perfecto, but we couldn't wait to break them in. So that's why I wanted the leather to be thin, nice, soft, and smooth. I chose a black and silver zebra pattern for the inside. The pants have studs on them because, when we started to play on the punk scene, at the CBGB, we couldn't get jeans with studs. We had to buy studs and put them on ourselves with a stud machine! So I figured I could make these jeans with a few studs on them, but tasteful. They are around the top of the back pockets, and also on the

# CREATIVE REVIEW

UNITED KINGDOM

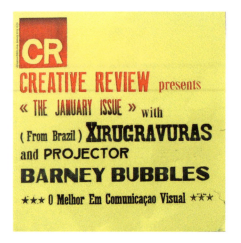

New ideas in visual communications, including graphic design, advertising and all related crafts.

**Where do you want your magazine to be in five years?**

There will always be a core of readers who will prefer the magazine in printed format, but the big shift for us will be in thinking of the magazine as an information source that can be delivered in a number of different ways, letting people choose the one that is best for them. I think that, as long as a magazine is based in part on entertainment and providing a rich experience, print will endure: it remains a wonderful, tactile medium. However, the growth for us will be in developing a worldwide audience and that will undoubtedly be led by the CR blog and a new website that is set to launch later this year.
—

Answered by Mark Sinclair
Deputy editor
www.creativereview.co.uk

Hand-set letterpress posters once covered the streets of São Paulo, Brazil. Gallery owner Baixo Ribeiro explains how he is attempting to revive this dying art by working with local artists on a new book

LAMBE LAMBE

DENMARK

Denmark's first international
fashion magazine.

Where do you want your magazine
to be in five years?
With a bigger audience and even-
better collaborators.
—
Answered by Kathrine Houe
Editor in chief
www.danskmagazine.com

# DIRTY FOUND

UNITED STATES

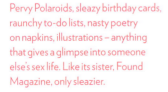

Pervy Polaroids, sleazy birthday cards, raunchy to-do lists, nasty poetry on napkins, illustrations – anything that gives a glimpse into someone else's sex life. Like its sister, Found Magazine, only sleazier.

Where do you want your magazine to be in five years?
In the hands of every man and woman over the age of 18.
—
Answered by Jason Bitner
Editor
www.dirtyfoundmagazine.com

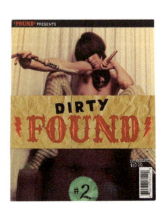

# ENCENS

FRANCE

90% fashion, 10% conceptual art.

Where do you want your magazine
to be in five years?
We always make each issue as if
it were the last.
—
Answered by
Samuel Drira and Sybille Walter
Editors
www.encensrevue.com

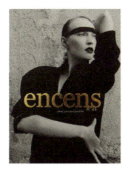

# EYEMAZING

NETHERLANDS

International contemporary
photography.

Where do you want your magazine
to be in five years?
Exactly where it is today.
—

Answered by Susan A. Zadeh
Founder/Editor/Photography
director/Designer/Publisher
www.eyemazing.com

# FUTU
POLAND

The design, photography and modern meaning of luxury.

<u>Where do you want your magazine to be in five years?</u>
I want it to be a well-recognised, international title and the most important Polish magazine about design and modern living. I would also love it to be a magazine that sets graphic-design standards – not only in Poland but also in the wider, international perspective.
—
Answered by Wojciech Ponikowski Managing director of Publishing and Design Group
*www.futu.pl*

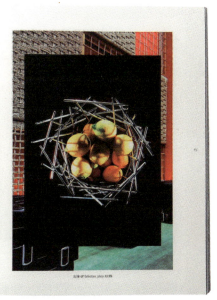

FUTU MAGAZINE
SELF/PEOPLE/SURROUND
NUMBER 7, LUXURY

# GRAFIK

UNITED KINGDOM

Graphic design and the things
that interest graphic designers:
typography, photography, illustration,
fashion, music, art.

Where do you want your magazine
to be in five years?
Still independent, with more pages,
more readers, a gallery space, a book-
publishing arm and a bakery.
—
Answered by Angharad Lewis
Deputy editor
www.grafikmagazine.co.uk

# KWANI?

KENYA

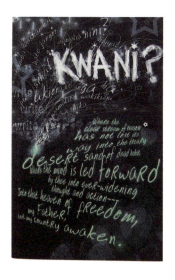

Cutting-edge new fiction, thought-provoking non fiction, photo essays and graphic narratives.

Where do you want your magazine to be in five years?
It is clear to us that Kenya has changed significantly over the years. In the 1970s, the emerging middle-class was the driving force of creativity in the country. Since 1990, the urban working class has dominated the arts, and the quality of music and fine arts has grown significantly.

Despite the current state of the economy, Kenyans are subscribing to a new wave of homegrown music, a clear indication that there is a demand for local, original cultural products. The new musicians have redefined what it means to be a Kenyan. English has been abandoned as a language that we use in popular culture. When it is used, it is broken down into rhythms that are completely Kenyan.

But the writing community lags behind. Over the next five years, we want to ensure that a new generation of writers from this pool of creativity are promoted, encouraged and read.
—
Answered by Angela Wachuka
Managing editor
www.kwani.org

# LODOWN

GERMANY

Leftfield pop culture and the art of movement.

Where do you want your magazine to be in five years?
Alive.
—

Answered by Sven Fortmann
Editor in chief
www.lodownmagazine.com

# METAL
SPAIN

Pretty things.

Where do you want your magazine
to be in five years?
At the top.
—

Answered by Yolanda Muelas
Editor
*www.revistametal.com*

# REVOLUTIONART

PERU

Fighting art fascism.

Where do you want your magazine
to be in five years?
On Mars, on the moon, and with our
logo on satellites.
—

Answered by Nelson Medina
Creative director
*www.revolutionart.publicistas.org*

# SLASH

UNITED STATES

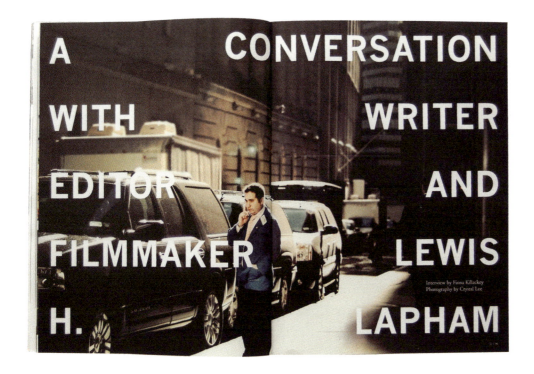

Art, politics, fashion and the crossovers in between.

Where do you want your magazine to be in five years?
I would like to see the magazine leave the constrains of mainstream public demands and become a bi-yearly book sold on the shelves, not the newsstand.
—
Answered by Kyle Hinton
Editor
www.slashmagazine.com

# STEREO

NETHERLANDS

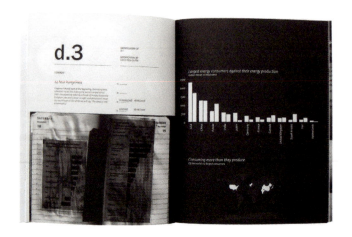

Breaking the boundaries between artistic disciplines.

Where do you want your magazine to be in five years?
In the Museum of Extinct Media, next to the Gutenburg bible.
—
Answered by Arjen de Jong
Art director/Co-ordinator
*www.stereopublication.com*

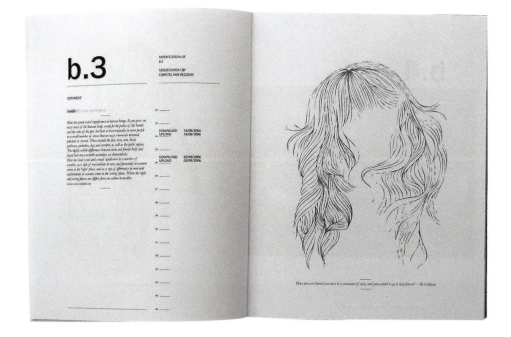

# SWINDLE

UNITED STATES

## GRILLED CHEESE

WHETHER YOU USE A HUNK OF GEWEY SHEEP'S MILK CHEESE OR A KRAFT SINGLES SLICE, THE GRILLED CHEESE SANDWICH IS ELEMENTALLY PLEASURABLE. AMERICAN COMFORT COULD NOT BE MORE EASILY DEFINED: BREAD, BUTTER, CHEESE.

All things pop culture.

Where do you want your magazine to be in five years?
If we're not out of ideas by then, we hope to have more advertisers, a larger circulation and a bigger staff.
—

Answered by Roger Gastman
Editor in chief
www.swindlemagazine.com

# THE DRAWBRIDGE

UNITED KINGDOM

Solid thoughts.

Where do you want your magazine
to be in five years?
Beijing.
—

Answered by Bigna Pfenninger
Editor
www.thedrawbridge.org.uk

# TOKION

UNITED STATES

Where art and fashion have a drink and a cigarette, and discuss art, film, travel and politics.

Where do you want your magazine to be in five years?
Alex: Launching Tokion TV.
Chris: Deciding on the color of Tokion's private jet and selecting the uniforms for the stewardesses.

—

Answered by
Alex Zafiris, Chris Ambrose
Editor, Publisher
*www.tokion.com*

# WHICH MAGAZINES HAVE INSPIRED YOU?

So many magazines, especially 1980s The Face and i-D magazine, 1950s Harper's Bazaar and Vogue.
**+ 81**

The German title Twen from the 1960s. Art Director Willy Fleckhaus introduced a whole new era in editorial approach and design.
**+Rosebud**

i-D, The Face, Vogue France, 10 magazine, Paradis, Qvest, Arena, Me, Vogue Italia, L' Uomo Vogue, Casa Vogue, Tar, Fantastic Man, Acne, Self Service.
**A**

Vogue Hommes International in the early 90s; The Face in the early 90s; Arena Homme +in the late 90s.
**Achtung**

Among my favourites: Flaunt, Surface, RayGun, i-D, Wired, This is a Magazine, Critique, Etapes, Baseline, Eye, Grafik, The Wire, tipoGrafica (from Argentina), No Zone, Rojo, Tiger and fanzines.
**Acido Surtido**

Jop van Bennekom (Re-, Butt, Fantastic Man) is a big inspiration.
**Afro**

Cabinet, Radical Philosophy, Wire, Screen (in the 1970s), Piktogram.
**Afterall**

Rojo, Code, BabyBabyBaby, Wow, Lodown, Ronda, Plan V, Carl's Cars, The End, Submag, Neo, Candy, Nylon, Clark. Now I have a little baby, so my favourite mag is Ahora Mamá (Now Mother).
**Atypica**

Interview, Details, i-D, The Face, Arena Homme+, Colors, Surface, Purple, Self Service, Wallpaper* in the beginning, Frame, Butt.
**b-guided**

Vice, WAD, i-D, Ptyuch (Russia), Dazed & Confused.
**B-East**

There are many, but some are Self Service, Purple, Fantastic Man, L'Officiel, V, Numéro, W, Black Book.
**BabyBabyBaby**

Oh gosh, so many, here are a few: Colors, The Face, i-D, Dazed & Confused, Mojo, Nova, Flair, Guardian Weekend, Paris Review, Life, Zembla, Times Style, Fortune, National Geographic, The New York Review of Books, Rolling Stone. On average, I read about 40 magazines a month. Me, a magazine maniac? Noooo.
**BON**

Aspen, Hermenaut, Finger, Zone, Re/Search, McSweeney's, and many niche zines. We get around 50 magazines a month at our office through subscription exchanges. It is always a thrill to get a magazine, a thrill which is both different and slightly more intense than receiving a book.
**Cabinet**

Artforum, ZG and Bomb have been important models, as well as the early days of Art News when the best art writing was being done by artists, and the American art scene was not unlike our own.
**Canadian Art**

The original Purple, i-D, Index, Interview, ANP Quarterly, Livrasion.
**Capricious**

40 years ago magazines like Vogue, Nova, Esquire, Playboy renewed art direction in a bold and elegant way. Now music magazines like Wire and outdoor titles like Huck put some new life into photography and layout. Unfortunately, the most interesting interior magazine ever, Nest, is closed down. We miss their unique stories.
**Carl's Cars**

Self Service, Purple, Fantastic Man, L'Officiel, V, Numéro, W, Black Book.
**Celeste**

Staffrider (South Africa), Transition (Uganda/Ghana), Black Orpheus (Nigeria). See www. chimurengalibrary.co.za for more.
**Chimurenga**

The Face in the mid eighties and early nineties, Interview in the eighties, Arena in the early nineties. And Dutch, which does not exist anymore. To me all of these magazines were iconic. Also Wired till this day, which I think is an incredibly well-made magazine. I enjoy GQ. But also Linda, which is one of the most successful (mass) titles for women in Holland is interesting. It's based on Oprah's magazine O, but one can only appreciate their bold editorial choices. These mass titles are extremely well-made magazines, with enormous amounts of passion and lots of creativity, though the content is not art or creativity linked. A good magazine surprises. It does not conform. Being independent or not has little to do with it being good or not. Furthermore: A magazine. Acne Paper. Juxtapoz, even though it lost its rough edge, is interesting. And I like V magazine. Also kids' wear is really really well done. Love that one.
**CODE**

Blitz, i-D, The Face, NME in the eighties.
**Crash**

Twen was a great inspiration, and so are Numéro and Spoon.
**Cream**

Zembla, i-D, The Face, Sleazenation, Wire, Private Eye, Colors, but in a more professional capacity, magazines like IDEA, Twen, ZOO, Kilimanjaro, 032c, Coupe, +81, Spin's self-published efforts, Thisisamagazine, Sarah Douglas' work on the Architect's Journal, Eye.
**Creative Review**

When it comes to content: from the beginning we have been concentrating on doing our own thing – not some spinoff or cheap copy. When it comes to editorial design: The New York Times Magazine (US), Weltwoche (Switzerland), Atlantic Monthly (US), the Sueddeutsche Magazin and brand eins (both from Germany).
**Datum**

Dazed & Confused, Purple, Número, Fantastic Man.
**Dansk**

Magazines don't inspire me as much as other designers – like David Carson, Vince Frost, Nathan Reddy, Peter Saville, Mark Farrow, Irma Boom, etc. I like designs that are simple. Even logo and poster designs can be inspiring for magazine layouts.
**Design Indaba**

WAD, Flaunt, Surface, Wallpaper etc.
**DIF**

I love what started with Andy Warhol's Interview, that is people, personalities, interviews. I like to read interesting conversations, see some unique pictures. I like those magazines that are a kind of art object. I like to touch them. I like the way how Warhol used the magazine as a part of his artistic concept, as a medium equal to paintings or film. It sounds very familiar to me.
**DIK Fagazine**

Found, Esopus, Sweet Action Magazine!
**Dirty Found**

Other than British kids' comics like the Beano, teenage pop magazines like Smash Hits, and adolescent music papers like the NME, I've never been interested in periodicals. The New Yorker is the only magazine I've ever subscribed to as an adult, and despite the content being so homogenic, I appreciate the editorial hardline, and its sense of being designed by time. Actually, recently I subscribed to Lapham's Quarterly, a new journal consisting of historical excerpts around a key theme (war, money, nature, education), founded by Lewis Lapham.
**Dot Dot Dot**

Colors, VF, Twen, Jasmin, brandeins.
**Dummy**

Twen. Diana Vreeland's writing. Maurizio Cattelan's magazine Permanent Food is just the best of the best.
**Editor&Art Director**

French Marie Claire 1976-1984, Avalanche, File.
**Encens**

Interview by Andy Warhol, Egoiste magazine.
**Eyemazing**

Old issues of Interview in the 90s. And sometimes copies of Vogue Per Lui. I don't know if it still exists today or if it became L'Uomo Vogue. But they should do it again.
**Fairy Tale**

Fantastic Man, kids' wear, Kilimanjaro, 032c, A Magazine, Purple, Colors, Useful Photography (not really a magazine but that makes it even nicer!), Ojodepez, Next Level, Aperture, Next Level, Capricious as well as Frame, Frieze, Domus and Art Review.
**Foam**

Domus, Wallpaper*, Dazed & Confused, Intersection, Fantastic Man, Another Magazine, to name a few.
**Frame / Mark**

I really like an old Polish magazine Projekt.
**Futu**

Colors, Spy, early Esquire, The New Yorker, modern New York, old Life, Mad, New York Times Magazine, early Wired, Might, Highlights, The Whole Earth Catalog, Brill's Content.
**Good**

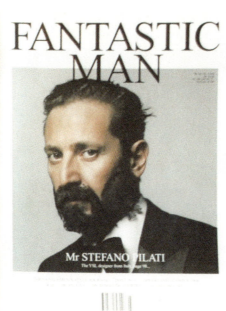

Index, Interview, The Manipulator, i-D, The Face.
**Girls Like Us**

Smash Hits, Jackie, The Face, i-D, 032c, Tate Etc, Wire, Interview.
**Grafik**

International press such as Les Inrockuptibles, Mojo, Billboard, NME, Premiere, Edge... and national press such as Rockdelux or Cahiers du cinema. And, obviously, a bunch of internet sites where you can find the newest information (such as Pitchfork Media). Our fashion editor's favourites are Nylon Magazine, Purple, Dazed & Confused, i-D and a lot of underground magazines.
**H**

Purple.
**Here and There**

Life, Zoom, Playboy, Purple, L'Uomo Vogue, Nest, Vanity Fair, Artforum, Interview.
**Hot Rod**

Oddly for someone living at the bottom of Africa, the best magazine on earth is The Rodder's Journal, and West Coast Hot Rod auto magazine published by hot rod fanatics. Quite superb! (and I'm not a hot rodder myself). I wasn't inspired by any particular magazine, but the closest would be Emigre.
**i-jusi**

All magazines.
**IdN**

Fairy Tale, Kasino A4, Werk, 032c, Re-Magazine, Idea, Straight to Hell.
**Kaiserin**

My local 'Gazette' magazine is a constant inspiration. It's full of little bits of news about the local community.
**Karen**

Farafina Magazine (Nigeria), Chimurenga (South Africa), Black Orpheus (Nigeria), Transition (Uganda), Harpers (Canada), The New Yorker (USA), Joe Magazine (Kenya), Straight Up No Chaser (UK) and Frank Talk (South Africa)
**Kwani?**

El Canto de la Tripulácin. It was an independent magazine in Madrid in the early 90s, made by a group of artists. Their only motivation was just to publish. Visual magazine (from Madrid, they still exist, www.visual.gi) is also important for us, we learnt a lot from them. Also a magazine from Beijing called O2, and from Chile: Kiltraza and La Nueva Grafica Chilena, two very experimental and fun projects. In Spain there is also La Lata, a wonderful magazine in a can.
**La Más Bella**

Ralph Ginzberg's Avant Garde (1968-1971) is the inspiration for our format. We like our friends at Swindle. Flaunt has beautiful covers too.
**Lemon**

All magazines that fight for sincerity in beauty and the beauty of sincerity.
**Liebling**

Jetzt and SZ Magazin, both weekly supplements of the German Süddeutsche Zeitung, although the former moved online years ago. Both of them taught me that you can treat your readers like intelligent human beings and be entertaining at the same time. Same for Dummy magazine (Germany). Bulgaria magazine (Finland) because of its amazing looks. Monocle (UK) for breaking new ground. And in the same line, obviously Esquire under Hayes, Colors under Kalman, and Rolling Stone in the 1970s.
**Ling**

Edge, adrenalin, Flaunt, The Face.
**Little White Lies**

Bikini, Tokion, Film Threat.
**Lodown**

Interview, The Face, Jackie, Vogue (French and Italian).
**Lula**

L'Illustration, Paris-Normandie, Le Point du Jour.
**Magazine**

Número, Wallpaper* (before Time Warner bought it), RayGun, Colors, Émigré, New York.
**Me**

Cabinet, Gastronomica, Esopus, Speak, Readymade, the New Yorker, McSweeney's, early Colors.
**Meatpaper**

i-D, The Face, Dutch, Purple, Self Service, Fantastic Man, Encens, Rolling Stone – in its beginnings – Vanity Fair and Interview.
**Metal**

Fantastic Man. We're ordering all the back issues from the Netherlands.
**MK Bruce/Lee**

Vanity Fair, Frame, Italian Vogue.
**Monument**

L'Autre Journal (France), Actuel and the first (quarterly) version of Les Inrockuptibles (France) – the three of them dating back to the 80s ; Wire (UK) , Weirdo(Robert Crumb's magazine, for its title ;-)
**Mouvement**

i-d and The Face, a long time ago.
**Neo2**

Dutch magazine. I still keep the Bye Bye issue!
**Neue Mode**

From the 80s: Interview, The Face, i-D, Tempo, as they were really different from what the magazine world had to offer. Today, I'm always looking for very strong visuals, good stories and a personal concept. Good erotica is still difficult to find, I really like S Magazine from Copenhagen and Paradis from Paris.
**Nico**

I used to read Peanuts and Vanity Fair, because that was the favourite magazine of my stepfather who was a journalist. Bamse magazine (Swedish 'socialist' cartoon for kids), some old Interviews. I guess The Face, i-D, Purple played a certain role.
**Nuke**

FMR, Worldsign.
**Nusign**

Volume, Wad, Archis, Pin-up, Re-magazine, KasinoA4 and many more...
**Omagiu**

Minotaure.
**Parkett**

Emigre, Mondo 2000, Avant Garde, Flair, RayGun, Maximum Rock 'n' Roll.
**Plazm**

My all-time favourite magazine is The Face and it is pretty much entirely responsible for my wanting to work in magazine publishing. Both the photography and the writing were always incredible, and it was an extraordinary document of British (and other) subcultures.
**Poster**

No single magazine, but rather the wide variety of all the different titles focused on fashion, art, culture, architecture, beauty and lifestyle. Our job is to buy, get and read as many magazines we can.
**QVEST**

Thrasher, Rip, Maxim, Vogue.
**Revolutionart**

Projections: John Boorman's filmmaker's magazine that is similarly interview-obsessed as we are. Cahiers du Cinema: The French legend, where film thinking and filmmaking used to be neighbours. Filmkritik: The only serious German film magazine; it died in 1983, but is still inspiring because of its precise use of language. Kunstforum: An open-minded art magazine that is truly independent.
**Revolver**

I was influenced by all magazines I read... so I decided to create a magazine that had nothing to do with the rest. I stopped looking for things in other magazines long ago – it is hard to look to the side when you are driving in the fast lane on a totally different road.
**Rojo**

The Beano, Vogue, Private Eye, The Onion, and the TV show Have I Got News For You.
**Rubbish**

New York Magazine (it's where I work). The occasional issue of Vice, eXile, Found, Grand Street, Granta, and a Russian biweekly called Bolshoi Gorod.
**Russia!**

Senhor and Realidade were magazines that represented a lot in terms of content and design in the country in the late 60s. Later in the 70s there was Pop. Those were the years when Brazil had a military government and photographers had to be very imaginative to deal with censorship. British magazines from the 80s such as Arena, Blitz, The Face and i-D were also important, as later were French Egoïste and Purple.
**s/n°**

Re-, the old programs of die Rote Fabrik (a famous club in Zürich) from the 90's, i-D, Self Service, 032c, A, Skin Shows, Editor & Art Director, lots of punk fanzines and. I also draw a lot of inspiration from art books and artists' catalogues, old type specimens etc. I guess the printed pieces that have inspired me the most are Décosterd & Rahm, Physiological Architectures, designed by Norm, and the catalogue of the famous exhibition "When Attitudes Become Form".
**Sang Bleu**

Conceptual magazines. Daring magazines. Experimental publications. Interesting thinking publications: Re-magazine for their fantastic monographic concept. Emigre for their experimentations. Point d'Ironie for their carte blanche concept and fantastic contributing artists, Eye and Parachute for their articles. Art4d, the Thai design magazine, for being a well-designed magazine offering interesting information on Asian design. In the beginning of shift! we were definitely influenced by Yps magazine, a 70s youth magazine that was playful and tactile and always contained a gimmick. I have absolutely always been bored to death by glossy style magazines.
**shift!**

Twen, Tempo, Rolling Stone, RayGun, U&lc, Eye, Emigre, ZEITmagazin,. i-D, Purple, brandeins. Fanzines and underground publications.
**Slanted**

I tend to find inspiration from the more mainstream magazines. I think it's interesting what established magazines are willing to do. I find that more interesting than most independent magazines that are simply trying too hard to ultimately be mainstream. Of course, the stories behind magazines like Dazed and i-D are inspiring but I see nothing inspirational about the magazines themselves.
**Slash**

Purple, Dazed & Confused, i-D.
**Sleek**

Purple has found a formula that works and works well – you might say the different issues have much the same feel/look to them, but since the quality and editorial voice are so strong, it carries through with bravura. Another one is Karen Magazine, a gem that deserves a much wider audience. Also I enjoy Rojo from Spain.
**S Magazine**

Definitely The Face. Also Wired and RayGun. Lately I've also become quite partial to Vanity Fair. You can see I'm a product of the nineties... but more than that, I buy magazines to read them, and the common thread with all those magazines I mentioned is that they look great, but they had a serious depth to the writing that is almost impossible to find these days. It was a sad day when The Face closed but it just goes to show that all magazines are a product of their times.
**Sneaker Freaker**

Wendingen (Dutch architectural magazine published between 1924 and 1950s), Lodown, Transworld Skateboarding (early editions).
**Stereo**

RayGun, Dazed and Confused, Adrenalin, Dave Cooper's Weasel.
**Stirato**

Oz, Avant Garde, The Face 1980-britpop, i-D 1980-present, Private Eye, Grazia.
**SuperSuper**

Teen Angels. Tiger Beat, F.E.D.S., Us Weekly, Hustler's Barely Legal, Garden & Gun, Domino, Girls and Corpses and three issues of the long-defunct Mary-Kate and Ashley magazine.
**Swindle**

Many and many more in parts.
**The Drawbridge**

Smash Hits. We gave our collection of zines to the DOCVA in Milan (open to the public). We don't consume so many magazines, like not wanting to eat chicken if you work in a KFC.
**This is a magazine**

The Face, NME, New Yorker, Paper, Interview, Purple, Private Eye. French Vogue, Monocle, Dazed and Confused, Purple, Audience (out of print). Q, Mojo, Vogue, National Geographic, Les Inrockuptibles, plus all those amazing band fanzines I'd subscribe to via mail. Sonic Youth, particularly. GAMES, Hustler.
**Tokion**

Colors, DU, Monocle, Foam.
**Truce**

Warm Red U, Harakiri, Pardon, Plamen, Revue svetovej literatury (until 1969), Vokno, National Geographic, 100+1 (until 1980), Zingmagazine.
**Umelec**

The Face, Self Service, Another Magazine, i-D, Pop, French Vogue, Interview.
**Vanidad**

Beautiful ones.
**Varoom**

Wired, Bidoun, Third Text, Permanent Food, Wallpaper* (at first), Nest, Arch Plus, Parkett.
**Volume**

Twen, Life, Harpers, Vogue France, Wallpaper*, Butt, Fantastic Man, AD Germany.
**Vorn**

i-D. Terry Jones is my hero.
**Yummy**

# MAGAZINE DIRECTORY

# A B
# C D

# ARGENTINA

**TIPOGRÀFICA**
Buenos Aires
Quaterly, founded in 1987
Spanish
www.tipografica.com

**BLANKET**
Uncovering Art Design and
Photography
Melbourne
Bi-monthly, founded in 2006
180 x 220 mm
English
www.blanketmagazine.com
Publisher: Bec Brown

**ACIDO SURTIDO**
100% Argentine product
Buenos Aires
Tri-Annual, founded in 2001
160 x 235 mm
Spanish
www.acidosurtido.com.ar
Editor (2001/2005): Diego
Cabello

# AUSTRALIA

**CRAFT ARTS
INTERNATIONAL**
Neutral Bay
Tri-Annual, founded in 1984
230 x 310 mm
English
www.craftarts.com.au
Editor: Ken Lockwood

**ATYPICA**
Art, culture and design
Rosario, Santa Fe
Every two months, founded in
2003
200 x 250 mm
40,000 copies
Spanish / English
www.atypica.com.ar

**ACCLAIM**
Street Lifestyle Magazine
Albert Park
Quarterly, founded in 2005
210 x 275 mm
30,000 copies
English
www.acclaimmag.com
Editor in chief and Publisher:
Andrew Montell

**CREAM MAGAZINE**
A cooler blend of pop culture.
Sydney
Quarterly, founded in 1997
235 x 325 mm
100,000 copies
English
www.creammagazine.com
Publisher and Editor: Antonino
Tati
Publisher: Future Perfect
Publications Pty Ltd.

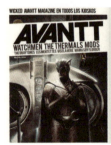

**AVANTT MAGAZINE**
avantt colophon magazine
indie art latin
Bernal
Monthly, founded in 2007
200 x 270 mm
Spanish / English / Basque
www.avanttmag.com/

**ARTLINES**
Art and people
Brisbane
Tri-Annual, founded in 2005
210 x 275 mm
12,000 copies
English
www.qag.qld.gov.au/artlines
Editor: Ian Were

**DESKTOP:**
St Kilda
Monthly,
English
www.desktopmag.com.au
Editor: Elise Goodwin
Publisher: Niche Media PTY,
Ltd.

**G7**
Buenos Aires
Monthly, founded in 2001
15,000 copies
Spanish
www.revistag7.com
Editor in chief: Francisco
Condorelli
Publisher: Gruposiete S.R.L.

**AUTORE**
Sydney
230 x 300 mm
English
www.pearlautore.com.au/
Editor: Louise Upton
Publisher: Louise Upton

**DNA**
Lidcombe
Monthly, founded in 2000
210 x 297 mm
English
www.dnamagazine.com.au
Editor and Publisher: Andrew
Creagh

**SUITE**
Design art
Buenos Aires
Annual, founded in 2004
140 x 155 mm
10,000 copies
Spanish / English
www.suiteintima.com.ar

**BLACK+WHITE**
East Sydney
Every two months,
240 x 323 mm
English
www.studiomagazines.com
Editor in chief: Eyre
Publisher: Studio Magazines
Pty Ltd.

**DOINGBIRD**
Fashion / Arts Publication
Bondi Beach
Bi-Annual, founded in 2001
210 x 275 mm
English
www.doingbird.com
Editor in chief: Max Doyle

**DUKE MAGAZINE**
Perfect toilet reading
Westgate N.S.W
Bi-Annual, founded in 2006
205 x 275 mm
4,000 copies
English
www.dukemag.com
Publisher: Raquel Welch
Publisher: Hunt & Welch

**LIFELOUNGE**
Life from a different angle
St Kilda
Every two months, founded in 2005
220 x 270 mm
150,000 copies
English
www.lifelounge.com
Editor in chief: Jamie Driver

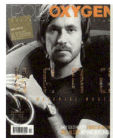

**POL OXYGEN**
Redfern
Every two months, founded in 2002
25,000 copies
English
www.poloxygen.com
Distribution & circulation:
Michelle Willis

**DUMBO FEATHER, PASS IT ON.**
NSW
Quarterly, founded in 2004
210 x 244 mm
20,000 copies
English
www.dumbofeather.com

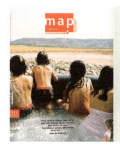

**MAP MAGAZINE**
Purveyors of pop culture with a conscience
Brisbane
Monthly, founded in 1999
275 x 220 mm
40,000 copies
English
www.mapmagazine.com.au
Editor in Chief: Carl Lindgren
Publisher: Map Creative

**POSTER**
Australia_s leading design, fashion, and art magazine.
Prahran
Quarterly, founded in 2001
220 x 285 mm
English
www.postermagazine.com.au
Founder & Creative Director:
Nicholas Meimaris
Publisher: Poster Australasia Ltd

**EMPTY**
Darlinghurst
Bi-Monthly, founded in 2003
210 x 275 mm
English
www.emptymag.com

**MONSTER CHILDREN**
NSW 2050
Quarterly,
210 x 297 mm
20,000 copies
English
www.monsterchildren.com
Publisher & Editor: Campbell Milliigan

**RUNWAY**
An Australian contemporary art magazine
Strawberry Hills
Tri-Annual, founded in 2002
200 x 250 mm
1,000 copies copies
English
www.runway.org.au
Managing Editor: Jaki Middleton
Publisher: The Invisible Inc.

**FRANKIE MAGAZINE**
change is something we're not afraid of
North Burleigh Heads
Bi-Monthly,
50,000 copies
English
www.frankie.com.au

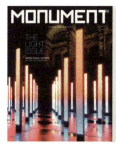

**MONUMENT**
Architecture & Design
Pyrmont
Every two months,
English
www.monumentmagazine.com.au
Editor: Leanne Amodeo

**RUSSH**
Sydney
Every two months, founded in 2004
236 x 303 mm
25,000 copies
English
www.russhaustralia.com
Editor: Charlotte Scott
Publisher: Russh Magazines & Publications

**HARVEST**
Fresh Australian writing
Melbourne
Quarterly, founded in 2008
210 x 250 mm
1,000 copies
English
www.harvestmagazine.wordpress.com

**NOI.SE MAGAZINE**
Balmain
Bi-Annual,
240 x 340 mm
English
Editor: Mark Stapleton

**SNEAKER FREAKER**
Collingwood 3066
Bi-Annual, founded in 2003
English
www.sneakerfreaker.com
Editor: Woody

**HIGHLIGHTS**
Hair Magazine
Balmain
Bi-Annual,
240 x 330 mm
English
www.highlightsmag.com
Editor: Mark Stapleton
Publisher: Highlights Publications

**OYSTER**
Surry Hills
Every two months,
240 x 325 mm
36,000 copies
English
www.oystermag.com
Creative director: Johnathan Morris

**T-WORLD**
The Art of T-shirt Culture
Melbourne
Bi-Annual, founded in 2005
185 x 280 mm
English
www.t-world.com.au
Founder / Publisher / Art Director: Eddie Zammit

**THEY SHOOT HOMOS DON'T THEY?**
Collingwood, Melbourne
Bi-Annual, founded in 2004
148 x 210 mm
1,000 copies
English
www.theyshoothomosdont-they.com

**DATUM**
Seiten der Zeit
Vienna
Monthly (11 x / year), founded in 2004
210 x 280 mm
10,000 copies
German
www.datum.at
Editor in chief: Klaus Stimeder
Publisher: Verein zur Förderung des Qualitätsjournalismus

**MODART**
Creative action breeds active creation
Insbruck
Every two months,
280 x 270 mm
English
www.modarteurope.com
Creative Director: Garry Maidment
Publisher: More Productions Ltd

**TORPEDO**
Fiction and illustration
Melbourne
Quarterly, founded in 2007
160 x 230 mm
4,000 copies
English
falconvsmonkey.com
Founder and Publisher: Chris Flynn

**EIKON**
International Magazine for Photography and Media Art
Vienna
Quarterly, founded in 1991
280 x 210 mm
German / English
www.eikon.at
Art Director: Florian Halm

**NULL ACHT**
Magazin für Rasenpflege
Vienna
founded in 2007
230 x 320 mm
German
www.nullacht.at
Publisher: Alois Gstoettner

**WON MAGAZINE**
Melbourne
Quarterly, founded in 2007
270 x 380 mm
English
nownow.com.au
Editor: Chris Barton
Publisher: NowNow

**EUROCITY**
Reise. Kultur. Literatur. Lebensart. Das internationale Magazin
Vienna
bimonthly, founded in
Founded in April 1991
185 x 250 mm
70,000 copies
German
www.eurocity.at

**POOL MAGAZINE**
Life & Culture
Vienna
Quarterly, founded in 2001
240 x 300 mm
28,000 copies
German / English
www.pool-mag.net
Editor in chief: Helmut Wolf
Publisher: pool verlags gmbh

# AUSTRIA

**FRAME**
The state of art.
Vienna
Quarterly, founded in 2000
230 x 290 mm
15,000 copies
German
Editor in chief: Alexander Pühringer
Publisher: Frame Projects
www.frameprojects.com

**SPIKE**
ART QUARTERLY
Vienna
Quarterly, founded in 2004
225 x 280 mm
20,000 copies
German / English
www.spikeart.at
Distribution: Christian Kobald
Publisher: Sportmagazin GmbH & Co KG/ New Art Club

**BIORAMA**
Magazine for Sustainable Lifestyle
Viena
Quarterly, founded in January 2009
170 x 240mm
40,000 copies copies
German
www.biorama.at

**LANDJÄGER**
Unhabängig seit Ewig
Egg
148 x 210 mm
German
www.landjaeger.at/
Editor: Martin Fetz, Sven Matt, Robert Hiller and Christian Feurstein

**SPRINGERIN**
Hefte für Gegenwartskunst
Vienna
Quarterly, founded in 1995
230 x 275 mm
5,000 copies
German
www.springerin.at
Editor: Christian Höller
Publisher: Springerin

**CAMERA AUSTRIA**
Graz
founded in 1980
www.camera-austria.at
Editor: Tanja Gassler

**LÜRZER'S ARCHIVE**
Ads and Posters worldwide
Salzburg
Every two months, founded in 1984
205 x 285 mm
9,000 copies
English
www.luerzersarchive.com
Publisher & Editor: Walter Lürzer
Publisher: Lürzer GmbH

**THE ALL SEASON FASHION PAPER**
Vienna
Bi-Annual,
325 x 480 mm
4,000 copies
German / English
www.fashionpaper.at
Editor in chief: Ulrike Tschabitzer
Publisher: Unit F assocation for contemporary fashion

**WEAR**
global magazine
Zell am See
Quaterly,
248 x 340 mm
15,000 copies
English / German / French /
Italian / Spanish / Russian /
Mandarin / Japanese
www.wear-magazine.com
Advertising: Sabine Strobl
Publisher: Klaus Vogel

**A PRIOR**
Brussels
Bi-Annual, founded in 1999
170 x 235 mm
2,000 copies
English
www.aprior.org
General Manager: Els
Roelandt
Publisher: vzw Mark

**DAMN**
A magazine on contemporary
culture
Brussels
Bimonthly,
220 x 280 mm
25,000 copies
English
www.damnmagazine.be
Editor: Emma Firmin
Publisher: DAMnation Ltd

**WIENERIN**
Das österreichische
Frauenmagazin
Vienna
Monthly, founded in 1984
74,000 copies
German
www.wienerin.at
Editor in chief: Karen Müller
Publisher: Lifestyle
Zeitschriften Verlag GmbH

**A+**
Revue Belge d'Architecture
Brussels
Every two months,
240 x 300 mm
14,078 copies
French / Dutch/English
www.a-plus.be
Editor in chief: Stefan
Devoldere
Publisher: CIAUD asbl

**DENG**
Antwerp
Monthly, founded in 2003
15,000 copies
Dutch

**X-RAY**
Global style + fashion
Salzburg-Anif
Quarterly,
220 x 300 mm
German / English
www.ucm-verlag.at/fash_xray.
php
Editors in chief: Stephan
Huber, Ina Köhler
Publisher: UCM Verlag

**AD!DICT**
Inspiration book
Brussels
Bi-Annual, founded in 1997
240 x 240 mm
English
www.addictlab.com
Editor in chief: Anja Samson
Publisher: Ad!dict Creative
Lab

**DITS**
La revue du Musée des arts
contemporains du
Grand-Hornu.
Hornu
Bi-Annual, founded in 2002
170 x 238 mm
French
www.mac-s.be
Editor in chief: Denis Gielen
Publisher: Mac's

# BELGIUM

**ADDMAGAZINE**
Magazine about print & other
media.
Brussels
Tri-Annual, founded in 2005
220 x 310 mm
Dutch / French / English
www.addmagazine.be
Editor in chief: Hugo Puttaert
Publisher: Papyrus Belgium &
Visionandfactory
Internationalelaan

**FREEZE**
Actionlifesytle magazine
Every two months,
www.freeze.be
Editor: Luc Van Ginneken
Publisher: L & M Publishing
Partners

**+1 MAGAZINE**
Created by the fourth year
students of the Antwerp
fashion department
Antwerp
Annual, founded in 2006
230 x 295 mm
English
www.antwerp-fashion.be
Idea & Concept: Demna
Gvasalia
Publisher: Artesis Hogeschool
Antwerp, Fashion Department

**CODE**
Life & Artstyle
Brussels
founded in 2005
170 x 250 mm
5,000 copies
French / English / Dutch
www.codemagazine.be
Development: Mariana Melo
Publisher: Stoemp asbl

**GUS**
Gay & Urban lifeStyle
magazine
Brussels
Every two months, founded in
2001
220 x 300 mm
French / English
www.gusmag.com
Editor in chief: Frédérick
Boutry
Publisher: DYP sprl

**A MAGAZINE**
A Magazine Curated by...
Antwerp
Bi-Annual, founded in 2004
230 x 295 mm
English
www.modenatie.com/
amagazine/
Editor: Hilde Bouchez
Publisher: A Publisher p/a
Fashionclub 70

**CULT OF CHIC**
Belgian niche magazine for
fashion addicts
Brussel
Bi-Annual,
230 x 265 mm
30,000 copies
Dutch / French
www.ppmg.be
Publisher: Hedwig Dethée
Publisher: PPMG

**JANUS**
Art & philosophy
Brussels
Bi-Annual, founded in 1998
226 x 300 mm
4,000 copies
English
www.janusonline.net
Editor in chief: Nicola Setari

**L'ART MÊME**
Bruxelles
Quarterly, founded in 1998
20 x 260 mm
7,500 copies
French
www.cfwb.be/lartmeme
Editor in chief: Christine
Jamart

**RUIS**
Gent
Monthly,
English
www.ruismagazine.net

**BRAZIL**

**LA PART DE L'OEIL**
Bruxelles
Annual, founded in 1985
210 x 297 mm
French
lapartdeloeil.be/
Editor in chief: Lucien
Massaert

**THE WORD**
Neighbourhood Life + Global
Style
Brussels
Bi-Monthly, founded in
January 2008
210 x 295 mm
15,000 copies copies
English
www.thewordmagazine.be
Founder and Managing Editor:
Nicholas Lewis
Publisher: JamPublishing

**ELEELA**
Sao Paulo
202 x 265 mm
Portuguese
www.revistaeleela.com.br
Editor in chief: Wagner Carelli

**LABEL**
Mortsel
8,000 copies
Dutch
Art director: Daniel Osuna

**TL MAGAZINE**
Textile & Living - Shaping
Tomorrow
Brussels
Quarterly, founded in January
2009
230 x 285 mm
French / Dutch / English
www.tlmagazine.be

**L.U.M.I.E.R.E ACCESS**
Sao Paulo
Every two months,
230 x 275 mm
Portuguese
Director of advertising &
marketing: Geraldo Park
Publisher: Marcos Park &
Ronaldo Gomez

**MOVE-X**
Trendy Underground
magazine
Brussels
Monthly,
265 x 210 mm
30,000 copies
French / Dutch
www.move-x.be
Editor: Miel Vanschoenbeek
Publisher: PPMG

**VICE**
Antwerp
Dutch / French
http://www.viceland.com

**S/N°**
Sao Paulo
Bi-Annual,
240 x 320 mm
5,000 copies
Portuguese / English
www.bobwolfenson.com.br
Editor In chief & Creative
Director: Bob Wolfenson
Publisher: Editora Livre

**PLASTIKS MAGAZINE**
Antwerp
243 x 278 mm
English
Editor in chief: Groove
Merchant
Publisher: Plastiks Magazine

**VIEW**
Photography Magazine
Brussels
Quarterly,
240 x 300 mm
English / French / German
www.viewmag.be

**SIMPLES**
Sociedade criativa
Sao Paulo
Every two months,
170 x 238 mm
Brazilian
www.revistasimples.com.br
Founder: Ale MC Falijone
Publisher: Wide Brand
Experience

**PULP**
International Mediaguide
Antwerp
Every two months (5 x / year),
150 x 210 mm
German
www.pulpwebsite.com
Publisher & Editor & Creative
Director: Emmanuelle
Verheyden

**TRIP**
São Paulo, SP
Monthly,
208 x 275 mm
40,000 copies
Portuguese
revistatrip.uol.com.br

**TUPIGRAFIA**
Sao Paulo
founded in 2000
160 x 224 mm
Portuguese
www.tupigrafia.com.br
Claudio Rocha

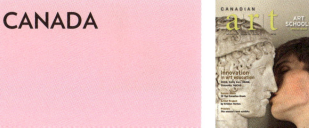

# CANADA

**CANADIAN ART**
Toronto
Quarterly, founded in 1984
81 x 108 mm
23,000 copies
English
www.canadianart.ca
Publisher: Melony Ward
Publisher: Canadian Art
Fondation

**WOOF!**
Sao Paulo
Every two months,
English
www.woofmagazine.net
Editor in chief: Eduardo Burger

**180 MAGAZINE**
Style art fashion art style
Ontario
Monthly, founded in 2005
200,000 copies
English
180mag.ca/
Editor & Publisher: Kim Taylor

**CINEMA SEWER**
Vancouver
167 x 260 mm
English
www.cinemasewer.com
Founder: Robin Bougie

**ZUPI**
"Design, illustration,
photography and street art"
São Paulo
Quarterly, founded in 2002
170 x 245 mm
15,000 copies
Portuguese / English / Spanish
www.zupi.com.br
Founder and Editor: Allan
Szacher

**ADBUSTERS**
Vancouver
Every two months, founded in
1992
230 x 272 mm
120,000 copies
English
www.adbusters.org
Editor in chief: Kalle Lasn'
Publisher: Abusters Media
Foundation

**COLOR MAGAZINE**
A Skateboard Culture
quarterly
Vancouver
Quarterly, founded in 2003
254 x 254 mm
90,000 copies
English
www.colormagazine.ca
Editor and Publisher: Sandro
Grison

# BULGARIA

**BETWEEN THE CRACKS**
Vancouver BC
founded in 2006
85 x 110 mm
English
www.btcracks.com
Publisher: Edward Drewitt

**COUPE**
Atmosphere. Image. Art.
Trash. All of it.
Toronto, Ontario
Bi-Annual, founded in 1999
245 x 294 mm
English
www.coupe-mag.com
Founder: Bill Douglas

**DOMYT MAGAZINE**
Interior Design & Architecture
Sofia
Monthly, founded in 1995
224 x 300 mm
10,000 copies
Bulgarian
www.thehome-bg.com
Publisher: Dom Media Ltd

**BUTTER**
Vancouver
15,000 copies
English
www.mmmbutter.com
Art Director: Reanna Evoy

**CV CIEL VARIABLE**
Art / Photo / Media / Culture
Montréal (Québec)
Quarterly,
240 x 293 mm
French / English
www.cielvariable.ca
Editor in chief: Jacques Doyon

**C MAGAZINE**
Toronto
Quarterly,
English
www.cmagazine.com
Editor: Rosemary Heather

**DAYJOB**
Toronto
Bi-Annual, founded in 2002
216 x 280 mm
English
www.dayjobmagazine.com
Grooming: Jodi Thibodeau
Publisher: Day Job Industries

**ESPACE SCULPTURE**
Montréal, Québec
Quarterly, founded in 1987
240 x 305 mm
26,000 copies
French / English
www.espace-sculpture.com
Editor in chief: Serge Fisette
Publisher: Le Centre de
Diffusion 3D

**LA RAMPA**
Toronto
Bi-Annual,
English
www.la-rampa.com
Publisher: Gethin James
Publisher: La Rampa
Publications Inc

**SEED**
Beneath the Surface
Montreal
205 x 275 mm
English
www.seedmagazine.com
Editor in chief: Adam Bly
Publisher: Seed Group

**ESSE**
arts + opinions
Montréal, Québec
Tri-Annual, founded in 1984
230 x 290 mm
2,600 copies
French / English
www.esse.ca
Editor: Sylvette Babin

**LUSH MAGAZINE**
Toronto
Quarterly,
20,000 copies
English
www.lushmag.com

**THIS MAGAZINE**
Because everything is political.
Toronto
Every two months, founded in
1966
English
www.thismagazine.ca
Editor: Emily Schultz

**ETC**
Revue de l'art actuel
Montréal
Quarterly, founded in 1987
211 x 298 mm
French / English
Editor in chief: Isabelle Lelarge

**NUVO**
Vancouver
Quarterly, founded in 1998
50,000 copies
English
www.nuvomagazine.com
Founder & Publisher: Pasquale
Cusano

**WORN**
Toronto
Bi-Annual,
English
www.wornjournal.com

**EVENT**
New & established writers.
New Westminster, BC
Tri-Annual, founded in 1971
152 x 229 mm
3,300 copies
English
www.event.douglas.bc.ca
Editor: Rick Maddocks

**PINNACLE**
Toronto
Quarterly, founded in 2008
195 x 252 mm
1,00 copies
English
www.pinnacle-magazine.com

**CHILE**

**HERBIVORE**
Vegetarian culture
Portland
Quarterly, founded in 2003
217 x 280 mm
English
www.herbivoreclothing.com
Editor: Josh Hooten

**PREFIX PHOTO**
A Publication of Prefix Institute
of Contemporary Art
Toronto
Bi-Annual, founded in 2000
229 x 267 mm
English / French
www.prefix.ca
Editor and Publisher: Scott
McLeod
Publisher: Prefix Institute of
Contemporary Art

**EXTRAVAGANZA**
Santiago
www.extravaganza.cl/
Editor in Chief: Fernando
Mujica M.

**HOBO MAGAZINE**
unf*ck the world
Vancouver BC
Published Occasionally,
founded in 2006
English
www.hobomagazine.com

**PYRAMID POWER**
The Journal of Art/Design/
Literature
Vancouver
www.pyramidpower.ca/

**VANIDADES**
Santiago
Monthly, founded in 1992
225 x 295 mm
Spanish
www.televisa.cl

# CHINA

# COLOMBIA

**TYPO**
Malesice
Every two months, founded in 2003
250 x 310 mm
Czech / English
www.magtypo.cz
Editor: Filip Blazek
Publisher: Vydavatelství Svt tisku, spol. s r. o.

**CREAM**
Hong Kong
Quarterly, founded in 2002
Variable format
5,000 copies
English
Founder: Takara Mak
Publisher: Media Nature Limited

**ICONIA**
Fashion Magazine
Bogota
Spanish / English
www.iconiamagazine.com/blog/
Director & Editor in Chief: Andres Rodriguez Villarreal
Publisher: Iconia Group

**UMELEC INTERNA- TIONAL**
Contemporary Art and Culture
Prague 8
Quarterly, founded in 1997
220 x 315 mm
6,000 copies
Czech / English / German / Spanish
www.divus.cz
Editor in chief: Alena Boika

**IDN**
International Designers Network
Hong Kong
Every two months, founded in 1992
235 x 297 mm
93,410 copies
English / Chinese / Japanese
www.idnworld.com
Editor: Bill Cranfield
Publisher: Systems Design Ltd

# CZECH REPUBLIC

**XMAG**
Technopop Magazine
Prague
Quarterly, founded in 1996
230 x 310 mm
10,000 copies
Czech
www.xmag.cz
Editor: Jakub Hrebenar
Publisher: Xpublishing

**PLUGZINE**
Beijing
Annual,
190 x 265 mm
2,000 copies
English / Chinese
www.plugzine.com
Editor in chief & Art Director: Jian Jiang

**GRAPHEION**
International review of contemporary prints, book and paper art.
Prague
Annual, founded in 1996
210 x 297 mm
1,300 copies
Czech / English
www.grapheion.cz
Editor in chief: Rachel de Candole

# DENMARK

**TIME OUT BEIJING**
Beijing
Monthly,
205 x 272 mm
English
www.timeout.com/cn/en/beijing/
Publisher: Time Out Group Ltd.

**HYPE MAGAZINE**
The magazine of the magazines
Prague
Bi-Annual, founded in 2002
210 x 260 mm
5,000 copies copies
Czech
www.xpublishing.cz
Founder and Editor: Tomas Zilvar
Publisher: Xpublishing

**BOOM BOOM**
Copenhague
founded in 2006
10,000 copies
Danish
dup.nu
Publisher: DUP

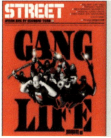

**STREET**
Urban Mag
Prague
5 x / year,
17,000 copies
www.xpublishing.cz
Editor in chief: Mickey Talls
Publisher: Xpublishing

**COVER**
Copenhagen
230 x 300 mm
Danish
www.cover.dk
Editorial Director: Frederik Bjerregaard
Publisher: Malling Publications

**DANSK**
Copenhagen
Quarterly, founded in 2002
240 x 300 mm
20,000 copies
English
www.danskmagazine.com/
Head of Marketing: Anette
Kjaergaard
Publisher: Style Counsel

**VS**
Copenhagen
Bi-Annual,
English / Danish / Swedish /
Norwegian
www.vspublications.com
Editor in chief: Jakob Forup
Stubkjaer

**ESTONIA**

**DOWNTOWN
MAGAZINE**
Music, Theatre, Art, Film,
Design, Shopping, Nightlife,
Gastronomy
Copenhagen K
Monthly (10 x / year), founded
in 2008
210 x 270 mm
30,000 copies
Danish
www.downtownmag.dk

**WONDERLAND**
Art.People.Culture
Copenhagen
Tri-Annual, founded in 2005
230 x 300 mm
Danish/English
www.wonderlandonline.dk
Art director: Simon Nygaard

**B EAST**
Fashion / Culture / Attitude
Tallinn
Quarterly, founded in 2005
240 x 310 mm
30,000 copies
English
www.beastnation.com
Publisher: Vijai Maheshwari
Publisher: Xpublishing

**FAT MAGAZINE**
English
www.fat-magazine.com
Editor in chief: Mette
Andersen

**DOMINICAN
REPUBLIC**

**FINLAND**

**KBH MAGAZINE**
Multi award winning magazine
on Copenhagen's urban
culture and architecture
Copenhagen
Monthly (11 x / year), founded
in 2005
210 x 270 mm
352,000 copies
Danish
www.kbhmagasin.dk
Publisher: Anders Ojgaard

**ADDICT**
Sumacultura
Santo Domingo
Every two months, founded in
01/02/2008
203.2 x 279.40
6,000 copies
Spanish
www.addict.com.do

**FRAMEWORK**
Helsinki
Bi-Annual, founded in 2004
240 x 340 mm
English
www.frame-fund.fi
Editorial Director: Marketta
Seppälä
Publisher: Frame Finnish Fund
for Art Exchange

**ROMEO + JULIET**
The leading danish lifestyle &
fashion magazine for men &
women.
Roskilde
Monthly,
223 x 297 mm
Danish
Editor in chief: Anders Hjort

**ECUADOR**

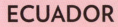

**KASINO A4**
The Most Melancholy
Magazine
Helsinki
Bi-Annual, founded in 2005
210 x 297 mm
6,000 copies
English
WeAreKasino.com
Photographer: Jussi Puikkonen
Publisher: WeAreKasino

**S MAGAZINE**
Copenhagen
Bi-Annual,
230 x 297 mm
30,000 copies
English
www.spublication.com
Editor in chief: Jens Stoltze

**BG MAGAZINE**
Cuenca
8 x / year, founded in 2002
210 x 297 mm
10,000 copies copies
Spanish / English
www.bgmagazine.com.ec
Assitant director: Jenny
Garate

**PÀPMAGAZINE**
Helsinki
Every two months, founded in
2001
210 x 285 mm
English
Editor in chief and Creative
Director: Tiina Alvesalo
Publisher: Oy Modabox Ltd

**PTAH**
Helsinki
Annual,
200 x 270 mm
English / Finnish
www.alvaraalto.fi
Editor in chief: Esa Laaksonen
Publisher: The Alvar Aalto
Academy

**ART ACTUEL**
Le Magazine des Arts
Contemporains
Every two months,
220 x 280 mm
French
www.artactuel.info
Editor in chief: Jean-Pierre
Frimbois
Publisher: Artoday sarl

**BLACKPOOL**
Paris
Quarterly, founded in 2005
230 x 280 mm
20,000 copies
French
www.blackpoolmagazine.com

# FRANCE

**ART PRESS**
La revue d'art contemporain
Paris
Monthly, founded in 1972
240 x 300 mm
French / English
www.artpress.com
Editor in chief: Catherine
Millet
Publisher: art press sarl

**BLAST**
Paris
Quarterly,
232 x 280 mm
French
www.blast.fr
Editor in chief: Julien
Millanvoye
Publisher: ICI Editions

**ACNE PAPER**
Paris
Bi-Annual, founded in 2005
280 x 375 mm
English
www.acnepaper.com
Editor at large: Johny
Johansson

**BAM**
Beaux-Arts Magazine
Paris
220 x 290 mm
French
www.beauxartsmagazine.com
Editor in chief: Fabrice
Bousteau
Publisher: TTM Editions

**C & G**
Concept & Graphisme
Paris
Quarterly, founded in 2004
270 x 355 mm
30.000 copies
French
www.idbmedia.com
Fashion & Beauty Editor &
Creative Director: Catherine
Rochette
Publisher: IDB Luxe SARL

**AE**
Aspire and emerge.
founded in 2005
English
www.ae-magazine.com/lit.htm
Editor: Don Duncan

**BANG!**
Le Meilleur de la BD
Paris
Quarterly, founded in 2005
230 x 300 mm
French
www.bangtz.com/
Editor in chief: Vincent
Bernière
Publisher: Les Editions
Indépendantes SA

**CHALLENGES**
Paris
Weekly, founded in 2005
200 x 265 mm
French
Editor in chief: Brigitte
Gry-Régent
Publisher: Editions Croque
Futur Sarl

**AMAAN**
The subversive avant-garde of
international luxury magazine
Paris
Quarterly,
English
www.amaanmagazine.com
Publisher: Paul Steinitz

**BESTIAIRE**
Animal Politik Magazine-
culture urbaine
208 x 270 mm
15,000 copies
French
Publisher & Editor in chief:
Olivier Braizat

**CHECKPOINT**
Review of art and
contemporary reflection
Paris
Annual, founded in 2006
297 x 420 mm
2,000 copies
Arabic / French
www.revuecheckpoint.fr
Chief editor and art director:
Djamel Kokene
Publisher: LAPLATEFORME
Editions

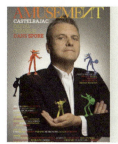

**AMUSEMENT**
Videogames, interaction, style,
inspiration
Paris
Quaterly, founded in 2008
220 x 300 mm
150, 000 copies
French / English
www.amusement.fr

**BIBA**
Paris Cedex 15
Monthly,
216 x 280 mm
French
www.bibamagazine.fr
Editor in chief: Christine Leiritz
Publisher: Mondadori

**CITIZEN K INTERNA-
TIONAL**
Paris
Quarterly,
240 x 295 mm
French
www.citizen-k.com/
Editor in chief: Vincent
Bergerat
Publisher: BMJ Ltd

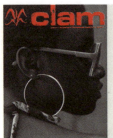

**CLAM**
Local everywhere
Paris
Bi-Annual, founded in 1999
210 x 280 mm
www.clammag.com
Creative director and fashion
director: Andy Okoroafor
Publisher: Clam sarl

**DEALER DE LUXE**
Paris
Annual,
English / French /
shop.dealerdeluxe.fr
Advertising Director:
Alexandre MAKOWSKI

**EGOÏSTE**
Paris
300 x 400 mm
French
www.egothemag.com
Founder: Nicole Wisniak
Publisher: Editions Cassini

**CLARK**
Street cultures-graphisme-
musique
Paris
Every two months, founded in
2001
225 x 300 mm
35,000 copies
French
www.clarkmagazine.com
Publisher: Guillaume Le Goff

**DEDICATE**
Un autre regard sur les
passions modernes
Paris
founded in 2002
230 x 285 mm
40,000 copies
French
www.dedicatemagazine.com
Publisher: Olivier Bouché
Publisher: DEdiCate
publishing

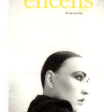

**ENCENS**
Epernay
Bi-Annual,
220 x 300 mm
20,000 copies
English / French
www.encensrevue.com/
Creative Director & Publisher:
Samuel Drira

**COMING UP**
Urban Guide: fashion / music /
arts / sports & hang out.
Marseille
Quarterly, founded in 2002
230 x 300 mm
15,000 copies
French / English
www.comingup.net
Editor in chief & Managing
Director: Eric Foucher
Publisher: Pimp Style sarl

**DONG**
Fashion Fanzine
Paris
Bi-Annual,
210 x 297 mm
3,000 copies
French / English/ German
www.dongmag.de
Publisher & Editor in chief:
Nicole Hardt

**ENVILLE**
City Magazine pour urbains
curieux
Boulogne-Billancourt
Monthly, founded in 2005
265 x 380 mm
150,000 copies
French
Editor in chief: Fanny Triboulet
Publisher: Urban France sarl

**CRASH**
Mode/Style/Beauty/Art/
Music/Design/Food/Ideas
Paris
Quarterly,
207 x 270 mm
French / English
www.crash.fr
Creative Director: Frank Perrin
Publisher: Crash Production
sarl

**DOUBLE**
Paris
Quarterly,
297 x 228 mm
French / English
www.lemagazinedouble.com
Fashion Director: Alexandra
Elbim
Publisher: All Publishing
French

**ETAPES GRAPHIQUES**
Graphisme design image
création
Paris
Monthly, founded in 1994
French
www.etapes.com
Editor in chief and art director:
Michel Chanaud
Publisher: Pyramyd NTCV

**CULTURES**
Le magazine des cultures
populaires
Monthly, founded in 2005
230 x 300 mm
French
www.culturesmag.com

**DUTCH**
Paris
Every two months, founded in
1995
230 x 292 mm
English
Editor in chief & Publisher:
Sandor Lubbe
Publisher: Art View bv

**Etapes:International**
Paris
Quarterly, founded in 2004
212 x 275 mm
English
www.etapes-international.com
Editor in chief & art director:
Michel Chanaud
Publisher: Pyramyd NTCV

**DE L'AIR**
Reportages d'un monde à
l'autre
Paris
Monthly,
260 x 320 mm
Editor in chief: Stéphane
Brasca
Publisher: Médina sarl

**EDGAR**
Le premier magazine du luxe
au masculin
Cannes
Every two months,
230 x 280 mm
French
www.luxmediagroup.com/
Editor in chief: Isabelle Garner-
one
Publisher: Lux Media Group

**FACE B**
Architecture from the other
side
Paris
Bi-Annual, founded in 2007
130 x 180 mm
English / French
www.faceb.fr
Editor: Aurélien Gillier

**FAIRY TALE**
Fashion magazine with a focus
on photography,
graphic-design and contempo-
rary typefaces.
Paris
Bi-Annual, founded in 2003
230 x 330 mm
English / German / French
www.fairytale-magazine.com
Editor: Achim Reichert
Publisher: VIER5

**FROG**
Dijon
Bi-Annual, founded in 2005
230 x 300 mm
French
www.frogmagazine.net
Publisher: Stéphanie Moisdon
Publisher: Frog sarl

**INK**
Lyon
founded in 2006
190 x 260 mm
French
www.ink-magazine.com

**FAKE-REAL MAGAZINE**
Paris
Quarterly, founded in 2006
200 x 280 mm
2,500 copies
French / English
www.fakerealmagazine.com
Production: Joel Dagès
Publisher: Tsunami-Addiction
for Plateforme Bureau

**GAULTMILLAU**
Clichy cedex
Every two months,
210 x 280 mm
French
www.guides-gaultmillau.fr/
Editor in chief & Director:
Patrick Mayenobe
Publisher: Société GaultMillau

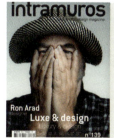

**INTRAMUROS**
Paris
Every two months,
225 x 300 mm
French / English
www.intramuros.fr
Editor in chief: Chantal
Hamaide

**FAMOUS**
Paris
Quarterly, founded in 2004
Variable
10,000 copies
French / English
www.tsunami-addiction.com
Editor in chief: Reiko
Underwater

**GLOSS**
Le magazine de la beauté et du
bien-être
Paris
Quarterly, founded in 2001
230 x 300 mm
90,000 copies
French / English
Editor: Thierry Taittinger
Publisher: Thierry Taittinger
SEPEM (a TTM Group
company)

**IT'S ROUGE**
Paris
230 x 310 mm
15,000 copies
English
Editor in chief & Creative
Director: Patrice Fuma Courtis
Publisher: It Publishing sarl

**FESTIV'ALL**
Le mensuel des événements
culturels en France et en
Europe.
Paris
Monthly, founded in 2006
210 x 297 mm
French
www.festivall.biz
Editor: Sylvain Florent

**HIAWATHA**
fashion books music
Paris
Quarterly,
150 x 210 mm
English
www.trans-id.be/Hiawatha.
html
Editor & Publisher: Jesse
Brouns
Publisher: Wig Wam Press

**J'AIME BEAUCOUP CE
QUE VOUS FAITES...**
Revue littéraire & artistique
Paris
Bi-Annual, founded in 2005
210 x 297 mm
1,000 copies
French
www.revueJBCQVF.com
Publishers: Christian Alandete,
Agnès Violeau
Publisher: Revue JBCQVF

**FLAVOR**
Paris
Every two months, founded in
2003
200 x 250 mm
200,000 copies
French
www.flavourmediagroup.com/

**ICONOFLY**
Diary of an accessory
Paris
Bi-Annual, founded in 2006
240 x 165 mm
80,000 copies
French / English
www.iconofly.com
Publisher: Olivia Bransbourg

**JALOUSE**
audace et modernité
Paris
Monthly (10 x / year), founded
in 1998
222 x 285 mm
French / English
www.jaloufashion.com
Editor in chief: Marie-José
Susskind-Jalou
Publisher: Les Editions Jalou
sarl

**FRENCH**
Revue de Modes
Paris
Bi-Annual, founded in 2005
230 x 300 mm
40,000 copies
English
www.frenchrevue.com
Editor at large: Lisa Tucker
Publisher: Thierry Le Gouès

**ICONOMIX**
Art, Brands and Business
Intelligence
Paris
Annual, founded in 2004
300 x 400 mm
30,000 copies
English
Founder: Eric Mézan
Publisher: art process

**JOHN MAGAZINE**
Paris
Bimonthly, founded in 2003
johnmagazine.free.fr
Publisher: Studio Jhon

JULES
Gentlemag
Paris
Monthly (11 x / year), founded
in 2005
204 x 275 mm
French
www.dm.net/~jules/magazine.
html
Editor in chief: Bruno Godard
Publisher: Buzzer Press

LADY CAPRICE
Paris
French
ladycapricemagazine.ning.com
Editor in chief: Emilie Janin

LIBÉRATION STYLE
Paris
240 x 340 mm
French
www.liberation.fr
Managing Editor: Vitorio De
Filippis

KAISERIN
A magazine for boys with
problems
Paris
Bi-Annual, founded in 2007
176 x 250 mm
3,000 copies
French / English
www.kaiserin-magazine.com
Publisher: Arnaud-Pierre
Fourtané

LE COLETTE
magalogue
Paris
Bi-Annual, founded in 2003
165 x 240 mm
10,000 copies
French / English
www.colette.fr

LIIÉ
Luxe et Culture Urbaine
Paris
Every two months, founded in
2005
210 x 275 mm
French
www.liiemag.com
Editor in chief: Rosemonde
Pierre-Louis
Publisher: LIIE Edition sarl

KARNET
Voyage-Mode-Lifestyle
Paris
Every two months, founded in
2005
210 x 285 mm
French / English/ German
Publisher: Pascale Costa
Publisher: Bleucom Editions
SAS

LE PURPLE JOURNAL
Paris
Quarterly, founded in 2003
210 x 275 mm
French / English
www.purple.fr
Publisher & Editor in chief:
Elein Fleiss
Publisher: Purple Institute

LIVRAISON
Revue d'art contemporain
contemporary arts journal
Strasbourg
Bi-Annual,
165 x 240 mm
French / English
www.r-livraison.org
Editor in chief: Nicolas Simonin
Publisher: Rhinocéros

KAUGUMMI MAGAZINE
Contemporary drawing and
photography
Rennes
Bi-Annual, founded in 2006
210 x 290 mm
500 copies copies
English
www.kaugummi.fr
Publisher: Bartolomé Sanson

LE RÉSERVOIR
Alimente gratuitement votre
curiosité
Saint-avertin
Quarterly, founded in 2003
150 x 210 mm
French
www.lereservoir.org
Managing Editor: Cédric
Neige

MAGAZINE
You are what you read
Paris
Every two months (5 x / year),
200 x 260 mm
French / English
www.acp.com.au
Founder: Angelo Cirimele
Publisher: ACP

L'OFFICIEL
De la couture et de la mode de
Paris
Paris
Monthly (10 x / year), founded
in 1921
220 x 282 mm
French
www.jaloufashion.com
Editor in chief & Managing
Director: Marie-José Jalou
Publisher: Les Editions Jalou
sarl

LE TIGRE
Paris
Monthly,
French
www.le-tigre.net

MAGIC
Revue pop moderne
Paris
Monthly,
230 x 300 mm
French
www.magicrpm.com
Directeur: Christophe Basterra
Publisher: Bonne Nouvelle
Editions sarl

L'OPTIMUM
Everything for Men
Paris
Monthly (8 x / year), founded
in 1996
227 x 275 mm
French
www.jaloufashion.com
Director & Publisher:
Marie-José Susskind-Jalou
Publisher: Les Editions Jalou
sarl

LES INROCKUPTIBLES
L'hebdo musique, cinéma,
livres, etc
Paris
Weekly, founded in 1986
230 x 280 mm
French
www.lesinrocks.com
Editor in chief: Christian Fevret

MÉDIAS
Lire entre les lignes
Paris
Quarterly, founded in 2004
195 x 255 mm
25,000 copies
French
www.revue-medias.com
Publisher: Pierre Hessler
Publisher: Minuit moins le
quart

MILK
Paris
Quarterly,
French
www.milkmagazine.net/
accueil_milk-Francais,m,1

NUKE
Paris
Bi-Annual,
240 x 340 mm
20,000 copies
French / English
www.nuke.fr
Founder & creative director:
Jenny Mannerheim

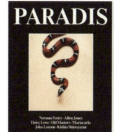

PARADIS
A Magazine for the
contemporary man
Paris
Bi-Annual,
45,000 copies
French / English
www.paradismagazine.com
Publisher: Thomas Lenthal
SARL

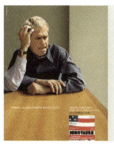

MINOTAURE
Paris
Quarterly, founded in 2003
210 x 275 mm
French
Director: Guillaume Dasquié
Publisher: Editions du
Minotaure
www.leminotaure.org

NUMÉRO
Le magazine international de
mode
Paris
Monthly, founded in 1998
230 x 300 mm
French
www.numero-magazine.com
Président Directeur général:
Alain Ayache
Publisher: Numéro PRESSE
SA

PARIS CAPITALE
Paris
Monthly,
210 x 275 mm
French
www.leclubparis.com
Publisher: Anne-Marie
Herrmann
Publisher: Sarl Paris 3S

MONSIEUR
Le magazine de l'Homme
élégant - Mode, accessoires,
beauté, luxe
Paris
Every two months, founded in
1920
230 x 300 mm
French
www.monsieur.fr
Editor in chief: François-Jean
Daehn
Publisher: Montaigne
Publications

NUMÉRO HOMME
Le magazine international de
mode pour homme
Paris
Quarterly, founded in 2000
230 x 300 mm
French
www.numero-magazine.com
Publisher: Alain Ayache
Publisher: Numéro PRESSE
SA

PARIS, LA
Paris
Bi-Annual,
English
http://paris-la.com/

MOUVEMENT
L'indisciplinaire des arts vivants
Paris
Every two months, founded in
1998
225 x 285 mm
French
www.mouvement.net
Editor in chief: Jean-Marc
Adolphe
Publisher: Editions du
mouvement

NUSIGN*
Art-in-progress magazine
Paris
Quarterly, founded in 2007
210 x 270 mm
3,000 copies
English / French
www.myspace.com/nusign
Publisher: L'ARAIGNEE
Publisher: L'araignee sarl

PERMANENT FOOD
Bi-Annual, founded in 1995
170 x 235 mm
French / English
Publisher: L'association des
temps libérés

MUTEEN
Il y a une vie avant vingt ans…
évidemment!
Paris
Monthly,
220 x 282 mm
French
www.muteen.com
Editor in chief: Catherin
Nerson
Publisher: Les Editions Jalou
sarl

OBLIK
lik(e) la culture
Saint-Avertin
Every two months, founded in
2005
French
www.oblikmag.com
Publishing director: Jeremy

PERSO
Paris
Monthly (10 x / year),
216 x 286 mm
French
Director: Jean-Yves Le Fur
Publisher: Groupe Alain
Ayache
www.groupe-ayache.com

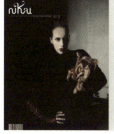

NIKAU
The New Face Of Design
La Ciotat
Quarterly, founded in 2007
225 x 300 mm
French / English
www.nikaumag.com
Publisher and founder:
Caroline Sehi
Publisher: Mon Quartier 13

PALAIS /
Le nouveau magazine
Paris
Tri-Annual, founded in 2006
210 x 280 mm
French / English
www.palaismagazine.com
Publisher: Marc-Olivier
Wahler
Publisher: Palais de Tokyo

PHILOSOPHIE
MAGAZINE
Paris
Monthly, founded in 2006
215 x 280 mm
French
www.philomag.com
Editor in chief: Alexandre
Lacroix

**PHOTO**
Levallois-Perret Cedex
Monthly,
230 x 297 mm
French
www.photo.fr
Managing Editor & Art
Director: Eric Colmet Daage
Publisher: Hachette Filipacchi
Associés

**REDUX**
Collectif Combo présente
Anglet
Quarterly,
170 x 250 mm
French / English
www.reduxmag.com
Editor & Art Director: Erwann
Lameignère
Publisher: Erwann Lameignère

**TECHNIKART**
Culture & Société
Paris
Monthly,
210 x 275 mm
French
www.technikart.com
Rédacteur en chef: Raphaël
Turcat
Publisher: Technikart sarl

**POINT D'IRONIE**
Paris
Quarterly,
305 x 430 mm
French / English
www.pointdironie.com
Managing Editor: Maria Inés
Rodriguez
Publisher: agnès b.

**RENDEZ-VOUS
MAGAZINE**
culture, fashion and society
Paris
Every two months (5 x / year),
founded in 2005
245 x 330 mm
150,000 copies
French
www.rendezvousmagazine.fr

**TECHNIKART
MADEMOISELLE**
99% fashion magazine
Paris
Quarterly, founded in Founded
in 2003
290 x 410 mm
French
www.technikart-mademoiselle.
com
Editor in chief: Raphaël Turcat
Publisher: Technikart sarl

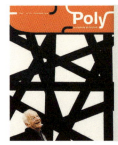

**POLY**
La culture se cultive !
Strasbourg
7 x / year,
200 x 270 mm
15,000 copies copies
French
www.bkn.fr
Art director: Mathieu Linotte
Publisher: BKN

**ROUGE GORGE**
Paris
Published Irregularly, founded
in 2003
French

**TÊTU**
Le magazine des gays et des
Lesbiennes
Paris
Monthly (11 x / year),
230 x 300 mm
French
www.tetu.com
Editor in chief: Thomas
Doustaly
Publisher: CPPD SAS

**PRÉFÉRENCES MAG**
Le magazine des nouveaux
genres
Levallois
Every two months,
210 x 278 mm
French
www.preferencesmag.com
Manager: Jean Gaspar
Publisher: Préférences Editions

**SELF SERVICE**
Paris
Bi-Annual, founded in 1995
235 x 305 mm
30,000 copies
English
www.selfservicemagazine.com
Fashion Director: Camille
Bidault Waddington
Publisher: Ezra Petronio sarl

**TOUS**
Des gens, des vies
Paris
Monthly (11 x / year), founded
in 2003
230 x 285 mm
French
Director: Stéphane Bauche

**PURPLE FASHION**
Paris
Bi-Annual, founded in 2004
230 x 300 mm
English
www.purple.fr
Editor in chief & Creative
Director: Olivier Zahm
Publisher: Purple Institute

**STANDARD**
Petits écrans et fins des grands
empires. Telle est la télé.
Paris
French
www.standardmagazine.com
Editor in Chief: Magali Aubert

**TRANSVERSALE**
Arts et sciences en recherche
transversale Erkundungen in
Kunst und wissenschaft
Paris
Annual, founded in 2004
170 X 240 mm
German / French
http://transversale.org

**R2 MAG**
Regards sur l'air(e) Locale
Quarterly, founded in 2001
260 x 210 mm
15,000 copies copies
French
Publisher, Editor in chief & Art
Director: Bernard Sébastien
Publisher: B&M

**STILETTO**
Paris
Tri-Annual, founded in 2003
230 x 300 mm
35,000 copies
French / English
www.stiletto.fr
Publisher & Editor in chief:
Laurence Benaïm
Publisher: Stiletto Editions

**TRAX**
Paris
Monthly,
230 x 300 mm
French
Editor in chief: Alexandre
Jaillon
Publisher: IXO Publishing SA

**TRUBLYON**
le magazine des scratch papiers
Quarterly, founded in 2003
210 x 250 mm
20,000 copies
French
www.trublyon.com
Publisher & Editor in chief: Emma Hebert
Publisher: Trublyon Association

**VOGUE PARIS**
Paris
Monthly (10 x / year),
220 x 285 mm
French
www.vogue.fr
Editor in chief: Carine Roitfeld
Publisher: Condé Nast Publications

**+ROSEBUD**
Ammerndorf
Every 15 months, founded in 1998
Various format
4,000 copies
English
www.rosebudmagazine.com
Founder & Publisher: Ralf Herms
Publisher: Rosebud, Inc., Herms & Magistris Design OG

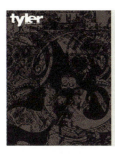

**TYLER**
Sports & Cultures Urbaines
Paris
Tri-Annual, founded in 2001
210 x 275 mm
French
www.tylerstudio.com
Managing editor: François Bocquier

**WAD**
We're different: le magazine des modes et cultures urbaines
Paris
Quarterly, founded in 1999
230 x 300 mm
200,000 copies
French / English
www.wadmag.com
Publisher: Bruno Collin
Publisher: Les Editions Trevilly & Family

**032C**
Fashion, art & conflict
Berlin
Bi-Annual, founded in 2000
200 x 270 mm
English
www.032c.com
Editor in chief: Sandra Von Mayer
Publisher: 032c workshop

**UN**
Paris
Quarterly,
230 x 260 mm
French / English
www.unsixhuit.com
Director & Publisher: Michel Rivière
Publisher: Publications 3+

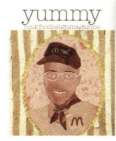

**YUMMY**
fastfooddesignmagazine
Paris
Annual, founded in 2005
212 x 275 mm
1,000 copies
French / English
www.eat-fast.net
Art Director & Publisher: Alexandra Jean

**11FREUNDE**
Magazin für Fussball-Kultur
Berlin
Monthly, founded in 2000
210 x 280 mm
German
www.11freunde.de
Editor: Dirk Brichzi
Publisher: INTRO Verlag GmbH & Co

**UNDER THE INFLUENCE**
Paris
Quarterly, founded in 2007
240 x 340
10,000 copies
English
www.undertheinfluencemaga-zine.com/
Editor and Creative Director: Mark O'Sullivan

**ZEUXIS**
Magazine international du Film sur l'Art.
Paris
Monthly, founded in 2000
210 x 270 mm
4,000 copies
French
www.zeuxis.fr
Editor in chief, Creative Director & Publisher: Gisèle Breteau Skira

**33 GRAD NORD 44 GRAD OST**
594 x 841 mm
200 copies
German
www.33gradnord44gradost.de
Publisher: Florian Conradi

**VIEW ON COLOUR**
Paris
Quarterly,
240 x 305 mm
English
www.edelkoort.com
Art Director: Lidewij Edelkoort
Publisher: United Publishers SA

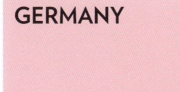

# GERMANY

**ACHTUNG**
Zeitschrift für Mode
Berlin
Bi-Annual, founded in 2003
225 x 300 mm
10,000 copies
German / English
www.achtung-mode.com
Editor in chief & Creative director: Markus Ebner
Publisher: Markus Ebner

**VOGUE HOMMES INTER-NATIONAL**
Paris
Bi-Annual,
230 x 297 mm
English
www.voguehommes.com
Editor in chief & Creative Director: Bruno Danto
Publisher: Condé Nast Publications

**\*FUSION**
experimental magazine
Cologne
Irregularly published,
140 x 190 mm
English
www.khm.de/mg/seminare/fusion

**ALERT**
Berlin
Every two months,
235 x 295 mm
German
www.alertmagazin.de
Art Director: Sibylle Trenck

**AM13**
Kampf!
Stuttgart
founded in 2008
240 x 320 mm
1,500 copies
German / English
www.am13.de
Publisher: Manuel Dollt

**BAILGUN MAGAZINE**
Skateboarding, photography,
art, culture, traveling
Münster
Every two months, founded in
2005
English
www.bailgun.com
Editor in chief: Gerd Rieger

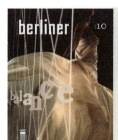

**BERLINER**
Urbanity Culture Politics
Berlin
Quarterly, founded in 2002
200 x 267 mm
English
www.berlinermagazine.com
Publisher & Editor in chief:
Boris Moshkovits

**AMORE POSTER
MAGAZINE**
Munich
founded in 2003
297 x 420 mm
German
www.gomma.de

**BALKON & GARTEN**
Das Gartenmagazin aus Berlin
/ The gardening magazine
from Berlin
Berlin
Every two months, founded in
2004
148 x 210 mm
150 copies
German
www.balkon-garten.de
Publisher and graphic
designer: Anke Wulffen

**BLOND MAGAZIN**
We are one step ahead
Hamburg
Monthly,
230 x 300 mm
German
www.blondmag.com
Editor in chief: Sven Bergmann
Publisher: blond Media GmbH

**ANYWAY**
There is no other way to travel
Berlin
Every two months, founded in
2005
200 x 250 mm
German / English
www.anyway-magazine.com/
Editor & Creative Director:
Alexander Geringer
Publisher: Ahead Media
GmbH

**BANG BANG BERLIN**
Berlin
German / English
bangbangberlin.com

**BOOKLET**
Magazin für Fotografie
Cologne
Bi-Annual, founded in 2004
190 x 230 mm
30,000 copies
German / English
www.booklet.ws
Publisher: home made GmbH

**ARCH+**
Journal for architecture
Berlin
Quarterly, founded in 1967
235 x 297 mm
32,000 copies
German
www.archplus.net
Art director: Mike Meiré
Publisher: ARCH+ Verlag
GmbH

**BASTARD**
Art, Design & Culture
Bottrop
Published Irregularly, founded
in 2005
German / English
www.bastardmagazine.net

**BOXHORN**
das Magazin aus dem
Fachbereich Gestaltung in
Aachen
Aachen
Bi-Annual, founded in 1998
Various format
German
www.boxhorn-magazin.de

**ARTINVESTOR**
Herzberg / Harz
230 x 298 mm
German
www.artinvestor.de
Publisher: ARTinvestor /
artpartners GmbH

**BAUMEISTER**
Zeitschrift für Architektur
Munich
German
www.baumeister.de
Editor in chief: Dr. Ing.
Wolfgang Bachmann
Publisher: Georg D.W. Callwey
GmbH & Co KG

**BRAND EINS**
Wirtschaftsmagazin
Hamburg
Monthly, founded in 1999
212 x 280 mm
German
www.brandeins.de
Editor in chief: Gabriele
Fischer
Publisher: brand eins Verlag
GmbH & co

**AUF ABWEGEN**
Cologne
Annual,
1,000 copies copies
German
www.aufabwegen.de

**BAUWELT**
Berlin
235 x 297 mm
German
www.bauwelt.de
Editor in chief: Felix Zwoch

**BRANSCH**
Hamburg
Annual, founded in 2002
230 x 300 mm
20,000 copies
English
www.branschmagazine.com
Publisher: Susanne Abatenni
Publisher: Abatenni Verlag

**C'EST LA VIE**
Berlin
founded in 2004
210 x 280 mm
German / French
Editor: Nicolas Bourquin
Publisher: etc. publications
www.etc-publications.com

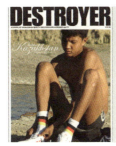

**DESTROYER**
Journal of Apollonian Beauty
and Dionysian Sexuality
Berlin
Tri-Annual, founded in May
2006
148 x 210 mm
4,500 copies copies
English
www.destroyermag.com
Editor in chief: Karl Andersson

**ETC. PEACE**
Issues that matter
Berlin
Irregular, founded in 2002
420 x 600 mm
1,000 copies
English / German
www.etc-publications.com
Publisher: etc. publications

**CICERO**
Magazin für politische Kultur
Berlin
Monthly,
210 x 286 mm
German
www.cicero.de
Editor in chief: Dr. Wolfram
Weimer
Publisher: Ringier Publishing
GmbH

**DEUTSCH**
Berlin
230 x 300 mm
German
www.deutschmagazine.org
Editor in chief: Bülent
Publisher: Art Berlin Verlag

**EUROPEAN PHOTOGRA-PHY**
Berlin
Bi-Annual, founded in 1980
240 x 300 mm
German / English
www.equivalence.com
Editor and publisher: Andreas
Müller-Pohle
Publisher: European
Photography

**DE:BUG**
Berlin
Monthly,
German
www.de-bug.de
Publisher: DE:BUG Verlags
GmbH

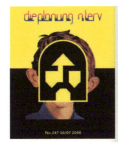

**DIE PLANUNG / A TERV**
Berlin
founded in 2007
198 x 258
German / Hungarian / English
www.dieplanung.org
Editors and Publishers: Sandra
Bartoli, Martin Conrads, Silvan
Linden, Levente Polyák,
Katarina _evic

**FELD HOMMES**
Hamburg
Quarterly,
German
www.feld-magazine.com
Creative Director: Mieke
Haase
Publisher: Feld Verlag

**DER FREUND**
Fire walk with me
Hamburg
Quarterly, founded in 2004
210 x 250 mm
German
www.derfreund.com
Editor in chief: Dr Eckhart
Nickel
Publisher: Axel Springer AG

**DIENACHT**
Trier
Bi-Annual, founded in 2007
150 x 180 mm
1,000 copies
German / English
www.dienacht-magazine.com
Founder and Publisher: Calin
Kruse

**FRAU BÖHM**
Photography now.
Düsseldorf
Quarterly, founded in 1999
210 x 297 mm
No text
www.frau-boehm.de

**DER WEDDING**
Das Kulturmagazin
Berlin
Bi-annual, founded in 2008
210 x 270 mm
5,000 copies copies
German
www.derwedding.de
Publisher & Creative Director:
Axel Völcker
Publisher: Axel Völcker

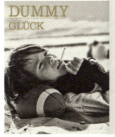

**DUMMY**
Das Gesellschaftsmagazin
Berlin
Quarterly,
230 x 270 mm
30,000 copies
German
www.dummy-magazin.de
Editor: Oliver Gehrs
Publisher: Schön & Gut

**FREIER**
Berlin
Monthly (11 x / year),
195 x 260 mm
German/English text supply
www.neuedokumente.de
Publisher: Neue Dokumente

**DESIGNERS DIGEST**
The international artwork
magazine
Hamburg
Quarterly, founded in 2008
240 x 330 mm
25,000 copies
German / English
www.designers-digest.de

**ELECTRONIC BEATS**
Berlin
Quarterly, founded in 2005
216 x 280 mm
50,000 copies
English
www.electronicbeats.net
Editor in chief: Liz McGrath
Publisher: Commandante
Berlin GmbH

**GALORE**
Das Interview Magazin
Dortmund
Monthly (10 x / year), founded
in 2003
225 x 300 mm
90,000 copies
German
www.galore.de
Editor: Michael Lohrmann
Publisher: Dialog GmbH

**H.O.M.E.**
Das Magazin fürs Leben
Berlin
Monthly,
223 x 290 mm
German
Editor in chief: Gerald Sturz
Publisher: Ahead Media
GmbH

**HUSK MAGAZINE**
A fucking good Zine about
music, style, art and everything
else.
Peissenberg
Published irregularly, founded
in 2007
1,000 copies
German / English
www.huskmagazine.de

**KID'S WEAR (INTERNA-TIONAL)**
Cologne
Bi-Annual, founded in 1995
230 x 300 mm
32,000 copies
English / German / Italian
www.kidswear-magazine.com
Managing Editor &
Advertising Director:
Ann-Katrin Weiner
Publisher: kid's wear verlag

**HATE**
Magazin für Relevanz und Stil
Berlin
Tri-Annual, founded in 2008
210 x 300 mm
6,000 copies
German
www.hate-mag.com
Publisher: Nina Scholz

**INSIDE ARTZINE**
Artcore since 1990: Graphical
fevervisions from the depth of
the creativ underground: The
sewer!
Trier
Bi-Annual, founded in 1990
210 x 297 mm
600-800 copies
English
www.inside-artzine.de

**LACE**
Sneakers Magazine
Mülheim/Ruhr
Bi-Annual, founded in 2003
German / English
www.lace-mag.de
Publisher: lace Verlag

**HEKMAG**
Berlin
Bi-Annual, founded in 2005
245 x 335 mm
50,000 copies
English/German
www.hekmag.com
Editor in chief & Creative
Director: André Aimaq
Publisher: Aimaq Rapp Stolle
GmbH

**J'N'C**
Fashion Trend Magazine
Langenfeld
Quarterly, founded in 1992
230 x 300 mm
8,000 - 15,000 copies
German
www.jnc-net.de
Director: Rainer Schlatmann
Publisher: J&C Publishing
Services GmbH

**LASER MAGAZINE**
Living in a magazine
German / English
www.lasermag.de
Editors: Michael Satter, Tina
Schott, Nicole Klein and Tina
Kohlmann

**HERE COMES
IRREGULAR**
Results, byproducts, leftovers,
findings
Berlin
founded in 2008
210 x 270 mm
200 copies
English
www.ilikeyourbadbreathdaddy.
blogspot.com/2008/04/
here-comes-irregular.html
Publisher: Martin Müller

**JAM**
Jam Der Bücherscout/The
Book Scout
Hamburg
Bi-Annual, founded in 2003
123 x 142 mm
28,000 copies
German / English
www.jam-publications.com
Director & Editor in Chief:
Enja Jans

**LEICA FOTOGRAFIE
INTERNATIONAL**
Hamburg
Monthly (8 x / year),
217 x 280 mm
German
www.lfi-online.de/ceemes/
Editor in chief: Frank P.
Lohstöter
Publisher: Image Division
Publishing GmbH

**HOW TO MAGAZINE**
Das kritische Themenmagazin
Leipzig
Bi-Annual,
230 x 300 mm
750 copies
German
www.howtomag.com
Publisher: Tim Klinger

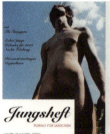

**JUNGSHEFT**
rude, nude, cute ...
Cologne
Published irregularly, founded
in 2005
150 x 210 mm
4,000 copies
German / English
www.jungsheft.de
Founder: Nicole Rüdiger

**LIDO**
Das Magazin von KIT - Kunst
im Tunnel
Düsseldorf
Quaterly, founded in 2008
220 x 280 mm
1,000 copies
German
www.kunst-im-tunnel.de
Editor in chief: Gertrud Peters

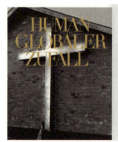

**HUMANGLOBALER
ZUFALL**
Berlin
Quarterly, founded in October
2007
205 x 255 mm
German
www.humanglobalerzufall.de

**KATJA**
It's zine
Berlin
Bi-Annual, founded in 2005
266 x 362 mm
500 copies
German / English
Art Director: Matthias
Ernstberger

**LIEBLING**
Berlin
Every two months, founded in
2005
305 x 470 mm
75,000 copies
German
www.liebling-zeitung.com
Editor in chief: Anne Urbauer,
Moritz von Uslar
Publisher: Fifteen Minutes
GmbH

**LIESCHEN**
Revolution of assiduity
Dortmund
Annual, founded in 2006
335 x 215 mm
1,000 -1,200 copies
German
www.lieschen.net
Publisher: University of
Applied Sciences & Arts,
Dortmund

**MONOPOL**
Magazin für Kunst und Leben
Berlin
Monthly, founded in 2004
220 x 280 mm
55,000 copies
German
www.monopol-magazin.de
Editor: Florian Illies
Publisher: Juno Verlag GmbH

**NOVUM**
World of Graphic Design
Munich
Monthly,
230 x 297 mm
German / English
www.novumnet.de
Editor in chief: Bettina Ulrich
Publisher: New Media
Magazine Verlag GmbH

**LODOWN**
pop relevant subjects before
art
Berlin
Every two months (5 x /year),
265 x 232 mm
English
www.lodownmagazine.com
Publisher & Editor: Thomas
Marecki

**NATURFREUNDIN**
Zeitschrift für nachhaltige
Entwicklung sozial- ökologisch
-demokratisch
Berlin
Quarterly, founded in 1930
210 x 297 mm
German
www.naturfreundin.
naturfreunde.de/

**ODDS AND ENDS**
Magazine for eclectic
treasuries
Berlin
English
odds-and-ends.eu

**LOOM**
Walking with the speed of light
Weimar
founded in 2007
297 x 210 mm
English / German
www.loom-mag.net

**NEID**
Berlin
founded in 1992
German
www.thing.de/neid
Co-Founder / Editor: Ina
Wudtke

**PAGE**
Hamburg
Monthly, founded in 1986
210 x 297 mm
German
www.page-online.de
Editor in chief: Gabriele
Günder
Publisher: Ebner Verlag
GmbH & Co. KG

**LUNA MAGAZINE**
The first german kidsfashion
magazine
Cologne
Quarterly, founded in 2005
210 x 280 mm
German
www.luna-magazin.de

**NEON**
Munich
Monthly, founded in 2003
212 x 287 mm
190,000 copies
German
www.neon.de
Editor in chief: Michael Ebert
Publisher: Gruner + Jahr AG &
Co KG

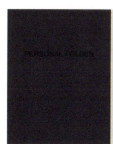

**PERSONAL FOLDER**
Art-Project
Cologne
Published irregularly, founded
in 2004
170 x 230 mm
10-30 copies
No Text
www.personal-folder.com
Founder and Editor: John
Harten
Publisher: John Harten

**MINIINTERNATIONAL**
Quarterly, founded in 2001
207 x 264 mm
200,000 copies
German / English / French /
Japanese/ Chinese
www.MINIspace.com/
magazine
Creative Director: Mike Meiré
Publisher: Bayerische Motoren
Werke AG, MINI Brand
Management

**NEUE MODE MAGAZINE**
Frankfurt Main
Bi-Annual, founded in 2003
235 x 295 mm
35,000 copies
English
www.neuemodemagazine.com
Editor in Chief & Creative
Director: Oliver Daxenbichler
Publisher: Oliver Daxenbichler
& Nada Nadia Vagioka

**PLUG**
ex.tensions
Berlin
founded in 2005
200 x 260 mm
200 copies
English / German
www.ilikeyourbadbreathdaddy.
blogspot.com/2005/06/
plug-zine.html
Publisher: Martin Müller

**MONO.KULTUR**
Berlin
Quarterly, founded in 2005
150 x 200 mm
5,000 copies
English
www.mono-kultur.com
Publisher: Kai Von Rabenau

**NEUE PROBLEME**
Das Magazin mit heißen
Geschichten
Cologne
Annual, founded in 2006
150 x 210 mm
500 copies
German / English
www.neue-probleme.de

**POLENPLUS**
Life, art & economy
Berlin
Quarterly, founded in 2006
210 x 280 mm
German
www.polenplus.eu
Editor in chief: Antje
Ritter-Jasinska

**PONY**
Göttingen
Monthly (10 x / year), founded
in February 2005
105 x 148 mm
60,000 copies
German
www.readmypony.com
Publisher: Pony medien

**ROGER**
Design People Questions
Cologne
founded in 2004
191 x 297 mm
10,000 copies
German / English
www.rogermagazine.net
Publisher: daab GmbH

**SPATIUM**
Magazin für Typografie
Offenbach
Annual,
150 x 230 mm
German / English
www.typosition.de
Editor: Peter Reichard
Publisher: Peter Reichard

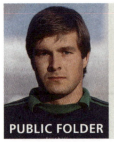

**PUBLIC FOLDER**
Cologne
Published irregularly, founded
in 2004
170 x 230 mm
1,000 copies
English / German
www.public-folder.com
Founder and Editor: John
Harten
Publisher: John Harten

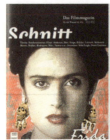

**SCHNITT**
Das Filmmagazin
Cologne
Quarterly,
210 x 297 mm
German
www.schnitt.de
Editor in chief: Olivier
Baumgarten

**SPECTOR CUT+PASTE**
A spectre is hunting Europe
Leipzig
Published irregularly, founded
in 2001
230 x 296 mm
3,000 copies
German / English
www.spectormag.net
Founder & Publisher: Tilo
Schulz

**QVEST**
Berlin
Every two months,
230 x 285 mm
80,000 copies copies
German / English
www.qvest.de
Publisher: Lothar Eckstein
Publisher: B20 publishing
GmbH

**SHIFT!**
Berlin
Published Irregularly, founded
in 1996
Variable format
English
www.shift.de
Art Director: Anja Lutz
Publisher: gutentagverlag

**SPEX**
Das Magazin für Popkultur
Cologne
Monthly,
230 x 295 mm
German
www.spex.de
Editor in chief: Uwe Viehmann
Publisher: Piranha Media
GmbH

**RAKETE**
The Poster Design Magazin
Duesseldorf
Annual, founded in 2005
160 x 220 mm
1,500 copies
German / English
www.raketemag.de
Editor in chief & Direction:
Kathrin Spohr

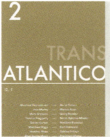

**SITE MAGAZINE**
Duesseldorf
Bi-Annual, founded in 1998
210 x 280 mm
1,300 copies
German / English
www.sitesite.de
Founders & directors: Petra
Rinck and Ralf Brög
Publisher: Hausammeer
Productions

**SQUINT**
Hamburg
220 x 278 mm
English
www.squintmagazine.com
Publisher and Creative
Director: Anita Mrusek
Publisher: Squint Magazine
GmbH

**REGINA**
Berlin
Monthly, founded in 1994
210 x 275 mm
English
www.regina-magazine.de
Founder & Editor: Regina
Möller
Publisher: artranspennine 98

**SLANTED**
Typography
Karlsruhe
Quarterly, founded in 2005
205 x 255 mm
10,000 copies
German / English
www.slanted.de
Director: Lars Harmsen

**STREETWEAR TODAY**
International Styles
Bochum
Quarterly,
240 x 340 mm
German / English
www.streetwear-today.de
Editor in Chief: Martin
Magielka
Publisher: Magseven GmbH

**REVOLVER**
Zeitschrift für Film
Berlin
Bi-Annual, founded in 1998
105 x 145 mm
1,800 copies
German
www.revolver-film.de
Editors: Jens Börner, Benjamin
Heisenberg, Nicolas
Wackerbarth, Christoph
Hochhäusler
Publisher: Verlag der Autoren
GmbH & Co KG

**SLEEK**
Magazine for art and fashion
Berlin
Quarterly, founded in 2002
220 x 280 mm
English / German
www.sleekmag.com
Publisher: Lothar Eckstein
Publisher: B20 publishing
GmbH

**SW MAGAZIN**
Flensburg
Annual, founded in 1993
German
www.sw-magazin.com

**TUSH**
Beauty all over
Hamburg
Quarterly, founded in 2005
220 x 285 mm
German
www.tushmagazine.com
Director & Editor in chief:
Armin Morbach

**GREECE**

**GUATEMALA**

**VIER**
Das Magazin der Hochschule
für Künste Bremen
Bremen
Bi-Annual, founded in 2007
210 x 277 mm
German
www.vier.hfk-bremen.de
Publisher: Peter Rautmann

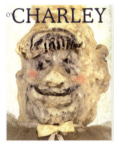

**CHARLEY**
Athens
Published irregularly, founded
in 2000
Various format
English
www.deste.gr
Founder & Editor: Maurizio
Cattelan

**TAXI**
Guatemala
Every two months, founded in
2004
10,000 copies
Spanish / English
www.revistataxi.com
Founder & Director: Juan
Manuel Alvarado
Publisher: Sin Título S.A.

**VON HERZEN**
German
www.vonherzenweb.de/
Founder: Jonas Natterer

**OZON**
Athens
Monthly, founded in 1996
235 x 280 mm
40,000 copies
Greek / English
www.ozonweb.com

**HUNGARY**

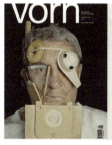

**VORN**
Berlin
Annual,
210 x 296 mm
German / English
www.vornmagazine.com
Publisher: Joachim Baldauf
Publisher: Printkultur Gbr

**PARALLAXI**
Ideas,Stories, Trends, People,
City
Thessaloniki
Monthly, founded in 1989
270 x 325 mm
25,000 copies
Greek
www.parallaximag.gr
Founder & Editor in Chief:
George Toulas
Publisher: Katerina
Karamfilidou

**BALKON**
Art, magazine, contemporary
Budapest
Monthly, founded in 1993
235 x 305 mm
8,000 copies
Hungarian
www.balkon.hu

**ZOO MAGAZINE**
Berlin
Bi-Annual, founded in 2003
230 x 298 mm
German
www.zoomagazine.de
Editor in chief: Sandor Lubbe
Publisher: Melon Collie

**SOUL**
Secrets Of Urban Life
Thessaloniki
Monthly, founded in 2006
235 x 330 mm
Greek
www.soulmag.gr

**PEP! MAGAZINE**
Budapest
Quarterly, founded in 2003
216 x 279 mm
12,000 copies
Hungarian
www.pepmagazin.hu
Managing Editor in chief:
Zsuzsanna Karpati
Publisher: Optimal Marketing
Bt.

**ZWIEBELFISCH**
Magazin für Gestaltung
Freiburg
Annual, founded in 2002
220 x 280 mm
1,500 copies
German
www.zwiebelfisch-magazin.de/
Editor: Wolfgang Wick
Publisher: Freie Hochschule
für Grafik-Design & Bildende
Kunst e.V

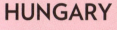

# INDIA

# ISRAEL

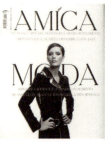

**AMICA**
Milan
Monthly,
215 x 285 mm
Italian
www.luluguinness.com/
amica_magazine_july.php
Editor: Daniela Bianchini
Publisher: RCS Mediagroup

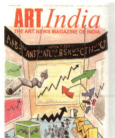

**ART INDIA**
Mumbai
founded in 1990
220 x 290 mm
English
www.artindiamag.com
Publisher: Art India Publishing
Co. Pvt. Ltd.

**(H)EARAT SHULAYM**
(Note in the Margin)
Jerusalem
Published irregularly, founded
in 2001
240 x 325 mm
1,000 -1,200 copies
English
no-org.net
Editor: Lea Mauas
Publisher: Sala-Manca Group

**BANG ART**
Art _ Illustration _
Photography _ Toys - Cool-
hunting
Rome
Every two months, founded in
2009
195 x 265 mm
Italian
www.bangart.it

**KYOORIUS DESIGN
MAGAZINE**
A Design magazine by
Kyoorius Exchange
Mumbai
Quarterly, founded in 2006
5,000 copies
English
www.kyooriusexchange.com/
exchange/
Publisher: Kyoorius Exchange

**A5 MAGAZINE**
Graphic design, art and
creative stuff
Tel-Aviv
Tri-Annual, founded in 2007
148 x 210 mm
Hebrew / English
www.thea5magazine.com
Editor and Designer: Golan
Gafni
Publisher: Keren and Golan

**BASEMENT**
Lanciano (Ch)
Monthly, founded in 2006
285,000 copies
Italian
www.basementmag.it
Editor in Chief: Marco Di
Batista
Publisher: MOVE Editore

**THE LITTLE MAGAZINE**
Dehli
Every two months, founded in
2000
210 x 297 mm
English
www.littlemag.com
Editor: Antara Dev Sen

**BLOCK**
Architecture / City / Media /
Theory
Tel Aviv
Tri-Annual, founded in 2005
185 x 250 mm
6,000 copies
Hebrew / English
www.blockmagazine.net
Founders & Editors in chief:
Carmella Jacoby Volk, Iftach
Alonl

**BEAUTIFUL FREAKS**
A passionate voice for the
independent culture
Rome
Quarterly, founded in 2001
135 x 190 mm
5,000 copies
Italian
www.beautifulfreaks.org
Founder and Publisher:
Alessandro Pollastrini

# IRELAND

# ITALY

**BOILER**
Contemporary Art and
Cultural (R)evolutions
Milan
Bi-Annual, founded in 2001
170 x 240 mm
15,000 copies
English
www.boilermag.it
Creative Director: Susanna
Cucco
Publisher: Boiler Corporation

**PRINTED PROJECT**
Dublin 7
Bi-Annual,
English
www.visualartists.ie/AP_
printed_project.html
Publisher: Visual Artists Ireland

**800ZINE**
Milan
297 x 420 mm
100 copies
Italian
www.800zine.org
Sara Bianchi

**CARNET**
Milan
Monthly,
110 x 145 mm
Italian
Managing Editor: Fausto
Tatarella

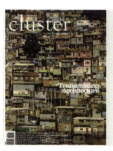

**CLUSTER**
City, Design, Innovation
Turin
founded in 2003
12,000 copies copies
Italian / English
www.cluster.eu
Editor in chief: Giulia Vola
Publisher: Cluster s.r.l.

**EGO[N]**
The magazine with multiple personalities
Firenze
Bi-Annual, founded in 2007
160 x 220 mm
1,000 copies
English / Italian
www.egonmagazine.com
Founder and art director:
Debora Manetti, Francesco Canovaro and Cosimo Lorenzo Pancini
Publisher: RED Publishing

**HOT**
Milan
Monthly, founded in 2003
190 x 260 mm
Italian
Director: Doriano Zunino

**COLLEZIONI**
Modena
English / Italian
www.logos.info
General manager: Mauro Cagnoni
Publisher: Logos Publishing, Srl.

**FAB MAGAZINE**
Catena di Villorba
Quarterly, founded in 2004
199 x 270 mm
English
www.fabrica.it
Editor in chief: Sara Beltrame
Publisher: Fabrica

**KULT**
Fashion - Art - Music - Film - Talents
Milano
Monthly, founded in 1998
230 x 280 mm
110,000 copies
Italian / English
www.kultmagazine.com
Dirretor: Enrico Cammarota
Publisher: Edizioni Pem srl

**COLORS**
Catena di Villorba (Tv)
Monthly, founded in 1991
228 x 287 mm
English / Spanish / French / Italian
www.colorsmagazine.com
Creative Director: Erik Oberman
Publisher: Colors Magazine s.r.l.

**FEFÈ VISUAL MAGAZINE**
Rome
Tri-Annual, founded in 2007
240 x 300 mm
Italian / English
www.fefeproject.com

**L'ARCA**
Milano
Monthly, founded in 1986
240 x 340 mm
41,600 copies
Italian
www.arcadata.com
Editor in chief: Cesare M. Casati
Publisher: Cesare Maria Casati

**COOLISSIMO**
Stay-up-magazine
Ravenna
founded in 2001
126 x 165 mm
10,000 copies
Italian
www.coolissimo.it
Director: Luca Bendandi

**FLASH ART**
The world's leading art magazine
Milano
Every two months,
205 x 270 mm
Italian / English
www.flashartonline.it
Editor: Chiara Leoni
Publisher: Giancarlo Politi Editore sas

**LA PATRIE DAL FRIÛL**
Par un Friûl plui furlan (To make a Friuli more friulian)
Gemona del Friuli (UD)
Monthly, founded in 1946
240 x 320 mm
22.000 copies copies
Friulian
www.lapatriedalfriul.org

**DEFRAG**
Art | Music | Urban Culture
Lanciano
Bi-Annual, founded in 1997
297 x 210 mm
10,000 copies
Italian / English
www.defragmag.com
Art Director: Francesco Galluppi
Publisher: MOVE Editore

**GARAGE MAGAZINE**
Pavia
Bi-Annual, founded in 1998
210 x 297 mm
12,000 copies
Italian / English
www.garagemagazine.net
Federico Chiozzi

**MUSE**
The Fashion and visual culture magazine
Milan
Quarterly, founded in 2005
230 x 300 mm
English / Italian
www.magmuse.com
Editor in chief: Fabio Crovi
Publisher: Mag Srl

**DROME MAGAZINE**
The Contemporary Art magazine based on Integrity and Visions
Rome
Quarterly, founded in 2004
210 x 297 mm
50,000 copies
Italian / English
www.dromemagazine.com
Creative director: Stefan Pollak
Publisher: PHLEGMATICS

**GRAB**
Contemporary Subjects
Rome
Every three months, founded in 2006
245 x 220 mm
15,000 copies
Italian / English
www.grabmagazine.it
Art director: Luca Panzieri
Publisher: Pnzap snc

**NEO HEAD**
Street Magazine
Torino
English / Italian
www.neo-head.net
Director & Photographer:
Enrico Frignani

**NEURAL**
new media art, electronic
music, hacktivism
Bari
Tri-Annual, founded in 1993
210 x 275 mm
6,000 copies
English
www.neural.it
Founder and Publisher:
Alessandro Ludovico
Publisher: Neural

**RODEO**
Milan
Monthly, founded in 2003
265 x 380 mm
215,000 copies
Italian / English
www.rodeomagazine.it
Founder & Publisher: Simona
Varchi

**TAKE IT EASY**
Livorno
Quarterly, founded in 2004
210 x 297 mm
Italian
www.takeiteasy.it

**NEXT EXIT**
Creatività e Lavoro
Roma
Monthly, founded in 2002
240 x 280 mm
Italian
www.nextexit.it
Art director: Luigi Vernieri
Publisher: Soc.Coop Next Exit

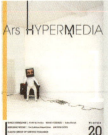

**SIMULTANEITA**
Roma
Tri-Annual, founded in 1997
150 x 210 mm
English
www.simultaneita.net
Editor and publisher: Giulio
Lotti

**TEMA CELESTE**
Contemporaryart
Milan
Every two months, founded in
1983
Italian / English
Executive Director: Simona
Vendrame
Publisher: ACS Editore S.r.l.

**NEXT MAG**
For creative people
Rome
Bimonthly, founded in 2008
240 x 280
Italian
www.nextexit.it
Publisher: Soc.Coop Next Exit

**SPORTSWEAR
INTERNATIONAL**
Milan
Every two months, founded in
1975
265 x 330 mm
German / English
www.sportswearnet.com
Executive Editor: Sabine Kühnl
Publisher: Klaus N. Hang

**THE END.**
Milano
Every two months, founded in
2006
220 x 284 mm
Italian / English
www.theendmagazine.com

**PIG**
Milano
Monthly, founded in 2002
Italian / English
www.pigmag.com
Managing Editor: Daniel
Beckerman

**STIRATO**
Poster Magazine
Rome
Quarterly, founded in 2003
150 x 210 mm
7,000 copies
Italian
www.stirato.net

**THIS IS A MAGAZINE**
This is not a Magazine
Milan
Published irregularly, founded
in 2002
Various format
1,400 copies
English
www.thisisamagazine.com
Founder & Publisher: Andy
Simionato
Publisher: Studio Donnachie/
Simionato Milan

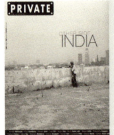

**PRIVATE**
International review of black
and white photographs and
texts.
Bologna
Quarterly, founded in 1992
240 x 280 mm
Italian / English / French
www.privatephotoreview.com
Editor in chief: Oriano Sportelli

**SUGO**
Venice
Bi-Annual, founded in 2003
230 x 300 mm
Italian / English
www.sugomagazine.com
Editor in chief: Giorgio
Camuffo

**UOVO**
an independent voice for
contemporary art
Torino
Quarterly, founded in 2003
170 x 240 mm
10,000 copies
English / Italian
www.uovo.tv
Publisher: chiara figone

**PURPLE MAGAZINE**
We write about books and
magazines.
Rome
founded in 2008
240 x 330 mm
2008 copies
Italian
www.purplepress.it

**SUPERFLY**
Roots, Style and Culture: An
Italian Perspective
Rome
Every two months, founded in
2003
210 x 270 mm
30,000 copies
Italian
www.superflymag.com
Publisher: Sylvia Volpato
Publisher: Stile Suoni Visioni
s.n.c

**VOGUE**
Milano
Monthly,
205 x 274 mm
Italian
www.voguevanity.it
Publisher: Condé Nast
Publications

**YESPLEASE**
The fashionable luxury lifestyle
magazine
Milan
Quarterly, founded in 1990
230 x 300 mm
English / Italian
www.yesplease.it/yesplease/
index.html
Editor in chief: Trevor Albert
Panton
Publisher: yesplease

**CASA BRUTUS**
www.brutusonline.com/casa/
index.jsp
Publisher: Magazinehouse Ltd

**ECOCOLO**
Monthly,
www.ecocolo.com
Publisher: Espre

**ZA!REVUE**
Independent graphic magazine
Milano
founded in 2003
160 x 160 mm
100,000 copies
English / Italian / German
www.zarevue.org
Filippo Anglano

**CAWAII**
Japanese
www.e-cawaii.net

**FRAU**
170,000 copies
Japanese
www.watashi-frau.com

# JAPAN

**COMMONS & SENSE**
Bi-annual, founded in 1997
225 x 297 mm
English / Japanese
www.commons-sense.net
Editor in chief & Creative
Director: Kaoru Sasaki
Publisher: Kaoru Sasaki- Cube
Inc.

**FRUITS**
Tokyo
Monthly, founded in 1997
190 x 264 mm
Japanese / English
www.fruits-mg.com
Director: Aoki Shoichi

**+81**
Tokyo
Quarterly, founded in 1997
210 x 297 mm
Japanese / English
www.plus81.com
Director: Satoru Yamashita
Publisher: D.D.Wave CO.LTD

**CROISSANT**
Fortnightly, founded in 1977
400,000 copies
Publisher: Indoor Media sl

**H**
Tokyo
Every two months,
Japanese
www.rock-net.jp
Publisher: Rockin'on

**ANAN**
Monthly,
Japanese
www.magazineworld.jp

**CUT**
Tokyo
Monthly,
www.rock-net.jp

**HAPPY NUTS**
Monthly,
Japanese
www.h-nuts.com

**BRUTUS**
210 x 285 mm
Japanese
www.brutusonline.com
Editor in chief: Takefumi
Ishiwatari
Publisher: Magazinehouse Ltd

**DIGMEOUT**
Osaka
founded in 2001
English / Japanese
www.digmeout.net
Editor in Chief & Creative
Director: Yoshihiro Taniguchi
Publisher: Petit Grand
Publishing

**HERE AND THERE**
Tokyo
Published irregularly, founded
in 2002
210 x 297 mm
Japanese / English
www.nakakobooks.com
Publisher & Author: Nakako
Hayashi

**HIGH FASHION**
Japanese
www.highfashion.cc

**POPEYE**
Monthly,
Japanese
www.magazineworld.jp
Publisher: Magazine World

**SIGHT**
Tokyo
Quarterly, founded in 1999
Japanese / English
www.rock-net.jp

**MILK**
Le Magazine de Mode
Enfantine
founded in 2003
Japanese
www.milkjapon.com

**RELAX**
Let's be adulty!
Tokyo
Monthly,
210 x 298 mm
Japanese

**SPOON**
Tokyo
Japanese / English
www.spoon01.com

**NEUT**
Tokyo
Japanese
www.altdesigners.com

**ROCKIN'ON**
Tokyo
Monthly,
English / Japanese
www.rock-net.jp
Publisher: Rockin'on

**STREET**
Photography magazine of
foreign STREET fashion.
Tokyo
Monthly, founded in 1985
205 x 275 mm
Japanese / English
www.street-mg.com
Director: Aoki Shoichi

**NYLON JAPAN**
founded in 2003
Japanese
www.nylon.jp
Publisher: NYLON LLC

**ROCKIN'ON JAPAN**
Tokyo
founded in 1986
English / Japanese
www.rock-net.jp
Publisher: Rockin'on

**TARZAN**
Monthly,
Japanese
www.magazineworld.jp

**OK FRED**
Meguro, Tokyo
Quarterly, founded in 2001
210 x 296 mm
20,000 copies
English
www.okfred.com
Editor In chief: Yoshi Tsujimura
Publisher: LittleMore

**RYUKO TSUSHIN**
Monthly,
Japanese
www.infaspub.co.jp/
ryuko-tsushin/rt.html
Publisher: Infas Publications

**TUNE**
Tokyo real culture photographs
magazine focus on boys
fashion
Tokyo
Monthly, founded in 2004
210 x 297 mm
Japanese
www.street-mg.com
Director: Aoki Shoichi

**OZONE ROCKS**
Let's feel more of your nature
3,000 copies
Japanese
www.ozonerocks.com
Editor in chief: Fumihiro
Hayashi
Publisher: Ozone Community

**SAVVY**
Monthly,
Japanese
www.lmagazine.jp

**UTB**
Monthly,
Japanese
www.wani.co.jp

**VOGUE NIPPON**
Tokyo
Monthly,
230 x 298 mm
Japanese
www.vogue.co.jp
Editor in chief: Kazuhiro Saito
Publisher: Condé Nast
Publications

# KUWAIT

# LITHUANIA

# JORDAN

**ALEF**
Shuwaikh
Quarterly, founded in 2006
230 x 300 mm
40,000 copies
English/ Arabic
www.alefmag.com

**PRAVDA**
Truth free of charge about
what? where? when?
Vilnius
Monthly, founded in 2004
170 x 240 mm
30,000 copies
Lithuanian
www.pravda.lt
Editor in chief: Inga Norke

**SKIN**
Fashion art design
Amman 11194
Monthly,
230 x 300
15,000 copies
English
www.skin-online.com

# LATVIA

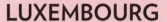
# LUXEMBOURG

# KENYA

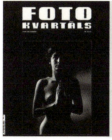

**FOTO KVARTALS**
Contemporary photography
Riga
Every two months, founded in
2006
228 x 240 mm
2,600 copies
Latvian / English
www.fotokvartals.lv
Editor in chief: Alise Tifentale

**DÉSIRS**
Mode Intérieurs Luxembourg
Luxembourg
Bi-annual, founded in 2004
238 x 300 mm
20,000 copies
French / English
www.desirsmagazine.com/
Fashion and design editor:
Céline Coubray
Publisher: Mike Koedinger
Editions SA

**KWANI?**
Africa's best Creative Writing
Nairobi
Annual,
65 x 96 mm
3,000 copies
English / Swahili
www.kwani.org

**VETO MAGAZINE**
Music & Art
Riga
Every two months, founded in
01.02.2007
230 x 320
12 000 copies
Latvian
www.vetomagazine.lv

**FLYDOSCOPE**
Luxair's inflight magazine
Luxembourg
Every two months, founded in
1975
210 x 297 mm
30.000 copies
English / French / German
www.flydoscope.lu
Managing Editor: Alexis
Juncosa
Publisher: Mike Koedinger
Editions SA

**LUXURIANT**
Le magazine gratuit du
Luxembourg
Luxembourg
20,000 copies
French / English
www.luxuriant.lu

**NICO INTERNATIONAL**
Interviews & fashion
Luxembourg
Bi-Annual, founded in 2003
230 x 280 mm
20,000 copies
English / French
www.nicomagazine.com
Founder and publisher: Mike
Koedinger
Publisher: Mike Koedinger
Editions SA

# MEXICO

**PODER**
Inteligencia para la elite de
Negocios
Mexico
founded in 2000
215 x 280 mm
1,200 copies
Spanish / English
www.poder360.com

**PAPERJAM**
média économique et financier
Luxembourg
Monthly, founded in 2000
238 x 300 mm
20,000 copies
French / English
www.paperjam.lu
Editor in chief: Jean-Michel
Gaudron
Publisher: Mike Koedinger
Editions SA

**BABYBABYBABY**
Mexico City
Bi-Annual, founded in 2004
213 x 270 mm
10,000 copies
English
www.babybabybaby.com.mx
Editor in chief: Paola Viloria
Publisher: Grupo Editorial
Celeste S.A. de C.V.

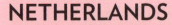

# NETHERLANDS

**RENDEZ-VOUS**
City Magazine Luxembourg
Luxembourg
Monthly (11 x / year),
230 x 300 mm
35,000 copies
French / English / German
www.rendez-vous.lu
Editor: Corinne Briault
Publisher: Ville de
Luxembourg / Mike Koedinger
SA

**CELESTE**
El tiempo Celeste
Mexico
Quarterly, founded in 2001
220 x 290 mm
25,000 copies
Spanish / English
www.celeste.com.mx
Director: Aldo Chaparro
Publisher: Grupo Editorial
Celeste S.A. de C.V.

**200%**
Amsterdam
Annual, founded in 2006
230 x 300 mm
English
www.200-percent.com

**SALZINSEL**
Luxembourg
founded in 2004
180 x 295 mm
1,000 copies
French
Editor in chief: Karolina
Markiewicz

**CODIGO06140**
México,DF
Bimonthly, founded in 2001
165 x 225 mm
Spanish
www.codigo06140.com
Founder, Creative Director,
Editor in Chief: Ricardo
Porrero

**BLAADJE**
Tijdschrift over Tijdschriften
Amsterdam
Annual, founded in 2004
230 x 300 mm
36,000 copies
Dutch
www.blaadje.nl
Publisher: Ernst Coenen
Publisher: Stichting The Black
Tiger

# MALAYSIA

**ETEL MAGAZINE**
Design, illustration,
photography, cinema, art,
architecture, music
Hermosillo
Quarterly, founded in 2007
Spanish / English
www.etelmagazine.com
Publisher: Laura Rodriguez

**BLEND**
Mode, mensen, media, muziek
en kunst
Amsterdam
Monthly (10 x / year), founded
in 2004
225 x 280 mm
20,000 copies
Dutch
www.blend.nl
Publisher: Jurriaan Bakker

**STIMULI**
Compendium of Creativity
Kuala Lumpur
Bi-Annual, founded in 2007
220 x 286 mm
English

**PICNIC**
Supervivencia y bienestar
Mexico City
Every two months, founded in
2004
230 x 286 mm
Spanish
www.picnic-mag.com
Editor-in-chief: Ana Echeverri

**BRIGHT**
Innovative Lifestyle
Amsterdam
Every two months,
185 x 245 mm
25,000 copies
Dutch
www.bright.nl

## BUTT
International magazine for homosexuals
Amsterdam
Quarterly, founded in 2001
165 x 234 mm
English
www.buttmagazine.com
Publisher: Gert Jonkers
Publisher: TOP Publishers BV

## FRAME
The Great Indoors
Amsterdam
Every two months,
236 x 303 mm
34,000 copies
English
www.framemag.com
Editor in chief: Robert Thiemann
Publisher: Peter Huiberts

## ITEMS
Amsterdam
Every two months,
8,000 copies
Dutch
www.items.nl
Publisher: BIS Publishers

## CODE MAGAZINE
documenting style
Amsterdam
Quarterly, founded in 2005
244 x 305 mm
22,000 copies
Dutch / English
www.code-mag.nl
Editor in chief: Peter Van Rhoon
Publisher: CODE Magazine bv

## GIRLS LIKE US
Lesbian Quarterly
Amsterdam
Tri-Annual, founded in 2005
165 x 228 mm
3,000 copies
English
www.glumagazine.com
Editor: Jessica Gysel
Publisher: Capricious Inc.

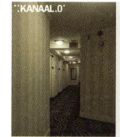

## KANAAL 0
Electronic music and art magazine
Den Haag
Published Irregularly, founded in 2006
Various Format
300 copies
Dutch / English
www.kanaal-0.com
Publishing and Photography: Iris Uffen
Publisher: Platform Kanaal 0

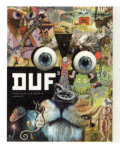

## DUF
onafhankelijk gedurfd
Den Haag
Annual, founded in 2006
200 x 245 mm
Dutch
www.duf.nu
Publisher, Design & Art Direction: Suzanne Hertogs

## GLAMCULT
Amsterdam
Dutch
www.glamcult.com
Publisher & Editor in chief: Rogier Vlaming
Publisher: Glamcult

## MARK
Another Architecture
Amsterdam
Quarterly, founded in 2005
240 x 320 mm
15,000 copies
English
www.mark-magazine.com
Publisher: Peter Huiberts

## EYEMAZING
Amsterdam
Quarterly, founded in 2003
245 x 340 mm
12,000 copies
English
www.eyemazing.com
Founder & Publisher: Susan Zadeh
Publisher: Picture Booklets Publishers B.V.

## GONZO CIRCUS
Independent Soundgenerating Magazine on Experimental Music & Culture
Amsterdam
Every two months, founded in 1991
210 x 275 mm
3,000 copies
Dutch
www.gonzocircus.com

## MISTER MOTLEY
Magazine over kunst
Amsterdam
Quarterly,
168 x 222 mm
Dutch
www.mistermotley.nl
Editor in chief: Hanne Hagenaars

## FANTASTIC MAN
Amsterdam
Bi-Annual, founded in 2005
240 x 300 mm
English
www.fantasticman.com
Editor: Jop Van Bennekom
Publisher: TOP Publishers BV

## HUNCH
Rotterdam
Bi-Annual, founded in 1999
240 x 300 mm
English
www.berlage-institute.nl
Editor: Salomon Frausto
Publisher: NAi Publishers

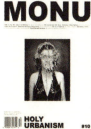

## MONU
Magazine on urbanism
Rotterdam
Bi-Annual, founded in 2004
200 x 270 mm
2,800 copies
English
www.monu-magazine.com

## FOAM MAGAZINE
Quarterly Photography Magazine
Amsterdam
Quarterly, founded in 2002
230 x 300 mm
10,000 copies
English
www.foammagazine.nl
Editor In chief: Marloes Krijnen
Publisher: Foam Magazine

## INTERMEDIAIR
weet wat werkt
Haarlem
Weekly,
250 x 350 mm
300,000 copies
Dutch
www.intermediair.nl
Editor in chief: Peter ter Horst

## MORF
Tijdschrift voor vormgeving
Amsterdam
Bi-Annual, founded in 2004
Dutch / English
www.morf.nl
Editor: Marjan Unger
Publisher: Premsela, Stichting voor Nederlandse vormgeving

## O.K. PERIODICALS
O.K. Collections, graphic
design, dutch, collaboration,
thematic,
Arnhem
Bi-Annual, founded in 1,500
170 x 240 mm
2008 copies
English
www.ok-periodicals.com
Publisher: O.K. Parking

## THE ISSUE MAGAZINE
Amsterdam
245 x 325 mm
English
www.the-issue-magazine.com
Publisher: Mets & Schlit
Publishers

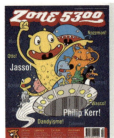

## ZONE5300
Rotterdam
Quarterly, founded in 1994
210 x 275 mm
Dutch
www.zone5300.nl/530
Editor in chief: Marcel Ruijters

## OASE
Journal for Architecture
Rotterdam
170 x 240 mm
Dutch /English
www.oase.archined.nl
Publisher: NAi Publishers

## USEFUL PHOTOGRAPHY
Amsterdam
Annual, founded in 2000
210 x 297 mm
English
www.usefulphotography.com

# NEW ZEALAND

## ONE PAGE MAGAZINE
Amsterdam
founded in 2008
English
www.onepagemagazine.com

## VIEWPOINT
The trends brands futures and
ideas magazine
Amsterdam
Bi-Annual,
215 x 284 mm
English
www.view-publications.com
Editor: Martin Raymon
Publisher: Metropolitan
Publishing

## FLURO MAGAZINE
Some music, some fashion,
some art, some more ...
Wellington
Quarely, founded in 2007
150 x 210 mm
English
www.fluromag.com/

## OPEN
Cahier on art and the public
domain
Amsterdam
Bi-Annual,
170 x 240 mm
English
www. opencahier.nl
Editor in chief: Jorinde Seijdel
Publisher: NAi Publishers

## VOLUME
To beyond or not to be
Amsterdam
Quarterly,
English
www.volumeproject.org
Contributing editor: Ole
Bouman
Publisher: Stichting Archis

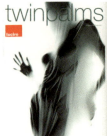

## LUCIRE
The global fashion magazine
Wellington
Bi-monthly, founded in 1997
235 x 335 mm
40,000 copies
English/Romanian
www.lucire.com
Publisher: JY&A Media

## PAGES
Rotterdam
Published Irregularly, founded
in 2006
240 x 330 mm
1,000 copies
Farsi / English
www.pagesmagazine.net
Distributor: episode publishers

## YDN
Eindhoven
Quarterly, founded in 2003
230 x 297 mm
3,000 copies
English
www.ydn.nl
Editor: Robert Andriessen
Publisher: Designlab

## NO.
No magazine. Yes.
Auckland
Quarterly, founded in 2008
235 x 285 mm
40,000 copies
English
www.nomagazine.co.nz
Creative Director and
Publisher: Delaney Tabron

## RE-MAGAZINE
A magazine about one person
Amsterdam
Bi-Annual,
Variable format
English
www.re-magazine.com
Chief Editor: Jop Van
Bennekom
Publisher: ARTIMO

## YVI MAGAZINE
Den Haag
Bi-Annual, founded in 2007
230 x 300 mm
English
www.yvimag.com
Editor / Designer / Publisher:
Welmer Keesmaat

## WHITE FUNGUS
Wellington
English
www.whitefungus.com/
Editor: Ron Hanson

# NORWAY

# PHILLIPINES

**KWARTALNIK FOTOGRAFIA**
Wrzesnia
Quarterly, founded in 2000
230 x 290 mm
3,000 copies
Polish / English
www.fotografia.net.pl
Editor in chief: Waldemar Sliwczynski
Publisher: Wydawnictwo Kropka

**CARL'S CARS**
A magazine about people
Oslo
Quarterly, founded in 2001
230 x 280 mm
25,000 copies
English
www.carls-cars.com
Founders: Stéphanie Dumont, Karl Eirik Haug
Publisher: Carl's Car

**MANUAL MAGAZINE**
Assembling the man
Ortigas Center Pasig
English
www.manualmag.com
Editor in chief: RJ Ledesma
Publisher: Mega Magazines

**PIKTOGRAM**
Talking Pictures Magazine
Warsaw
Quarterly,
210 x 263 mm
English / Polish
www.piktogram.org
Design: Janek Bersz

**HOT ROD**
Oslo
Quarterly, founded in 1998
235 x 295 mm
2,000 - 5,000 copies
English
www.hotrod.com/index.html
Editor: Jan Walaker
Publisher: Jan Walaker

# POLAND

# PORTUGAL

# PARAGUAY

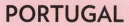

**A4**
Fashion, art, coulture, design - in a no commercial style
Warsaw
founded in 2003
210 x 297 mm
Polish / English
www.a4mag.com
Editor in Chief and Publisher: Iwona Czempinska
Publisher: Iwona Czempinska

**DIF**
Lisbon
Monthly (10 x / year), founded in 2002
210 x 260 mm
25,000 copies
Portuguese
www.difmag.com
Editor in chief: Trevenen Morris-Grantham

**GUARARA**
Otros Ruidos
Asuncion
Monthly, founded in 2005
210 x 310 mm
1,500 copies
Spanish / Guarani
guarara.com/

**DIK FAGAZINE**
Arts & Men
Warsaw
Bi-Annual, founded in 2005
210 x 285 mm
1,000 copies copies
Polish / English
www.dikfagazine.com
Founder / Publisher / Editor in chief: Karol Radziszewski
Publisher: Karol Radziszewski

**EGOÍSTA**
Lisbon
Monthly, founded in 2000
230 x 290 mm
40,000 copies
Portuguese
www.egoista.pt

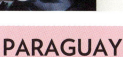

http://images.google.com/imgres?imgurl=http://www.ic.sunysb.edu/Stu/vdavidyu/sergey_bride_jpg&imgrefurl=http://www.ic.sunysb.edu/Stu/vdavidyu&h=432&w=800&sz=82&hl=en&start=28&um=_$w=u_epO8UXU3PLCt KY_W%V2Go=&tbnid=tmkNxyGqI-m1M:&tbnh=93&tbnw=143&prev=/images%3Fq%3DsUrry%2Bpage%2Bnd%2BSergey%2BBrin%26sa rt%3D20%26ndsp%3D20%26hl%3Den%26sa fe%3Doff%26ndl%3DN

**FUTU MAGAZINE**
SELF/PEOPLE/SURROUND
NUMBER 7, LUXURY

**FUTU MAGAZINE**
Warsaw
Bimonthly, founded in 2006
230 x 280 mm
6,500 copies
English / Polish
www.futumag.com
Editor in chief: Martyna Bednarska-Cwiek
Publisher: Publishing and Design Group Sp.zo.o

**FARFALLA**
Visual essays on communication design
Lisbon
Published irregularly, founded in 2008
Various format
Portuguese / English
www.farfallamag.com/

**NADA**
Lisbon
Quarterly, founded in 2003
Portuguese
www.nada.com.pt
Co-ordinatior: Joao Urbano
Publisher: Urbanidade Real
Lda

**OMAGIU**
Bucharest
Quarterly, founded in 2005
240 x 278 mm
Romanian / English
www.omagiu.com
Editor in chief: Ioana Isopescu

**MONITOR**
All Contemporary Design
Magazine
Moscow
Every two months, founded in
2000
230 x 300 mm
English / Russian
www.monitorunlimited.com
Editor in chief: Rem Khassiev

**PARQ**
Lisbon
Monthly, founded in 2008
20,000 copies
Portuguese / English
www.parqmag.com
Editor: Carla Isidoro

**OTAKU MAGAZINE**
Otaku manga anime music
film fashion design illustration
comics toys exhibition
Purcareni, Brasov
Bi-Annual, founded in 2006
140 x 210 mm
2,000 copies
English / Romanian
www.otakumag.com
Founder and Publisher:
Bogdan Gorganeanu

# SCOTLAND

# REPUBLIC
# OF PANAMA

**PAVILION**
Contemporary art & culture
magazine
Bucharest
Bi-Annual, founded in 2001
145 x 195 mm
6,500 copies
English
www.pavilionmagazine.org
Editors and Founders: Razvan
Ion and Eugen Radescu

**ARTESIAN**
Edinburgh
Bi-Annual,
7,000 copies
English
www.gotogetherpress.com

**BLANK**
Design, Trends & Fashion
Panama
Monthly, founded in 2003
230 x 300 mm
15,000 copies copies
Spanish
www.grupoblank.com
Publisher / CEO: Rafa
Candanedo
Publisher: Grupoblank

# RUSSIA

# SERBIA

# ROMANIA

**AFISHA**
Urban lifestyle and city listings
bible.
St Petersburg
Fortnightly, founded in 1999
212 x 290 mm
Russian
www.afisha.ru

**QUICK LOOK**
Pancevo
Monthly, founded in 2006
233 x 281 mm
Serbian
www.quicklook.co.yu

**AOOLEU**
Bucharest
Monthly, founded in 2008
297 x 420 mm
English/Romanian
www.aooleu.ro
Editor in chief: Tim Wislon
Publisher: Milos Jovanovic

**KAK**
Moscow
Quarterly, founded in 1996
Russian
www.kak.ru
Editor in chief: Peter Bankov
Publisher: Design Depot

# SINGAPORE

# SLOVENIA

**CHIMURENGA**
Who no know go know
Cape Town
Bi-Annual, founded in 2002
164 x 235 mm
English / French / Portugues /
Xhosa / Swahili
www.chimurenga.co.za
Copy Editor: Karen Press
Publisher: Kalakuta Trust

**TERRITORY**
International Designers
Territory
Singapore
Quarterly, founded in 2003
241 x 292 mm
24,000 copies
English
www.bigbrosworkshop.com

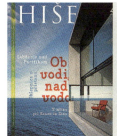

**HISE**
architecture, interiors
Ljubljana
Every two months, founded in
1999
227 x 273 mm
5,000 copies copies
Slovenian / English
www.zavodbig.com
Editorial Director: Ivan
Ferjancic
Publisher: Zavod Big

**DESIGN INDABA**
A better world through creativity
Cape Town
Quarterly,
234 x 285 mm
3,500 copies
English
www.designindabamag.com
Publisher / Editor: Ravi Naidoo
Publisher: Interactive Africa

**WERK**
Singapore
English
www.workwerk.com
Publisher: Work

# SOUTH
# AFRICA

**MK BRUCE LEE**
Cap Town
Quarterly,
197 x 280 mm
English
www.thepresident.co.za

# SLOVAK
# REPUBLIC

**A. MAGAZINE**
Nonfiction narratives of africa
Hoedspruit
founded in 2007
210 x 260 mm
5,000 copies
English
www.amagazine.org

**ONE SMALL SEED**
The south african
contemporary culture
magazine
Cape Town
Quarterly, founded in 2005
174 x 246 mm
5,000 copies
English
www.onesmallseed.com
Founder and creative director:
Giuseppe Russo

**3/4**
Arts, culture, media magazine
Bratislava
Tri-Annual, founded in 1999
215 x 287 mm
1,000 copies
Slovak, Czech
www.34.sk
Editor in chief: Slavo Krekovic

**AFRO MAGAZINE**
Cape Town
Variable format
www.thepresident.co.za

**SNAPPED**
Cape Town
Quarterly, founded in 2008
170 x 210 mm
English
www.snapped.co.za/

**ART SOUTH AFRICA**
Cape Town
Quarterly, founded in 2002
220 x 280 mm
10,000 copies
English
www.artsouthafrica.com

# SPAIN

**BLANK MAGAZINE**
Madrid
Spanish
www.blankmgz.com
Creative Director: Salvador
Cuenca Fromesta
Publisher: Dos Click S.L.

**ETAPES : DISEÑO Y CULTURA VISUAL**
Barcelona
Quarterly, founded in 2008
206 x 266 mm
4,000 copies
Spanish
www.etapes.es
Editor: Maria Serrano
Publisher: Editorial Gustavo
Gili, SL

**ACTITUDES**
Revista trimestral y gratuita de
vanguardias culturales
Bilbao
Tri-Annual,
200 x 210 mm
12,000 copies
Spanish
www.espacioactitudes.com/
am/index.php
Director: Fernando Sanz
Publisher: Espacio Actitudes

**CALLE 20**
La revista de la nueva cultura
Madrid
Monthly (10 x / year),
200 x 260 mm
Spanish
www.calle20.es
Director: Juan Carlos Avilès
Publisher: Multiprensa y Más,
S.L.

**EXIT**
Image & Culture
Madrid
Quarterly,
210 x 260 mm
Spanish / English
www.exitmedia.net
Editor in chief: Celia Díez
Huertas
Publisher: Olivarez &
Asociados SL

**APARTAMENTO**
An everyday life interiors
magazine
Barcelona
founded in 2008
English
www.apartamentomagazine.
com/

**CLONE**
Urban Art & Music Magazine
Sevilla
Every two months, founded in
2003
167 x 215 mm
15,000 copies
Spanish
www.clonemagazine.com
Director: Jose M. Maraver

**FAKE**
Madrid
Published irregularly, founded
in 2003
295 x 240 mm
20,000 copies
Spanish
www.fakeonline.com
Director: John Smith

**AZ/MAGAZINE**
Places
Igualada (Barcelona)
Bi-Annual, founded in 2004
225 x 280 mm
20,000 copies
Spanish / Catalan / English
www.escucurucuc.com

**D-PALMA**
Progressive Urban Culture
Palma de Mallorca
Every two months, founded in
2001
252 x 335 mm
18,000 copies
Spanish / German
www.d-palma.com
Publisher & Creative Director:
Gori Vicens
Publisher: DP de Palma

**FANZINE137**
An International Fanzine made
in Spain
Madrid
1,137 copies
www.fanzine137.com
Editor, Creative Director ,
Publisher: Luis Venegas

**B-GUIDED**
Barcelona
Quarterly, founded in 1999
165,5 x 211,5 mm
Spanish / English
www.b-guided.com
Editor and art director: Juan
Montenegro
Publisher: b-guided S.L.

**D(X)I MAGAZINE**
Culture & post-design
Valencia
Quarterly, founded in 2000
290 x 420 mm
25,000 copies
Spanish / English
www.dximagazine.com
Director: Alejandro Benavent

**FEW MAGAZINE**
Barcelona
Monthly, founded in 2008
215 x 290 mm
15,000 copies
English/Spanish
www.fewmagazine.es

**BELIO**
Madrid
Tri-Annual, founded in 1999
210 x 200 mm
Spanish / English
www.beliomagazine.com
Direction: Pablo Iglesias
Algora
Publisher: Belio Magazine sl

**ESFORÇ**
La força de l'equip
Torrelles de Llob.
Monthly, founded in 2006
220 x 280 mm
Catalan
www.esforc.com

**GO**
Discover the real meanng of
cutting edge music
Barcelona
Monthly, founded in 2000
230 x 300 mm
60,000 copies
Spanish
www.go-mag.com
Director: Janina Canet

**GRRR**
Barcelona
Bi-Annual, founded in 1994
165 x 235 mm
Spanish / English
www.grrr.ws

**LA MÁS BELLA**
Magazine of art
Madrid
Annual, founded in 1993
1,000 copies
Spanish / English
www.lamasbella.org
Publisher: Diego Ortiz
Publisher: Pepe Murciego and
Diego Ortiz

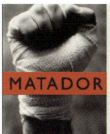

**MATADOR**
Journal of Culture, Ideas and
Trends 1995 - 2022
Madrid
Annual, founded in 1994
300 x 400 mm
English
www.lafabrica.com
Editor in chief: Camino Brasa
Publisher: La Fabrica

**H MAGAZINE**
Don't Believe The Hype
Barcelona
Monthly (10 x / year), founded
in 1998
230 x 270 mm
45,000 copies
Spanish
www.hmagazine.com
Editor: José Manuel Bejarano

**LAMILK**
Trend Magazine, music,
desing, fashion and more..
Valencia
Monthly (10 x / year), founded
in 2006
205 x 245 mm
150,000 copies
Spanish
www.lamilk.com

**METAL**
Barcelona
Every two months, founded in
2006
225 x 300 mm
15,000 copies
Spanish / English
www.revistametal.com
Editor: Yolanda Muelas
Publisher: Jazzmetal SL

**HERCULES**
About men fashion & people
Barcelona
Bi-Annual, founded in 2007
230 x 330
60,000 copies
Spanish / English
www.herculesmag.com
Editor & Creative Director:
Francesco Sourigues
Publisher: Magna Productions
S.L.

**LAMONO**
Barcelona
Monthly
170 x 210 mm
Spanish
www.lamono.net
Director: Eva Villazala
Publisher: Edicions La Nit

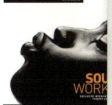

**MODERN DESIGN
MAGAZINE**
Smart magazine for Intelligent
People
Málaga
Monthly, founded in 2007
230 x 270
240.000 copies
English
modern-design.d-earle.com/
magazine-downloads.php

**ICONOGRAPHIC
MAGAZINE**
Graphic design & typography
Valencia
Bi-Annual, founded in 2008
220 x 286 mm
1,500 copies
Spanish
www.iconographicmagazine.
org
Content editor: Elena Veguillas

**LING**
A magazine about people and
their cities
Barcelona
Monthly, founded in 2007
217 x 280 mm
35,000 copies
English
lingmagazine.com
Publisher: Le Cool Publishing
and La Fabrica

**NAIF**
A new look at the universe of
children
Valencia
Quartely, founded in 2008
215 x 300 mm
Spanish
www.naifmagazine.com
Founder and designer: Silvana
Catazine
Publisher: Curry producciones

**KINGDOM MAGAZINE**
Magazine, culture, trends,
fashion, design, cinema, music,
people
A Coruña
Every two months, founded in
2008
210 x 291 mm
2008 copies
Spanish
www.kimag.net

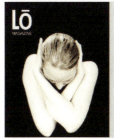

**LO MAGAZINE**
Barcelona
Monthly, founded in 2000
240 x 330 mm
Spanish
www.lomagazine.com
Director: Carlos Hernando
Publisher: Prensa y
comunicacion Agrip-Pina SL

**NEO**
design + art + architecture +
nature + fashion + living
240 x 300 mm
English / Spanish
www.neotabu.com
Art Director: Pepe Barroso
Publisher: Ibermaison Home
Designers

**KINK**
Barcelona
founded in 2006
Castellano / Enlish
www.pacoymanolo.com/kink

**LOOK DE BOOK**
Barcelona
Quartely, founded in 2007
210 x 265 mm
2007 copies
English / Spanish
www.lookdebook.com
Publisher: JUAN PEIRO
RUBEN

**NEO2**
Fashion po lo nuevo
Madrid
Monthly,
214 x 274 mm
Spanish / English
www.neo2.es
Director: Ruben Manrique
Publisher: Neo2

**NOX**
Vanguardia Singular
Madrid
Bi-Annual,
230 x 300 mm
Spanish / English
Director: Antonio Marquez
Coello
Publisher: Focus Ediciones

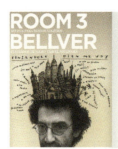

**ROOM**
Revista para buenos viajeros
Madrid
170 x 230 mm
Spanish
http://lafabrica.com/

**VERB**
Verb is ACTAR's main tool for
the investigation of current
architectural production.
Barcelona
Annual, founded in 2001
170 x 240 mm
5,000 copies
English / Spanish
www.actar.com

**OJODEPEZ**
Documentary Photography
Madrid
Quarterly,
235 x 300 mm
Spanish / English
www.ojodepez.org
Director and Publisher: Frank
Kalero
Publisher: La Fabrica

**SERIE B**
Underground Magazine
Madrid
Every two months, founded in
2004
210 x 280 mm
Spanish / English
www.sbum.com
Director: Antonio Garcia Mora
Publisher: Serie B Editores SL

**VIEW OF THE TIMES**
Madrid
Bi-Annual, founded in 2005
230 x 302 mm
Spanish / English
www.viewofthetimes.com
Editor & Creative Director:
Emilio Saliquet
Publisher: Egoiste
Publicaciones

**ORTODÒNCIA**
Revista independent de cultura
Barcelona
founded in 2004
170 x 240 mm
Catalan / Spanish
www.lallauna.biz/ortodoncia
Editor: Daniel Pujal
Publisher: Ortodoncia SCP

**SNOWPLANET**
Free snowboard magazine
since 1994
Barcelona
Every two months, founded in
1994
230 x 295 mm
15,000 copies
Spanish / English
www.snowplanetmag.com
Directors: Antonio Kobau,
Sebastian Saaavedra
Publisher: Snowplanetbase s.l.

**VISUAL**
Magazine de Diseno,
Creatividad Grafica y
Comunicacion
Madrid
Every two months,
Spanish
www.visual.gi
Publisher: Blur Ediciones, S.L.

**PAPERMIND**
The after 8 Fanzine
Barcelona
165 x 240 mm
Spanish
www.papermind.net

**THE BALDE**
Irunea
Every two months, founded in
2001
240 x 280 mm
20,000 copies
Euskera / English
www.thebalde.net
Director: Koldo Almandoz

**ZEHAR**
San Sebastian
Bi-Annual, founded in 1989
235 x 165 mm
7,000 copies
Spanish / English / Basque
www.zehar.net
Editor in chief: Maider Zilbeti
Publisher: Regional Council of
Gipuzkoa -Service of Visual
Arts-Arteleku

**ROCKET MAGAZINE**
Rocket Contemporary Culture
Magazine Barcelona
Barcelona
Every two months, founded in
2008
165 x 240 mm
Spanish
www.rocketmagazine.net

**UNO**
Freestyle culture and
skateboarding magazine
Barcelona
Every two months (5 x / year),
founded in 2000
200 x 265 mm
14,000 copies
Spanish
www.unopopmag.com
Art director: Sebastian
Saavedra

**ZONA DE OBRAS**
«Something as well as the bible
of the Latin Culture»
Zaragoza
Quarterly, founded in 1995
210 x 297 mm
8,000 copies
Spanish
www.zonadeobras.com
Editors: Rubén Scaramuzzino,
Daniela Rossi
Publisher: ZdeO / Bailanta, SL

**ROJO®MAGAZINE**
Emotionally structured textless
art magazine.
Barcelona
Quarterly, founded in 2001
210 x 280 mm
English (for credits only)
www.rojo-magazine.com
Founder & Director: David
Quiles Guilló
Publisher: Sintonison S.L.

**VANIDAD**
Madrid
Monthly, founded in 1992
230 x 300 mm
Spanish
www.vanidad.es
Editor and Creative Director:
Emilio Saliquet
Publisher: Egoiste
Publicaciones SL & Vanidad
SL

# SWEDEN

**LOYAL MAGAZINE**
Malmö
founded in 2000
235 x 305 mm
English
www.galleriloyal.com
Editor: Martin Lilja

**DU**
Zürich
Monthly (10 x / year), founded
in 1941
240 x 315 mm
German
www.du-magazin.com
Editor: Andreas Kläui

**BON (INTERNATIONAL ISSUE)**
Stockholm
Bi-Annual, founded in 2004
225 x 290 mm
45,000 copies
English
www.bonmagazine.com
Editor in chief: Madelaine Levy
Publisher: Letterhead AB _
BON INTL

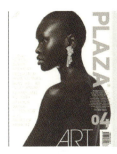

**PLAZA MAGAZINE**
Stockholm
9 x / year,
225 x 300 mm
35,000 copies
Swedish / English / German /
Arabic
www.plazamagazine.com
Publisher: Plaza Publishing
Group

**EDELWEISS**
Le magazine romand des
envies et des passions
Lausanne
Monthly,
French
www.edelweissmag.ch
Editor in chief: Laurence
Desbordes

**BON (SWEDISH ISSUE)**
Contemporary Fashion & Art
Stockholm
Every two months,
225 x 290 mm
25,000 copies
Swedish
www.bonmagazine.com
Editor in chief: Madelaine Levy
Publisher: Letterhead AB
-BON Sweden

**SWARTA**
242 x 335 mm
1,000 copies
www.swarta.com

**FORM**
The European Design
Magazine.
Basel
Every two months, founded in
1957
240 x 295 mm
English / German
www.form.de
Deputy Editor in chief: Gerrit
Terstiege
Publisher: Birkhäuser Verlag
AG

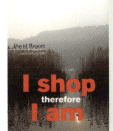

**DAVID REPORT**
Cutting-edge critical thoughts.
Falsterbo
Quarterly, founded in 2005
210 x 297 mm
English
www.davidreport.com
Publisher: David Carlson

**YKKY**
Stockholm
English
www.ykky.se
Co-editor: Tobias Rydin

**GATSBY MAGAZINE**
The supercilious assumption
that on Sunday afternoon you
have nothing better to do.
Zurich
Quarterly, founded in 2006
240 x 320 mm
45,000 copies
English
www.gatsbymagazine.com

**KÄNGURU**
Stockholm
Quarterly, founded in 1995
176 x 235 mm
Swedish
www.tidskriftenkanguru.se

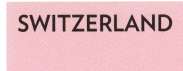

# SWITZERLAND

**ICÔN**
Expression visuelle
Carouge
Every two months,
245 x 310 mm
French / English
www.iconmagazine.ch/
Editor in chief & Creative
Director: Christophe Durand
Publisher: ADN sarl

**LIVRAISON**
Stockholm
Annual, founded in 2005
230 x 300 mm
2,000 copies
English
www.livraison.se
Director of the words: Marie
Birde

**BLUTT**
Magazin für Bildfolgen
Quarterly, founded in 2007
201 x 280 mm
500 copies
German
www.bluttmagazin.net/
Publisher: Konrad Beck, Simon
Schnellmann, Mathis Pfäffli

**IDPURE**
The Swiss magazine of graphic
design and visual creation
Morges
Quarterly,
220 x 280 mm
6,500 copies
French / English
www.idpure.ch
Publisher: Thierry Hausermann

**KINKI MAGAZINE**
St. Gallen
Monthly (11 x / year), founded
in 2008
225 x 280 mm
German
www.kinkimag.com

**TURBO MAGAZINE**
Biel/Bienne
Published irregularly, founded
in 2003
500 copies
French / English / German
www.turbomag.ch
Founder and Publisher: Adrien
Horni
Publisher: Adrien Horni

# TURKEY

**OUR MAGAZINE**
Zurich
Tri-Annual, founded in 2003
190 x 250 mm
2,000 copies
English
www.our-magazine.ch
Nick Widmer
Publisher: Our magazine

**ZOOMAGAZINE**
Lenzburg
Annual, founded in 1999
215 x 275 mm
English
Editor in chief: Benjamin
Sommerhalder
Publisher: Nieves Books
www.nieves.ch

**34**
Istanbul
Quarterly,
230 x 297 mm
60,000 copies
English
www.34mag.com
Fashion Director: Niki Brodie
Publisher: Otto Iletsim
Hizmetleri Ltd

**PARKETT**
Zurich
Tri-Annual, founded in 1991
270 x 320 mm
English / German
www.parkettart.com
Editor in chief: Bice Curiger
Publisher: Parkett Publishers

# TAIWAN

**BANT**
Music, art, cinema...
Istanbul
Monthly (10 x / year), founded
in 2003
205 x 255 mm
80,000 copies
Turkish
www.bantdergi.com

**SANG BLEU**
Lausanne
Bi-Annual, founded in 2006
240 x 330 mm
8,000 copies copies
English / French
www.sangbleu.com
Editor in chief: Maxime Buechi

**EGG+**
Tapei
Monthly, founded in 2003
210 x 280 mm
50,000 copies
www.eggmagazine.com

**FUTURISTIKA**
See. Think. Feel. Art.
Istanbul
Quarterly,
179.96 x 219.84 mm
English / Turkish
www.futuristikamag.com
Founder and Editor in Chief:
Baris Yarsel

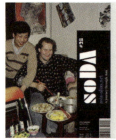

**SODA**
Zeitschrift / Zeitbild
Zürich
Quarterly, founded in 1996
220 x 270 mm
11,000 copies
German / English
www.soda.ch
Founder & Creative Director:
Martin Loetscher
Publisher: soDA Verlag s.A.

# THAILAND

**HILLSIDER**
Istanbul
Quarterly,
240 x 340 mm
14,000 copies
Turkish / English
www.hillside.com.tr

**TRUCE**
Celebrating Culture
Zurich
Annual, founded in 2005
230 x 290 mm
5,000 copies
German / English
www.truce.ch
Founding art director: Walter
Stähli

**VER MAGAZINE**
Bangkok
Published irregularly,
270 x 400 mm

**MAVIOLOGY**
Istanbul
Quarterly, founded in 2003
195 x 258 mm
Euskera / English
www.mavi.com
"Head": Ersin Akarlilar
Publisher: Maviology Inc.

**TRENDSETTER**
Istanbul
Monthly, founded in May 2002
220 x 300 mm
Turkish
www.mayailetisim.com
Editor: Zeynep Kun

**ABOVE MAGAZINE**
London
Bi-Annual,
210 x 300 mm
21,800 copies
English
www.above-magazine.com/
Editor in chief: Sascha Lilie
Publisher: SL Magazines Ltd

**ARENA**
Style for Men
London
Monthly,
218 x 279 mm
English
www.arenamagazine.co.uk/
Editor in chief: Anthony
Noguera

UK

**AFTERALL**
A Journal of Art, Context and
Enquiry
London
Tri-Annual, founded in 1998
190 x 295 mm
6,500 copies
English
www.afterall.org
Managing Editor: Pablo
Lafuente
Publisher: Central Saint
Martins College of Art &
Design

**ART MONTHLY**
Indispensable guide to today's
fast-moving artworld
London
Monthly (10 x / year), founded
in 1976
210 x 295 mm
English
www.artmonthly.co.uk
Editor: Patricia Bickers
Publisher: Jack Wendler

**_S3MAGAZINE**
style-led science
London
Every two months, founded in
2006
English
www.S3magazine.co.uk

**AG**
The art & craft of photography
Surrey
Quarterly, founded in 1991
English
www.ag-photo.co.uk
Editor: Chris Dickie

**BAD IDEA**
Modern Storytelling
London
Quarterly, founded in 2006
171 x 245 mm
22,000 copies
English
www.badidea.co.uk
Founding Editor: Jack Roberts
Publisher: Good Publishing
Ltd

**10 MAGAZINE**
Fashion and beauty for men
and women
Quarterly, founded in 2001
245 x 310 mm
English
www.10magazine.com/
Design and Art Direction:
Daren Ellis
Publisher: ZAC Publishing Ltd

**ANDROGYNY
MAGAZINE**
London
www.androgynymag.co.uk

**BASELINE**
Kent
founded in 1979
356 x 255 mm
English
www.baselinemagazine.com
Editor: Hans Dieter Reichert
Publisher: Bradbourne
Publishing Ltd

**125 MAGAZINE**
International photography
showcase
London
Bi-Annual, founded in 2003
230 x 300 mm
34,000 copies
English
www.125magazine.com
Editor in Chief: Perry Curties
Publisher: 125 World Ltd

**ANOTHER MAGAZINE**
The Luxury Fashion Bi-annual
London
Bi-Annual, founded in 2001
230 x 320 mm
175,000 copies
English
www.anothermag.com
Senior Editor: Mark Sanders
Publisher: Another Publishing
Ltd

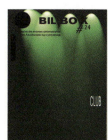

**BIL BO K INTERNA-
TIONAL**
Magazine des errances
contemporaines.
London
Bi-Annual, founded in 2008
165 x 240 mm
10,000 copies
French / English
www.bilbok.com
Publisher: BILBOK

**8**
London
Bi-Annual, founded in 1998
210 x 270 mm
5,000 copies
English
www.foto8.com
Editor: Jon Levy
Publisher: Jon Levy

**ANOTHER MAN**
London
Bi-Annual,
English

**BIZARRE**
It's about life in the extreme
London
English
www.bizarremag.com
Deputy editor: Kate Hodges
Publisher: Dennis Publishing
Ltd

**BLAG**
founded in 1992
30,000 copies
English
www.blagmagazine.com
Founder: Sally A. Edwards
Publisher: Blag UK Ltd.

**CO-OP**
London
founded in 2002
1,500 copies
English
www.cooperatewith.us

**DISTILL**
London
Bimonthly, founded in
September 2008
210 x 290 mm
84,500 copies copies
English
www.distilldigital.com
Creative & Publishing
Director: Christopher
Lockwood
Publisher: Craft Publishing Ltd

**BLUEPRINT**
London
Monthly,
270 x 337 mm
English
www.blueprintmagazine.co.uk
Editor: Vicky Richardson
Publisher: Wilmington Media
Ltd

**CONTAGIOUS**
London
Quarterly,
240 x 320 mm
2,000 copies copies
English
www.contaqiousmagazine.com
Production Editor: Emily Hare
Publisher: Xtreme Information
Publishing Division

**DRAFT**
London
Quarterly,
1,000 copies
English
www.draftmagazine.co.uk

**BOGEY**
Old Game, New Breed
London
Quarterly, founded in 2002
220 x 274 mm
German
Editorial Director: Michael
Fordham
Publisher: The Media Cell
LTD

**CREATIVE REVIEW**
London
Monthly, founded in 1980
280 x 280 mm
English
www.creativereview.co.uk
Editor: Patrick Burgoyne
Publisher: Centaur
Communications Ltd

**EXIT**
The award-winning art, fashion
and photography magazine
London
Bi-Annual, founded in 2000
20,000 copies
English
www.exitmagazine.co.uk
Publisher & Editor in chief:
Stephen Toner

**C**
International Photo Magazine
London
Bi-Annual,
230 x 337 mm
English / Japanese / Chinese /
Spanish
www.ivorypress.com
Publisher: Ivory Press

**CRYSTAL LIZED**
Crystal Fashion Components
by Swarovski
Bi-Annual, founded in 2002
216 x 310 mm
100,000 copies
English
www.crystallized.com
Editor: Stephen Todd
Publisher: John Brown

**EYE**
London
Quarterly,
237 x 297 mm
English
www.eyemagazine.com

**CENT MAGAZINE**
London
Bi-Annual, founded in 2003
297 x 210 mm
8,000 copies
English
www.centmagazine.co.uk/
Creative Director and
Publisher: Jo Phillips
Publisher: Onehundredper-
cent publishing ltd

**DAZED & CONFUSED**
Be the first to know
London
Monthly,
230 x 300 mm
English
Publisher: Jefferson Hack
Publisher: Dazed & Confused
www.confused.co.uk

**FRIEZE**
London
8 x / year, founded in 1991
English
www.frieze.com
Publisher: Amanda Sharp

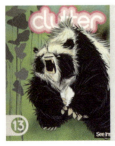

**CLUTTER**
Uttoxeter Staffordshire
Every two months, founded in
2004
English
www.cluttermagazine.com
Contributing editor &
photographer: Brian McCarty

**DESIGN WEEK**
London
Weekly,
256 x 341 mm
English
www.design-week.co.uk
Editor: Lynda Relph-Knight
Publisher: Morag Welham

**FUSED**
Birmingham
Quarterly, founded in 2000
297 x 210 mm
20,000 copies
English
www.fusedmagazine.com
Editor: David O'Coy

**GRAFIK.**
Essential reading for every
graphic designer.
London
Monthly,
225 x 310 mm
14,000 copies
English
www.grafikmagazine.co.uk
Editor: Caroline Roberts
Publisher: Grafik Ltd.

**IMAGE**
The magazine for professional
photographers
London
Monthly, founded in 1981
210 x 250 mm
3,000 copies
English
www.the-aop.org
Editor: Helena Rhodes

**KATALOGUE**
London
Annually, founded in 2005
297 x 420 mm
5,000 copies
English
www.katalogue.net
Founder and Publisher:
Wilhelm Finger

**GRAPHIC**
contemporary graphic culture
magazine
London
Quarterly,
220 x 280 mm
English
www.bispublishers.nl
Editor in chief: Marc-A Valli
Publisher: BIS Publishers

**INTELLIGENT LIFE**
London
Quarterly, founded in 2004
www.moreintelligentlife.com

**KILIMANJARO**
London
founded in 2003
480 x 640 mm
English
www.kilimag.com
Publisher, Founder & Creative
Director: Michael Olu
Odukoya

**GYM CLASS**
founded in 2008
148 x 210 mm
English
gymclassmagazine.com/

**INTERNATIONAL LIFE
MAGAZINE**
You, London, The World
London
Bi-monthly, founded in
October 2008
220 x 300 mm
240,000 copies
English
www.internationallife.tv

**KINGPIN**
Kingpin Skateboarding Europa
London
Monthly, founded in 2002
230 x 280 mm
80,000 copies
English / French / German /
Spanish
www.kingpinmag.com

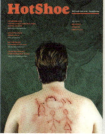

**HOTSHOE**
Fresh Perspectives on
Contemporary Photography.
London
167 x 240 mm
English
www.hotshoeinternational.com
Editor: Melissa DeWitt
Publisher: World Illustrated
Limited

**INTERSECTION**
Car Style Magazine
London
Quarterly, founded in 2001
227 x 276 mm
39,000 copies
English
www.intersection.com
Editor: Shiraz Randeria

**LEFTLION**
Nottingham Culture.
Nottingham
Every two months, founded in
2004
10,000 copies
English
http://www.leftlion.co.uk/
articles.cfm/id/2181

**I-D**
i-Deas
London
Monthly, founded in 1980
230 x 300 mm
English
www.i-dmagazine.com
Fashion Director: Edward
Emninful
Publisher: Levelprint Ltd.

**ISSUE ONE**
London
Quarterly, founded in 2006
245 x 310 mm
English
www.issue-one.com
Editor in chief: Paulus

**LET THEM EAT CAKE**
Quarterly, founded in 2006
250 x 190 mm
2,000 copies
English
www.letthemeatcakemagazine.
com

**ICON**
Essex
Monthly, founded in 2003
250 x 320 mm
English
www.icon-magazine.co.uk
Editor: Justin McGuirk
Publisher: Media 10 Ltd

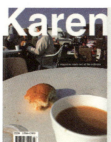

**KAREN**
Made out of the ordinary
Malmesbury, Wiltshire
Bi-Annual, founded in 2004
168 x 230 mm
English
www.karenmagazine.com
Publisher: Karen Lubbock

**LITTLE WHITE LIES**
Truth & Movies
London
founded in 2005
200 x 244 mm
English
www.littlewhitelies.co.uk
Managing Editor: Danny Miller

**LULA**
Girl of my Dreams
founded in 2005
210 x 297 mm
English
www.lulamag.com
Editor in chief: Leith Clark
Publisher: Lula Publishing Ltd

**MULTILINK**
Brighton
Bi-Annual, founded in 2004
English
www.multilinkmagazine.com

**PLASTIC RHINO**
Art, fashion, music, popular
culture.
Liverpool
Every two months, founded in
2004
260 x 300 mm
English
www.plasticrhino.com
Director: Chris Morris
Publisher: Peppered Sprout
Limited

**MAKING DO**
An independent publication
focusing on methods of
creative production
London
Irregularly, founded in 2007
205 x 255 mm
300 copies
English
www.makingdo.org.uk

**N.PARADOXA**
International feminist art
journal KT Press
East Greenwich, London
Bi-Annual, founded in 1998
210 x 260 mm
English
www.ktpress.co.uk
Editor in chief: Katy Deepwell
Publisher: KT Press

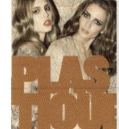

**PLASTIQUE**
London
Quarterly,
English
www.plastiquemagazine.com
Publisher: Plastique Magazine
Ltd

**MANZINE**
founded in 2009
English
www.themanzine.blogspot.
com

**NAKED**
The magazine for the weird
and the wonderful
Bristol
177 x 244 mm
English
www.hot-cherry.co.uk
Publisher: Hot Cherry

**PLUK**
London
Quarterly, founded in 2001
120 x 200 mm
10,000 copies
English
www.plukmagazine.com
Publisher: Daniel Newburg

**MEAT MAGAZINE**
Publish or Perish
London
Tri-Annual, founded in 2004
200 x 250 mm
2,000 copies
English
www.meatmagazine.co.uk

**NAKED PUNCH**
The engaged review of
contemporary art and thought
London
Quarterly, founded in 2002
176 _ 250 mm
8,000 copies copies
English
www.nakedpunch.com

**POP**
London
Bi-Annual, founded in 2000
230 x 300 mm
English
Art Director: Stuart Spalding

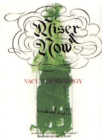

**MISER & NOW**
London
Quarterly,
210 x 265 mm
English
Art Director & Designer:
Christian Küsters
Publisher: Keith Talent Gallery
www.keithtalent.com

**NOTION MAGAZINE**
London
English
www.planetnotion.com
Culture Editor: Michael C
Lewin

**POST**
The journal for postgraduate
work & culture
Falmouth
Bi-annual, founded in 2006
20,000 copies
English / Gibberish
www.falmouth.ac.uk/majournal
Publisher: TEAM POST

**MONOCLE**
A briefing on global affairs,
business, culture & design
London
Monthly (10 x / year), founded
in 2007
English
www.monocle.com
Editor in chief & Chairman:
Tyler Brûlé

**PABLO INTERNACIONAL
MAGAZINE**
Macho not rough - art, men
and architecture
London
Bi-Annual, founded in 2005
140 x 215 mm
English
www.pablointernacionalmaga-
zine.com
Publisher: José Garcia Torres

**RANT MAGAZINE**
Quarterly, founded in 2003
Irregular
5,000-10,000 copies
English
www.rant-magazine.com
Founder, Publisher, Editor &
Art Director: Irene Rukerebuka
Publisher: Tilfeldig
Productions

**ROCK'N'REEL**
Roots, rock blues and beyond
Cleator Moor
Every two month, founded in
1988
220 x 297 mm
25,000 copies
English
www.rock-n-reel.co.uk

**TATE ETC.**
Visiting and Revisiting Art,
etcetera...
London
Tri-Annual,
210 x 270 mm
110,000 copies
English
www.tate.org.uk/tateetc
Associate publisher: Naomi
Richmond-Swift

**USELESS**
Because life is longer than you
think
London (also New York, USA)
Bi-Annual, founded in 2004
285 x 385 mm
English
www.uselessmagazine.com

**RUBBISH**
It's what everybody's talking
London
Annual,
215 x 280 mm
English
www.rubbishmag.com
Editor in chief: Jenny Dyson
Publisher: Rubbish Ltd

**THE**
London
Quarterly, founded in 2001
English
www.thefuturelaboratory.com

**V&A MAGAZINE**
London
Quarterly,
www.vam.ac.uk

**SCARLET CHEEK**
London
Bi-Annual, founded in 2006
170 x 210 mm
1,000 copies
English / Chinese
www.scarletcheek.com
Editor in chief: Cindy Chen

**THE DRAWBRIDGE**
London
Quarterly,
English
www.thedrawbridge.org.uk
Editor: Bigna Pfenninger

**VAROOM**
The journal of illustration and
mad images
London
Tri-Annual,
English
www.varoom-mag.com
Editor in chief: Adrian
Shaughnessy
Publisher: The Association of
Illustrators

**SONGLINES**
Discover a World of Music
London
8 x / year, founded in 1999
220 x 297 mm
18,000 copies
English
www.songlines.co.uk
Editor in chief: Simon
Broughton
Publisher: Songlines Publishing
Ltd

**THE ILLUSTRATED APE**
London
Tri-Annual, founded in 1998
240 x 300 mm
English
www.theillustratedape.com
Creative Director: Daren Ellis
Publisher: The Illustrated Ape
Company

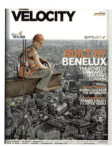

**VELOCITY**
London
Every two months,
210 x 265 mm
25,000 copies
English
www.vlmmagazine.com
Editor: Steve Watson
Publisher: INK

**SUPERSUPER**
Relentless Optimism!
London
Every two months, founded in
2006
230 x 300 mm
English
www.thesupersuper.com/
Creative & Editorial Director:
Steve Slocombe

**THE STOOL PIGEON**
London
founded in 2005
60,000 copies
English
www.thestoolpigeon.com
Editor: Phil Hebblethwaite

**VERY MAGAZINE**
London
Bi-Annual, founded in 1997
215 x 280 mm
100, 000 copies
English
www.verypublications.com
Publisher: Uscha Pohl
Publisher: Up&Co

**TANK**
Elitism for all
London
Quarterly,
230 x 300 mm
English
www.tankmagazine.com
Editor in chief & Creative
Director: Masoud Golsorkhi
Publisher: Tank Publications
Ltd

**UNTITLED**
London
Quarterly,
190 x 253 mm
English
www.untitledmag.co.uk

**VICE**
London
founded in 1994
210 x 275 mm
English
www.viceland.com
Founder: Suroosh Alvi
Publisher: Andrew Creighton

**VOLT**
London
Bi-Annual, founded in 2007
345 x 420 mm
12,000 copies
English
www.volt-mag.com
Editor: Rui Faria

# UNITED ARAB EMIRATES

**306090**
New York
Quarterly, founded in 2005
279 x 432 mm
15,000 copies
English
www.306090.org
Editor: Jonathan D. Solomon
Publisher: 306090, Inc.

**WALLPAPER\***
International Design Interiors
Fashion Travel
London
Monthly (11 x / year),
230 x 300 mm
English
www.wallpaper.com
Creative Director: Tony
Chambers
Publisher: The Wallpaper\*
Group

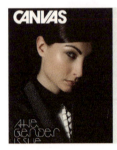

**CANVAS**
Art and Culture from the
middle east and arab world.
Dubai
Bi-Annual, founded in 2004
235 x 295 mm
30,000 copies
English
www.canvasonline.com
Editor in Chief: Ali Y Khadra

**3X3**
The magazine of
contemporary illustration
New York
Tri-Annual, founded in 2003
217 x 300 mm
4,300 copies
English
www.3x3mag.com
Publisher and Design Director:
Charles Hively
Publisher: 3x3 Magazine

**WHITE COLLAR**
London
English
www.whitecollar.org.uk/

**THE HANDBOOK**
Essential reading for male
survival
Dubai
Bi-monthly, founded in 2008
185 x 240 mm
English
Editor: Andrew Nagy

**ANP QUARTERLY**
Costa Mesa
Quarterly, founded in 2005
107 x 160 mm
English
www.rvcaanp.com
Publisher: PM Tenore
Publisher: RVCA

**WIRE**
London
Monthly, founded in 1982
230 x 280 mm
English
www.thewire.co.uk
Publisher & Editor in Chief &
Creative Director: Tony
Herrington

# USA

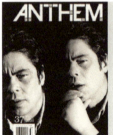

**ANTHEM**
Los Angeles
English
www.anthemmagazine.com/

**WONDERLAND**
London
Every two months,
220 x 285 mm
104,000 copies
English
www.wonderlandmagazine.
com

**(T)HERE**
New York
Bi-Annual, founded in 2000
235 x 304 mm
20,000 copies
English
www.t-here.com
Editorial Director: Jason
Makowski
Publisher: There Media, Inc.

**ARRAY**
Inside the New York Design
Center
New York
Quarterly,
English
www.arrayny.com
Editor in chief and Publisher:
Paul Millman

**WOUND**
London
Quarterly, founded in 2007
300 x 230 mm
English
www.woundmagazine.com

**2WICE**
New York
Bi-Annual, founded in 1997
English
www.2wice.org
Managing Editor: Jane Rosch
Publisher: 2wice Arts
Foundation

**ART ASIAPACIFIC**
Contemporary Visual Culture
New York
Every two months, founded in
1993
215.9 x 284.988 mm
English
www.aapmag.com
Editor: Elaine W. Ng
Publisher: Elaine W. Ng

**ART NEWS**
New York
Monthly (11 x / year), founded
in 1902
83,000 copies
English
www.artnews.com
Editor in chief & Creative
Director: Milton Esterow
Publisher: Milton Esterow

**BITCH MAGAZINE**
Feminist Response to Pop
Culture
Portland
Quarterly, founded in 1996
48,000 copies
English
www.bitchmagazine.com
Publisher: Debbie Rasmussen

**BREED**
Creative Freedom Mag
Pasadena
Quarterly, founded in 2006
165 x 197mm
English
www.breedmag.com

**ART PAPERS**
Art Papers is about
contemporary art.
Atlanta
Every two months, founded in
1976
230 x 296 mm
162,000 copies
English
www.artpapers.org
Creative Director: Jennifer
Smith

**BLACK BOOK**
Progressive Culture
New York
Quarterly, founded in 1996
225 x 274 mm
English
www.blackbookmag.com
Art Director: Tom Ackerman
Publisher: BlackBook Media
Corp

**BRILL'S CONTENT**
New York
Monthly,
204 x 265 mm
English
Editor in chief: David Kuhn
Publisher: Brill Media Ventures
L.P.

**BEAUTIFUL DECAY**
Culver City
founded in 1996
216 x 286 mm
45,000 copies
English
beautifuldecay.com

**BLENDER**
The ultimate guide to music
and more
Palm Coast
Monthly,
English
www.blender.com
Editor in chief: Craig Marks

**CABINET**
A Quarterly of Art and Culture
New York
Quarterly, founded in 2000
200 x 250 mm
English
www.cabinetmagazine.org
Editor in chief: Sina Najafi
Publisher: Immaterial
Incorporated

**BEE**
Dallas
English
www.beemag.com
CEO & Co-founding
Publisher: Celine Gumbiner
Publisher: Femme Publications

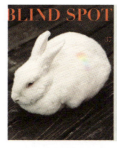

**BLIND SPOT**
The Premier Photography-
Based Fine Art Journal
New York
Tri-Annual, founded in 1992
230 x 265 mm
15,000 copies
English
www.blindspot.com
Associate Publisher: Evan
Forman
Publisher: Photo-Based Art

**CAMOUFLAGE**
New York
founded in 2008
English
camouflagemag.com
Owner: David Warren
Publisher: Tank Design, Inc.

**BIDOUN**
New York
Quarterly, founded in 2004
222 x 270 mm
18,000 copies
English
www.bidoun.com
Founder & Editor in chief: Lisa
Farjam
Publisher: Bidoun, Inc.

**BLOOM MAGAZINE**
Publication of Arts in Bloom
Project
New York
Bi-Annual,
English
www.bloommagazine.org/
Editor: Charles Flowers

**CAPRICIOUS**
New Photography
New York
Bi-Annual, founded in 2003
197 x 270 mm
4,000 copies
English
www.becapricious.com
Editor & Publisher: Sophie
Mörner

**BIG**
New York
230 x 290 mm
English
www.bigmagazine.com
Founder, Editor in chief and
creative director: Marcelo
Junemann
Publisher: BIG Communica-
tions

**BOMB**
A quarterly Arts & Culture
Magazine since 1981
Brooklyn
Quarterly,
English
www.bombsite.com
Publisher & Editor in chief:
Betty Sussler

**CLEAR**
Fashion / Design Magazine
Michigan
Every two months,
60,000 copies
English
www.clearmag.com
Publisher and creative director:
Emin Kadi

**CONTENT**
The Magazine of the Custom
Publishing Council
Rockport
Quarterly,
Staff Member: Patrick Mitchell

**EDITOR & ART
DIRECTOR - THE
GLOSSY ZINE**
Fashion, Pop & Art
New York
Bi-Annual, founded in 2004
1,500 copies
English / German
www.editorandartdirector.com
Editor & Art director: Katia
Kuethe
Publisher: Studio Von Birken

**FLAIR MAGAZINE**
The Tampa Tribune's
Magazine for Living
English
www.tampaflair.com

**DADDY**
Los Angeles
Quarterly, founded in 2000
English
www.daddythemagazine.com

**ESOPUS**
New York
Bi-Annual, founded in 2003
11,000 copies
English
www.esopusmag.com
Editor: Tod Lippy
Publisher: The Esopus
Foundation Ltd

**FLAUNT**
Los Angeles
Monthly,
230 x 275 mm
English
www.flaunt.com
Founder: Jim Turner
Publisher: Flaunt Magazine

**DETAILS**
New York
Monthly,
204 x 275 mm
English
www.details.com
Editor in chief: Joe Dolce
Publisher: Condé Nast
Publications

**ESQUIRE**
New York
Monthly,
English
www.esquire.com

**FLOSS**
Fashion / Celebrity / Lifestyle
Quarterly,
English
www.flossmagazine.com

**DIRTY FOUND**
Ann Arbor
English
Editor: Davy Rothbart

**FADER**
New York
English
www.thefader.com

**FOUND**
Ann Arbor
English
www.foundmagazine.com
Editor: Davy Rothbart

**DOT DOT DOT**
Arts journal
New York City
Bi-Annual, founded in 2000
165 x 235 mm
3,000 copies
English
www.dot-dot-dot.us/
Publisher: Dexter Sinister
Publisher: Dexter Sinister /
Just-In-Time Workshop &
Occasional Bookstor

**FAESTHETIC**
The fast aesthetic
Toledo, Ohio
Annual, founded in 1999
1,000 copies
English
www.faesthetic.com

**GASTRONOMICA**
The Journal of Food and
Culture
Williamstown
Quarterly, founded in 2001
English
www.gastronomica.org
Editor in chief: Darra Goldstein
Publisher: University of
California Press

**DWELL**
San Francisco
Monthly (10 x / year),
English
www.dwell.com
Editor in chief: Sam Grawe

**FASHION PROJECTS**
New York
Bi-Annual, founded in 2004
240 x 650 mm
7,000 copies
English
fashionprojects.org
Editor: Francesca Granata
Publisher: Francesca Granata

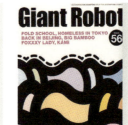

**GIANT ROBOT**
Los Angeles
English
www.giantrobot.com
Publisher: Eric Nakamura

**GLITTERATI MAGAZINE**
Changing the world one issue
at a time...
Los Angeles
Quarterly, founded in 2007
85 x 110 mm
English
www.glitteratimagazine.com
publisher: Nicholas Fahey
Publisher: Nicholas Fahey

**HEEB**
The new Jew Review
New York
Quarterly,
English
www.heebmagazine.com

**INICIATIVA COLECTIVA**
A collective for artists, by
artists. Tell everyone.
Pembroke Pines, Florida
Every two months, founded in
2006
177.8 x 228.6 mm
English
www.iniciativacolectiva.com
Publisher: Nicole Andujar

**GLOSS MAGAZINE**
San Francisco
127 x 203 mm,
English
glossmagazine.net

**HI FRUCTOSE**
Albany
Quarterly, founded in 2005
English
www.hifructose.com

**INKED**
Style, Culture, Art
New York
Monthly (10 x year), founded
in 2007
1,000,000 copies
English
www.inkedmag.com

**GOOD MAGAZINE**
West Hollywood
Every two months, founded in
2006
210 x 275 mm
65,000 copies
English
www.goodmagazine.com
Editor in chief: Zach Frechette

**HOOZDO**
Phoenix, Arizona
Quarterly, founded in 2006
133 x 204 mm
5,000 copies
English
www.hoozdo.org
Publisher: Nick Lehmans

**INTERVIEW**
The Crystal Ball of Pop
New York
Monthly, founded in 1969
255 x 305 mm
210,000 copies
English
www.interviewmagazine.com
Publisher: Sandra J. Brant
Publisher: Brant Publications
Inc.

**GOTHAM MAGAZINE**
New York
Monthly,
English
www.gotham-magazine.com
Editor in chief: Jason Oliver
Nixon
Publisher: Niche Media LLC

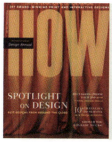

**HOW**
Cincinnati
Every two months, founded in
1985
English
www.howdesign.com
Editor: Bryn Mooth
Publisher: F&W Publications

**IQONS**
www.iqons.com
Editor in Chief: Diane Pernet

**GOTHIC BEAUTY**
underground fashion & pop
culture
Portland
founded in 2000
English
www.gothicbeauty.com
Publisher & Editor in chief:
Steven Holiday

**HYPHEN**
San Francisco
English
www.hyphenmagazine.com
Editor in Chief: Melissa Hung

**JPG MAGAZINE**
San Francisco
www.jpgmag.com

**HAMBURGER EYES**
Photo Magazine
San Francisco
Tri-Annual,
3,000 copies
English
www.hamburgereyes.com
Editor in chief: Ray Potes
Publisher: Burgerworld Media

**I.D.**
New York
Annual, founded in 1954
English
www.idonline.com
Editor in chief: Julie Lasky

**JUXTAPOZ**
Art & Culture Magazine
San Francisco
Monthly, founded in 1994
English
www.juxtapoz.com
Editor: Jamie O'Shea
Publisher: High Speed
Productions inc.

**LEMON**
Pop Culture with a Twist
Concord
Annual,
English
www.lemonland.net
Editor in chief & Creative
Director: Kevin Grady

**MEATPAPER**
Your journal of meat culture
San Francisco
Quarterly,
205 x 255 mm
English
www.meatpaper.com
Publisher / Editor in chief /
Co-founder / Art Director:
Sasha Wizansky

**NEW YORK**
New York
founded in 1968
English
www.nymag.com

**MAN ABOUT TOWN**
The biannual journal for men
Bi-Annual,
English
www.manabouttownonline.
com
Editors in chief and creative
directors: Jens Grede, Erik
Torstensson

**MEGAWORDS**
Exploring the modern
environment
Philadelphia
Quarterly, founded in 2005
15,000 copies
English
www.megawordsmagazine.
com
Founder & Publisher:: Dan
Murphy
Publisher: Megawords
Magazine

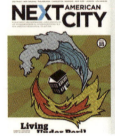

**NEXT AMERICAN CITY**
The Future of Urban Life
Philadelphia
Quarterly, founded in 2002
40,000 copies
English

**MAP MAGAZINE**
Music.Art.People.
Miami
Quarterly, founded in 2007
228 x 279 mm
English
www.themapmag.com

**METRO DOT POP**
The fashion magazine for the
rest of us
Long Beach
Every two months, founded in
2004
English
www.metrodotpop.com

**NYLON**
New York
Monthly (11 x / year),
230 x 273 mm
English
www.nylonmag.com
Art Director: Lina Kutsovskaya
Publisher: NYLON LLC

**MASS APPEAL**
Urban Lifestyle Magazine
Brooklyn
Every two months, founded in
1996
210 x 275 mm
English
www.massappealmag.com
Editorial Director: Sacha
Jenkins

**METROPOLIS**
New York
English
www.metropolismag.com
Publisher: Horace Havemeyer
III

**NYLON GUYS**
New York
Quarterly, founded in 2005
English
guys.nylonmag.com
Publisher: NYLON LLC

**MCSWEENEYS**
New York
Quarterly, founded in 1998
English
www.mcsweeneys.net
Editor in Chief & Creative
Director: Dave Eggers
Publisher: MCSweeneys

**MULE**
Chicago
Quarterly, founded in 2002
English
www.mulemagazine.com

**PAPER**
The Pervy Monthly with the
Curvy Readers
New York
Monthly (10 x / year),
215 x 275 mm
91,800 copies
English
www.papermag.com
Founder & Editor in chief:
David Hershkovits

**ME**
New York
Quarterly, founded in 2004
172 x 230 mm
English
www.memagazinenyc.com
Editor in chief & Creative
Director: Claudia Wu
Publisher: Me Publications Inc.

**NAZI KNIFE**
English
Publisher: Buenventure Press

**PIN_UP**
Magazine for Architectural
Entertainment
New York
Bi-Annual, founded in 2006
235 x 285 mm
10,000 copies
English
www.pinupmagazine.org
Editor & Creative Director:
Felix Burrichter
Publisher: FEBU Publishing
LLC

227

**PLANET**
Global Culture and Lifestyle
San Francisco
Quarterly, founded in 2001
215 x 270 mm
English
www.planet-mag.com
Editor & Publisher & Creative
Director: Derek Peck

**RELEVANT**
Orlando
founded in 2003
English
www.relevantmagazine.com
President & CEO: Cameron
Strang
Publisher: Relevant Media
Group

**SURFACE**
The american avant-garde
Brooklyn
230 x 274 mm
English
www.surfacemag.com
Publisher & Creative Director:
Riley John-donnell
Publisher: *Surface Publishing
LLC

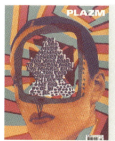

**PLAZM**
Portland
Annual, founded in 1991
228 x 305 mm
5,000 copies
English
www.plazm.com
Editor: Tiffany Lee Brown and
Raymond Jon
Publisher: Plazm Media, Inc.

**RES MAGAZINE**
Film / Music / Art / Design /
Culture
New York
Every two months,
230 x 277 mm
English
www.res.com
Editor: Jesse Ashlock
Publisher: RES Media Group

**SWINDLE**
Los Angeles
Every two months, founded in
2004
235 x 280 mm
English
www.swindlemagazine.com
Creative Director: Shepard
Fairey
Publisher: R. Rock Enterprises

**PLENTY**
It's easy being green
New York
Every two months, founded in
2004
130,000 copies
English
www.plentymag.com
Editor in chief: Mark Spellun

**RUSSIA!**
Since 882 A.D.
New York
Quarterly, founded in 2007
213 X 276 mm
35,000 copies
English
www.readrussia.com/
Associate Publisher: Nora
Liddell

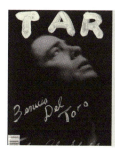

**TAR MAGAZINE**
New York
English
www.tar-art.com

**PRINT**
America's Graphic Design
Magazine
New York
Bi-monthly, founded in 1940
English
www.printmag.com
Editor in chief: Joyce Rutter
Kaye

**SHERBERT**
Brooklyn NY
founded in 2001
180 x 215 mm
English
www.sherbertmagazine.com
Publisher & Designer: Dan
Weise
Publisher: Sherbert LLC

**THE DRAMA**
Richmond
Quarterly, founded in 2000
229 x 229 mm
8,500 copies
English
www.thedrama.org
Editor in chief & Creative
Director: Joel Speasmaker
Publisher: Joel Speasmaker

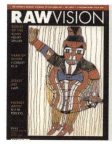

**RAW VISION**
New York
Quarterly,
English
www.rawvision.com

**SLASH MAGAZINE**
A Quarterly For The Extra
Observant
New York
Quarterly,
240 x 305 mm
English
www.slashmagazine.com
Editor: Kyle Hinton

**THE JOURNAL**
Contemporary culture
New York
Quarterly,
165 x 250 mm
25,000 copies
English
www.thejrnl.com

**RE:UP MAGAZINE**
San Diego
Quarterly, founded in 2002
English
www.reupmag.com

**SOMA**
Left coast culture.
San Francisco
Monthly,
214 x 275 mm
English
www.somamagazine.com
Art Director: Timothy
Peterson
Publisher: Soma Magazine

**THE JOURNAL OF
POPULAR NOISE**
Music and Sound Art
New York
Bi-Annual, founded in 2007
184 x 184 mm
300 copies
English
popularnoise.net

**THE LAST MAGAZINE**
www.thelastmagazine.com

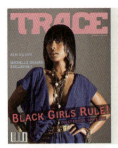

**TRACE**
Transcultural styles and ideas
New York
8 x / year, founded in 1995
English
www.trace212.com

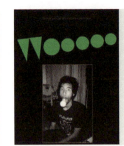

**WOOOOO MAGAZINE**
New York
Tri-Annual, founded in 2004
107.95 x 177.8 mm
10,000 copies
English
wooooomag.com
Publisher: Jason Crombie

**THE LOWBROW READER**
Of Lowbrow Comedy
New York
Annual, founded in 2001
2,000 copies
English
www.lowbrowreader.com
Editor: Jay Ruttenberg

**V MAGAZINE**
The biggest magazine in fashion
New York
Every two months, founded in 1999
295 x 415 mm
English
www.vmagazine.com
Publisher: V Magazine LLC.

**ZINGMAGAZINE**
New York
Annual, founded in 1995
217 x 280 mm
English
www.zingmagazine.com
Managing editor: Brandon Johnson
Publisher: Zing LLC

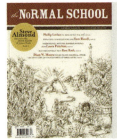

**THE NORMAL SCHOOL**
A literary magazine
Fresno
Bi-Annual,
English
www.thenormalschool.com
Editors: Steven Church, Sophie Beck, Matt Roberts

**V MAN**
New York
Bi-Annual, founded in 2003
225 x 295 mm
English
www.vman.com
Editor in chief & Creative Director: Stephen Gan
Publisher: V Magazine LLC.

**ZINK MAGAZINE**
New York
Monthly, founded in 2002
212 x 277 mm
English
www.zinkmag.com
Managing Editor: Casey Gillespie
Publisher: Jormic Media Group

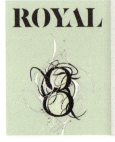

**THE ROYAL MAGAZINE**
New York
English
www.theroyalmagazine.com
Publisher: Keystone Design Union

**VISIONAIRE**
New York
Tri-Annual, founded in 1991
English
www.visionaireworld.com
Publisher: V Magazine LLC.

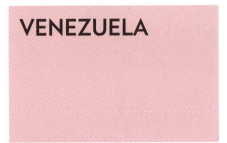

**VENEZUELA**

**THEME**
Asian Culture Quarterly
New York
Quarterly, founded in 2005
230 x 280 mm
English
www.thememagazine.com
Publisher & managing editor: John Lee
Publisher: Theme Publishing

**WHITEWALL**
New York
Quarterly, founded in 2006
45,000 copies
www.whitewallmag.com
Editor in chief & Creative director: Eve Therond
Publisher: Sky Art Media Inc.

**COMPLOT MAGAZINE**
Chic Latino
Caracas
Monthly, founded in 1998
230 x 300 mm
Spanish
www.complotmagazine.com

**TOKION MAGAZINE**
New York
Every two months, founded in 1996
250 mm x 300 mm
99,000 copies
English
www.tokion.com
Editor: Alex Zafiris
Publisher: Downtown Media Group

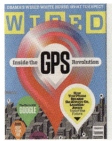

**WIRED**
San Francisco
Monthly,
205 x 278 mm
English
www.wired.com
Editor in chief: Chris Anderson
Publisher: Condé Nast Publications

**REVER**
Revista sin tinta / magazine without ink
Caracas
Every two months, founded in 2006
141 x 212 mm
Spanish
www.revermagazine.com
Editor: Eduarto Aguilera

# 1000 Words
## Photography

Contemporary
Photography
Magazine
Online

1000wordsmag.com

ng Qingsong, UN Party

1000 Words is an online magazine dedicated to highlighting the best work being produced internationally in photography today. It encourages critical awareness with photography through engaging articles from widely published arts writers across the world. We are committed to featuring portfolios of highly established photographers alongside those of emerging artists in the aim of bringing their work to a wider audience. Often incredibly diverse in terms of subjects, concepts, styles and techniques, yet by covering a wide spectrum of genres 1000 Words intends to make us reconsider the contemporary photograph.

**Editor in Chief:** Tim Clark
**Art Director:** Santiago Taccetti
**Web Design:** CCCH Creative Studio Barcelona

fantasy Nō2 פנטזיה

beginning Nō1 התחלה

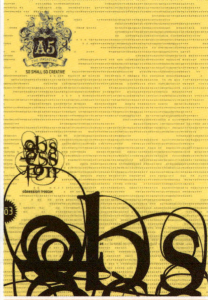

Nō4
PORTRAIT

Nō5
FUTURE :

A5 MAGAZINE: NO.6: SEX
WARNING!!!! THIS ISSUE CONTAINS
MATERIAL WHICH MAY OFFEND
AND MAY NOT BE DISTRIBUTED OR
CIRCULATED TO A PERSON UNDER
THE AGE OF 18. IT CONTAINS
A VARIETY OF UNPLEASANT
CONTENT, INCLUDING: PORN,
OFFENSIVE LANGUAGE, SEXUAL
AND EXPLICIT IMAGES AND MORE...
ENJOY !

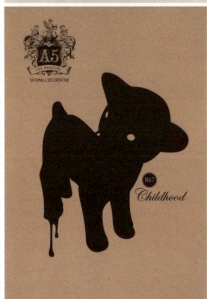

Nō7
Childhood

FRESH FROM TEL AVIV !

## THE A5 MAGAZINE

SO SMALL SO CREATIVE

GRAPHIC DESIGN // ILLUSTRATION

PHOTOGRAPHY // ART // TEXT

SPECIAL THEME // BLACK AND WHITE

FREE SUBMISSION

A5FORA5@GMAIL.COM

WWW.THEA5MAGAZINE.COM

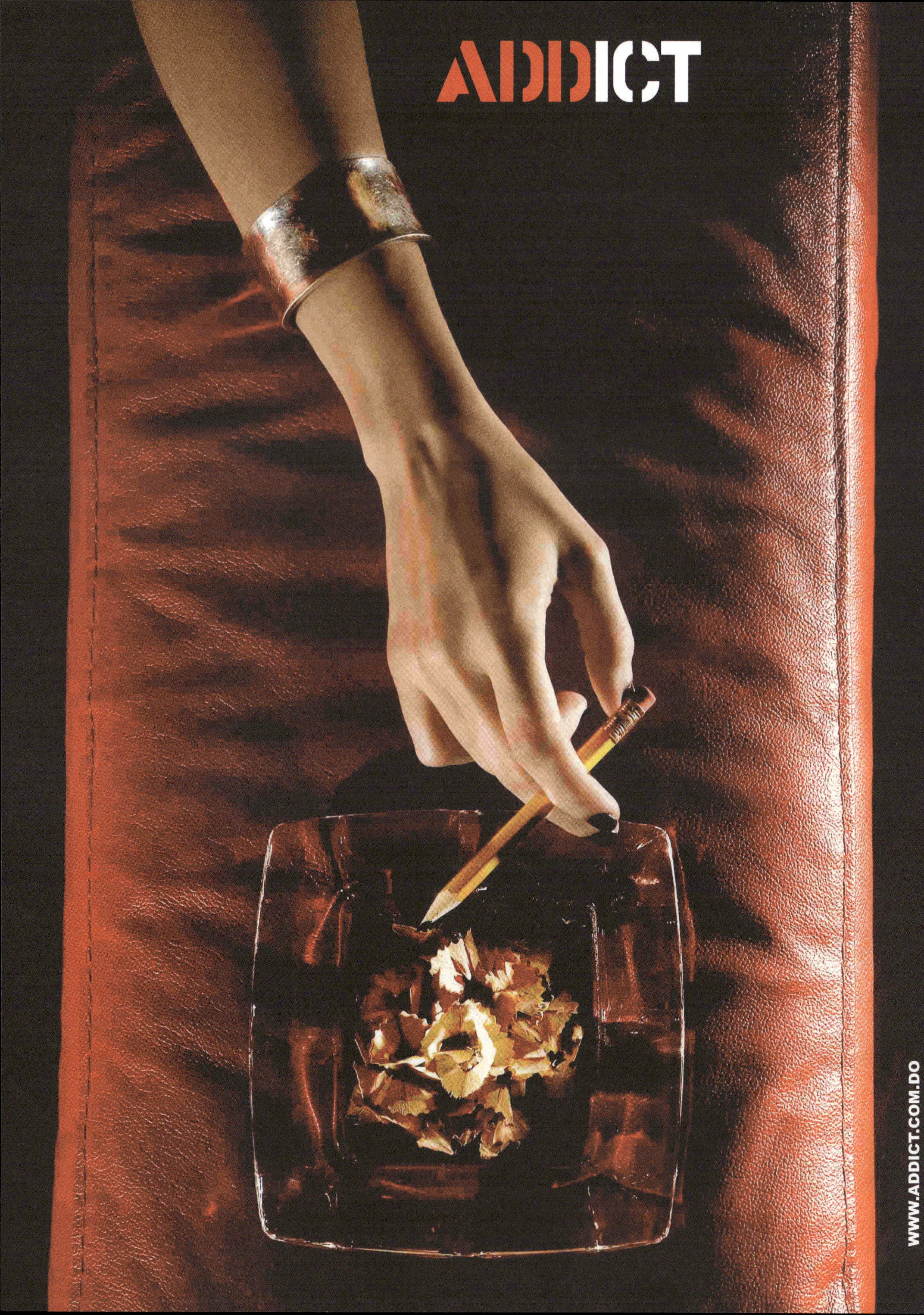
ADDICT
WWW.ADDICT.COM.DO

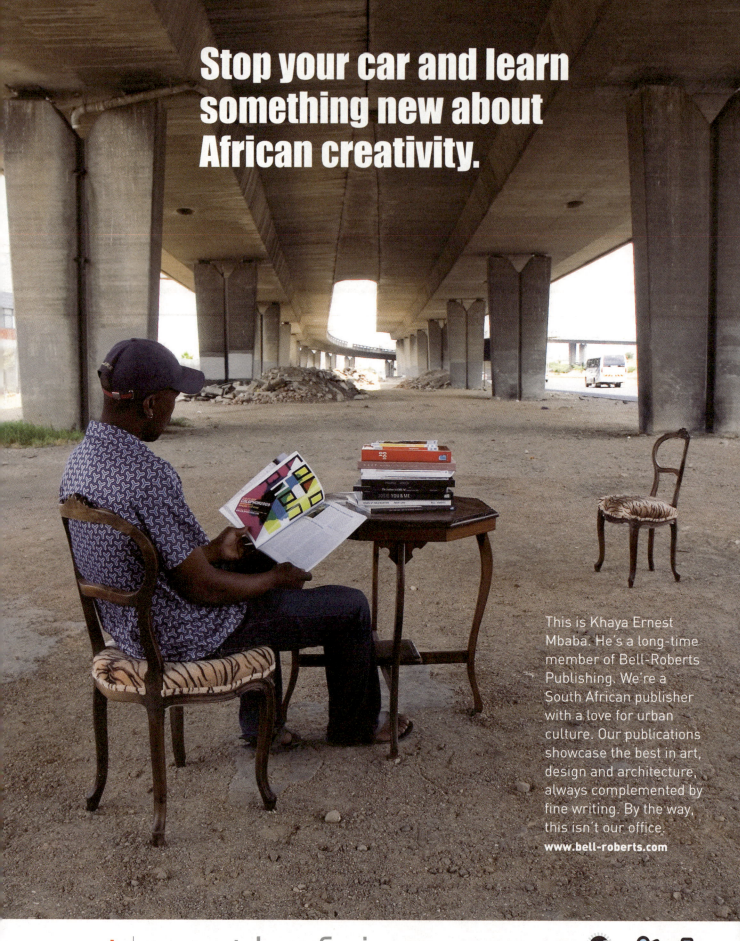

**Stop your car and learn something new about African creativity.**

This is Khaya Ernest Mbaba. He's a long-time member of Bell-Roberts Publishing. We're a South African publisher with a love for urban culture. Our publications showcase the best in art, design and architecture, always complemented by fine writing. By the way, this isn't our office.
**www.bell-roberts.com**

# atypica

www.**atypica**.com.ar

UNA REVISTA PARA GENTE QUE MASCA CHICLE
Y BAJA LA ESCALERA AL MISMO TIEMPO.

# BEAUTIFUL FREAKS

NUMERO 21 INVERNO 2006 / COPIA GRATUITA / WWW.BEAUTIFULFREAKS.ORG

ADHARMA / ALESSANDRO GRAZIAN / AQUEDUCT / B-BLAST / BLACK CIR-
CUS TAP... ...A / BLACK REBEL MOTORCYCLE CLUB / BLOC PARTY /
...POPULAR DEMAND / CAT POWER / CHAMPAGNE MONROE /
...ERGENCE/DIEFENBACH / DILAILA /E42/ ENNIO MORRICONE/
...LIGHT / FATHER MURPHY / FIONA APPLE / GEA / HELLACOPTERS
...A MEM... / MAGAZINE DU KAKAO / MALTOMINIMARCO
...MAXIMO PARK / MENS AGITAT MOLEM / ME-
...MONOLAKE / MR. WILSON / NOT MOVING /
...FLUIDO / SEARCHIN' GUITAR / SIKITIKIS /
...STORM OF DAMNATION / THE ANI-
...KELVINS / THE MIRRORS / THREE IN
...JACKSON / VOXTROT / WE ARE SCIEN-
...OLF PARADE ///// BEAUTIFUL AGONY
...AMA / IL CIELO SOPRA BERLINO / IL GABINET-
...A E LA PUTTANA / MAG&ZINES / SAN PIETRO...

---

# BEAUTIFUL FREAKS

NUMERO 22 PRIMAVERA 2006 / COPIA GRATUITA / WWW.BEAUTIFULFREAKS.ORG

...ANT... ...SQUE TREES / AURUM / BE-HIVE / BENNY GOODMAN /
...KEY / BUGO/ CONDIZIONE SONORA / CUT / DEVOR E GLI
...DRINK TO ME / ELU TEARS / EN ROCO / ENCHANDED /
...URADEI & MALACOMPAGINE / EURO CHILDS / FARMER
...YOU CAME / GRUPPO ELETTROGENO / HAND OF DOOM /
...IWA... I LOVE YOU BUT / I RATTI DELLA SABINA / JEAN DE
...JOHN PEEL / L'ESSENZA / LEITMOTIV / LUCA COR-
...KO / MASTICA / MATTA CLAST / MIRELLA LIPARI /
...NEKO CASE / NON TOCCATE MIRANDA / PEDRO
...SARAH BLACKWOOD (CLIENT) / SHABU / SIMONA
...S / THE HORMONAUTS / THE LUCKSMITHS / THE NAR-
...STICKS / YEAH YEAH YEAHS ///// DEEJAYRAMA / '60 E
...FUL AGONY / IL GABINETTO DEL DOTT. STARSKY /
...PATHY FOR THE DEVIL ////

---

(24)

AIUTACI A
DIFFONDERE

**BEAUTIFUL
FREAKS**

SE QUESTA FANZINE TI E
PIACIUTA A TROVARE DEI NUOVI
LETTORI.
NON BUTTARLA UNA VOLTA
FINITA DI LEGGERE MA
REGALALA AD UN AMICO, AD UN
CONOSCENTE O ABBANDONALA
IN BELLA VISTA SU QUALCHE
PANCHINA O DOVE TI PARE! SE
L'HAI LETTA E NON TI SERVE
ANZICHE ACCARTOCCIAR...
REGAL...
A QUAL...
DALL...
POSSIBI...
VUOI C...

# BEAUTIFUL FREAKS

NUMERO 24 AUTUNNO 2006 / COPIA GRATUITA / WWW.BEAUTIFULFREAKS.ORG

BADMASH / BLIND BIRDS / BUTTERFLY COLLECTORS / CADAVERI A PASSEGGIO / CANDY FOR
STRANGERS / CSS / DEVOCKA / DOWNTONONE / DR.JOE CASTELLANO BLUES BAND / EMILY
FOLKABBESTIA / GABRIEL STERNBERG / GERARDO ATTANASIO / HIKOBUSHA / I PENNELLI DI
VERMEE / INVISIBLES / IRA / ISTERICA / KESSLER / KILLIN'ALICE / KOOKS / LA GHENGA DEL FIL
DI FERRO / LEAVE HOME + RANCIDOS / LOVE IS ALL / MERCE VIVO / MIDORI / MODE9 / NETH-
ERS / OXFORD COLLAPSE / PAOLO SAPORITI / PECKSNIFF / REVHERTZ / SINCLEAR / SPASULATI
BAND / TAP TAP / THEEJONESBONES / TILT / TINKERBELL / VEILS / VITHRA / YOUNG KNIVES
...CTUS CLUB / CASIOTONE / ONE TWO / LITTLERUNNER - UN TEMPO TI AVREBBERO
...CLEMENTE BUTTATO IN UNA PIGNATTA E BOLLITO VIVO / BASTERD / IN UN TEMPO
...O / 33 GIRI DI PIACERE / 60 E DINTORNI / BEAUTIFUL AGONY / DEEJAYRAMA /
...ARSKY / MAG&ZINES ////

BETWEEN THE CRACKS Magazine
WWW.BTCRACKS.COM

CLONE

CLONE magazine
Art & Music Pop Mag

WWW.CLONEMAGAZINE.COM

photo_ Samuel Sánchez
illustration_ Adrián Blanca

# CO DE

**DOCUMENTING STYLE**
'Succes Revisited' issue

Sieradenspecial: de mooiste volgens CODE
Swagger is a state of mind: de beste pakken
Fransman in Tokio: interview Patrick Stephan
Imprint Culture Lab: de cult in culture
Brands: collecties S/S 09

ISSUE 13
WINTER 2008
PRIJS 8,95 EURO

# 4 times a year Documenting Style.

365 days a year: www.code-mag.nl myspace.com/codemagazine

**TRENDS**
**TENDANCES**
**TENDENCIAS**
倾向

SE HABLA ESPAÑOL
www.codigo06140.com

cÓdigo 06140
ARTE ARQUITECTURA MÚSICA MODA

DEdiCate

Passions
Art(s)
Life style
Mode
Design
Littérature
Cinéma
Musique

# DEdiCate

**DEdiCate** dedicate@dedicatemagazine.com  Tél. +33 6 11 18 79 53 / +33 1 48 01 65 50
45-47 rue des petites ecuries 75010 Paris France
**Magazine**

dΙenΙaΙcht

MAGAZINE
FOR
PHOTOGRAPHY,
DESIGN
AND
SUBCULTURE

MAGAZINES + BOOKS + ARTZINES:
WWW.DIENACHT-MAGAZINE.COM

PHOTO: © PETER FRANCK

info@difmag.com
difmag.com

Revista mensal de tendências
e guia cultural gratuito

# Distill

## The best of the international fashion and style press

**Second Issue** The hottest winter fashion shoots from the world's coolest magazines/**Plus** Will Self on style

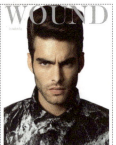

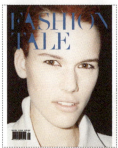

**Distill**
December/January
2009

UK £4.50
US $ 7.90
€    7.90

9 771755 720000   02>

distilldigital.com

**2**

## Inspiration for the creative elite

DOWNTOWN MAGAZINE #18 ↘ NOVEMBER 2008

DOWNTOWN MAGAZINE #18 ↘ NOVEMBER 2008

DOWNTOWN MAGAZINE #18 ↘ NOVEMBER 2008

// Mus
// Scene
// Kultur

DOWN
TOWN

Music
Theatre
Art
Film
Design
Shopping
Nightlife
Gastronomy
Downtown Magazine is a cultural magazine about Copenhagen

# DOWN
# TOWN

See you at **www.downtownmag.dk** where you can read all our backissues...
Downtown Magazine is proud to be Media Partner at Colophon 2009

# D

# DROME
## magazine

Kim Gordon (Sonic Youth) photographed by Cricchi+Ferrante for DROME magazine (#15 The LOVE Issue)

WWW.DROMEMAGAZINE.COM

**étapes:** diseño y cultura visual

© nimio arquitectos

¡La primera revista europea de diseño y cultura visual, ahora en español! Encuéntrala en las mejores librerías de España y América Latina y en www.etapes.es

The leading European graphic design magazine now also in Spanish! Find it at the best bookstores in Spain and Latin America and at www.etapes.es

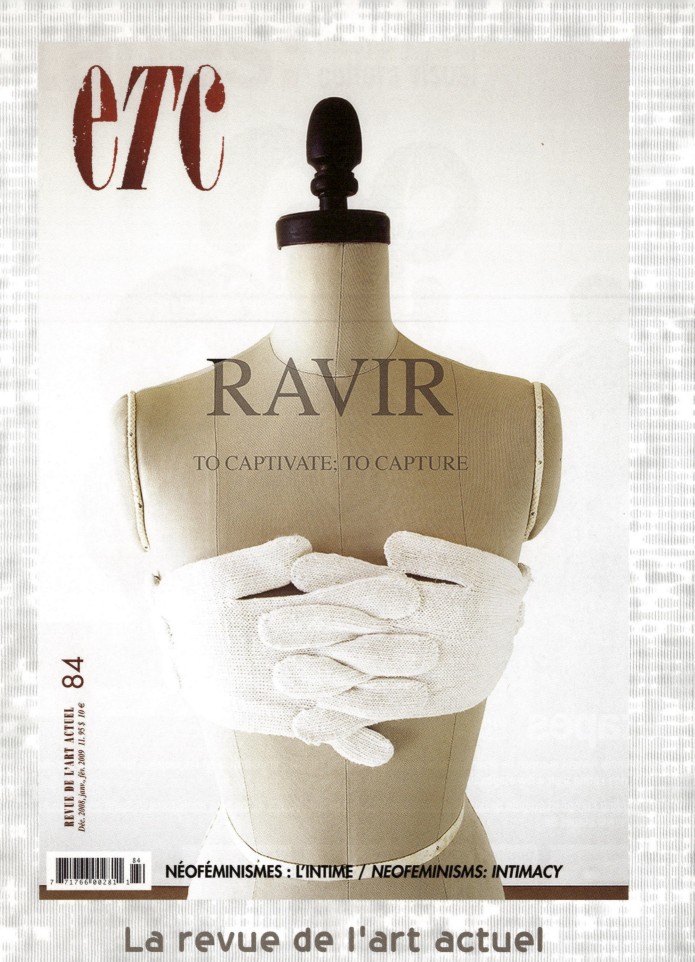

# etc

## RAVIR

### TO CAPTIVATE; TO CAPTURE

84

REVUE DE L'ART ACTUEL
Déc. 2008, janv., fév. 2009  11. 95 $ 10 €

**NÉOFÉMINISMES : L'INTIME / *NEOFEMINISMS: INTIMACY***

# La revue de l'art actuel

www.etcmontreal.com

# EUROPEAN PHOTOGRAPHY

ART MAGAZINE · NUMBER 83

9 770172 702002

# EYEMAZING

© Neon O'clocks Works

**Devoted to International Contemporary Photography**

## www.EYEMAZING.com

Picture Booklets Publishers
Naritaweg 14, 1043 BZ Amsterdam, The Netherlands
t +31(0)20 5849250, f +31(0)20 5849201,

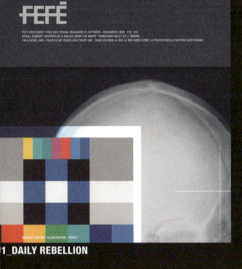

**#1_DAILY REBELLION**

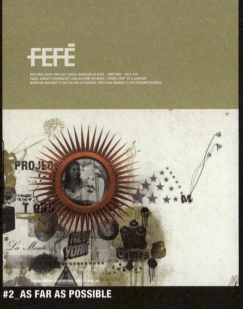

**#2_ AS FAR AS POSSIBLE**

**#3_I'M NOT BAD, I'M JUST DRAWN THAT WAY**

**4_WHO SAID THAT WE NEED TO BE STRONG?**

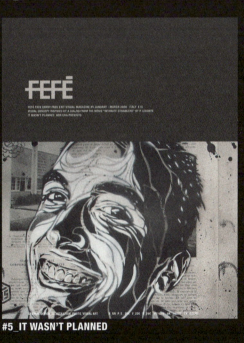

**#5_IT WASN'T PLANNED**

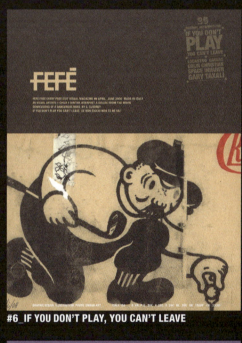

**#6_IF YOU DON'T PLAY, YOU CAN'T LEAVE**

**7_WHAT YOU OWN WILL FINALLY OWN YOU**

# FEFÉ
## VISUAL MAGAZINE

**25 VISUAL ARTISTS, 1 CHILD, 1 WRITER**
**INTERPRET A DIALOGUE FROM A MOVIE.**

**FEFEPROJECT.COM**

**#8_ I CAN'T SEE ANYTHING**

p 12

**STEPHEN WILTSHIRE**
Stephen Wiltshire's art work would be impressive even if one didn't know who he is. But his intricate and architecturally accurate pen and ink sketches are made all...

p.41

**PYCHODELIA AND APOCALIPSE**
September 2007. Miucca Prada presents a fashion show based on the young 29 year old American artist James Dean. The publicity will appear as...

p.65

**AMY WINEHOUSE**
She is the female voice of the moment. Winner of five Grammys she stands out because of her musical talent and her controversial life style...

# FEW #00

# foam

international
photography
magazine

*www.foammagazine.nl*

Simon Norfolk, Full-Spectrum Dominance

8 MAGAZINE — THE PHOTOGRAPHY BIANNUAL
WWW.FOTO8.COM

# FOTO KVARTĀLS

## Magazine on contemporary photography

Visit archive, order or subscribe online at www.fotokvartals.lv

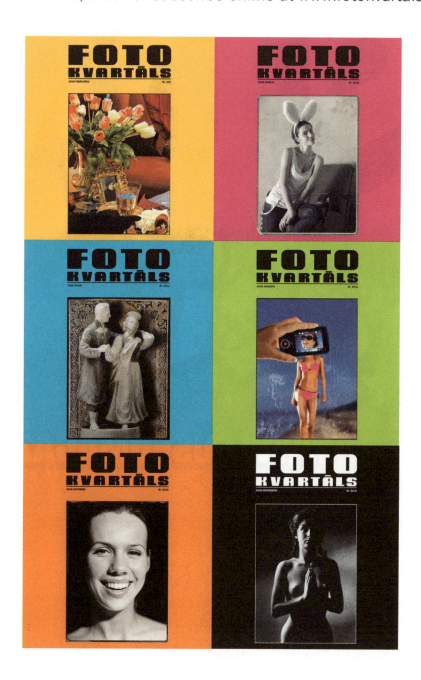

**WWW.FUSEDMAGAZINE.COM**

One of the Seven stars of the magazine world. ~ *Computer Arts Magazine*
Fused magazine is always forward-thinking and fresh. ~ *Smirnoff*
Fused Magazine are undoubtably the oracle on 'cool'. ~ *Levis*
Fused have been great supporters of our band from the start of our career.
We played a club show for them two years before we even signed a record deal.
It shows that they are believers in new music and have good taste ! Thanks Fused. ~ *Editors*

# Futuristika!

a <u>magazine</u> of extraordinary topics...

http://www.futuristikamag.com – english
http://www.futuristika.org – turkish

info@futuristika.org

# The supercilious assumption that on Sunday afternoon you have nothing better to do:

PH: Cesare Medri

## Subscribe now.

GlitteratiMagazine.com

## A FREE PRESS ABOUT STREET ART, ILLUSTRATION AND CONTEMPORARY SUBJECTS

For orders and informations please visit our website:
**http://www.grabmagazine.it**

Grab Magazine © is published by Pnzap Snc © - Via Monte Fumaiolo, 38 - 00139 - Rome - Italy - www.grabmagazine.it - www.pnzap.it

# GRRR

GRRR **és un**

## IS A COOL

**cool. but in per**

## ÆCTIVE

**la promoció**

## WHICH SUPPORTS
## & PROMOTES

**del disseny**

## GRAPHIC

**grafic**

## DESIGN

WE **HATE.** MAGAZINES

WWW.HATE-MAG.COM
MAGAZIN FÜR RELEVANZ UND STIL

WE ARE 10 X 10

Ilustración de Mijn Schatje (www.mijnschatje.fr)

www.hmagazine.tv es el punto de partida desde el que podrás acceder a todos los contenidos digitales de H en la red * Los contenidos del último número de H en formato vídeo: los últimos clips de los grupos entrevistados, trailers de los estrenos de cine, avances de los mejores videojuegos, fragmentos de los más recientes desfiles de moda... * Los blogs de H. * La página de Myspace de H. * Una sección de archivo en la que encontrarás los vídeos correspondientes a números anteriores de la revista.* Una sección en la que el staff de H cuelga regularmente sus vídeos preferidos, tengan o no relación con el contenido de la revista: una auténtica caja de Pandora en la que encontrarás lo más delirante y bizarro que puede. Una sección de noticias inéditas que no aparecen en la revista de papel. * Y, por supuesto, la propia página web de H: www.hmagazine.com, podrás descargarte completo el último número de la revista en formato pdf, o sólo aquellas de tus secciones preferidas, así como todos los números anteriores de H.

# HOTROD

I received recently here at the studio the new issue of HOTROD.
What a great surprise. I have been spoiled rotten by my publisher Steidl, who
does a superb job in reproducing my work.  But I have to confess being blown
away by the printing quality and paper choice of Hotrod- my chin dropped as I
opened your magazine.  Not to mention the great group of artists you selected.
Terrific! Thank you for the gorgeous exposure of my work in your magazine.
You made us all here at the studio very proud of it. Best wishes,
*Mona Kuhn. Photographer, USA*


*The most international and  beautiful magazine from Scandinavia.*
*Jan Gradvall. Writer, Dagens Industri, Sweden*

Art and style quarterly since 1998. Contact: jwalaker@frisurf.no

www.iconographicmagazine.org

info@iconographicmagazine.org

**THEORY AND CULTURE OF GRAPHIC AND TYPOGRAPHIC DESIGN MAGAZINE**

**REVISTA DE TEORÍA Y CULTURA DEL DISEÑO GRÁFICO Y TIPOGRÁFICO**

iconographic

essential for work.

# idnworld.com

wider creative resources for designers.

enquiry: info@idnworld.com

# SOMETHING IS MISSING IN IDP RE

**it's You!**
Subscribe to idpure magazine at **www.idpure.com**

**KAISERIN**
a magazine for boys with problems

**www.kaiserin-magazine.com**

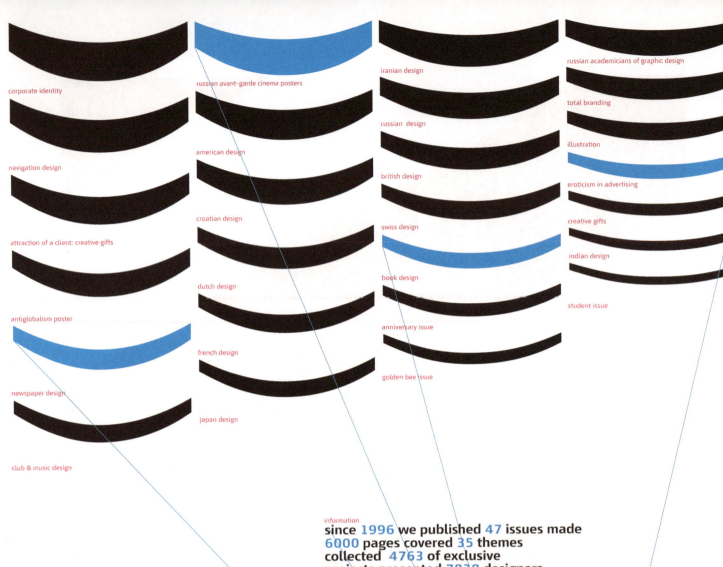

corporate identity

navigation design

attraction of a client: creative gifts

antiglobalism poster

newspaper design

club & music design

russian avant-garde cinema posters

american design

croatian design

dutch design

french design

japan design

iranian design

russian design

british design

swiss design

book design

anniversary issue

golden bee issue

russian academicians of graphic design

total branding

illustration

eroticism in advertising

creative gifts

indian design

student issue

information
**since 1996 we published 47 issues made**
**6000 pages covered 35 themes**
**collected 4763 of exclusive**
**projects presented 7820 designers**

address
**magazine [kAk)** bolshaya novodmitrovskaya st.
14/1, office 222, moscow. russia. 127015, e-mail:
info@kak.ru, www.kak.ru, +7(495) 73 933 73

magazine

the only illustrated periodical issue devoted to
professional graphic design in russia

# MADE OF PAPER.

Kasino A4 is biannual melancholy. WeAreKasino.com

**Made in Switzerland**
kinkimag.com

# BAR SAN ROMÁN

## LISTA DE PRECIOS.

### BOCADILLOS.

PTAS.

ANCHOAS...........
BOQUERONES.......
CHORIZO...........
JAMON.............
LACON.............
LOMO..............
QUESO.............
SALCHICHAS........
SALCHICHÓN........
SARDINAS..........

### RACIONES.

ANCHOAS...........
ASADURILLA........
BACALAO...........
BOQUERONES........
CALAMARES.........
CALLOS............

### RACIONES.

PTAS.

CANGREJOS..........
CARACOLES..........
CIGALAS............
CHICHIKIS..........
CHORIZO............
CHULETAS...........
GAMBAS.............
JAMÓN..............
LACÓN..............
MEJILLONES.........
NÉCORAS............
PULPO..............
QUESO..............
RIÑONES............
SALCHICHÓN.........
TORTILLA...........

## LA MÁS BELLA
## WWW.LAMASBELLA.ORG

# OLD TIRE

*photographed by Christopher Griffith*
*featured in LIEBLING # 5/08*

# NEW PAPER

*published bi-monthly*
*www.liebling-zeitung.com*

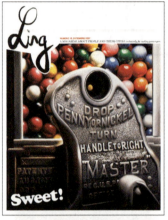

# POSSIBLY THE WORLD'S MOST EXTRAORDINARY INFLIGHT MAGAZINE

www.lingmagazine.com

Created by LE COOL Publishing Designed by Feriche Black Published by La Fábrica.

le magazine gratuit du Luxembourg

# luxuriant

‡ culture ‡ voyage ‡ mode ‡ clubbing ‡ musique ‡ voiture ‡ interviews ‡ agenda ‡

photography : Erwin Olaf / design : ill-studio

# MAGAZINE

NUMÉRO 47 ◆ DÉCEMBRE 2008 / JANVIER 2009

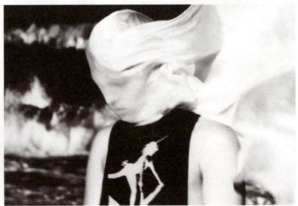

# METAL

ANTONIO BERTONE
+ eureka special

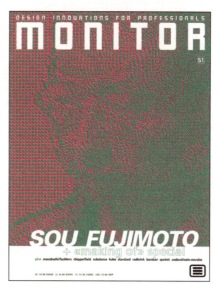

DESIGN INNOVATIONS FOR PROFESSIONALS

SOU FUJIMOTO
+ «making of» special

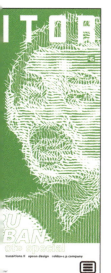

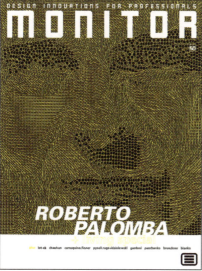

ROBERTO PALOMBA

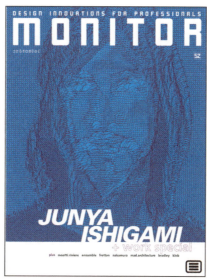

DESIGN INNOVATIONS FOR PROFESSIONALS

JUNYA ISHIGAMI
+ work special

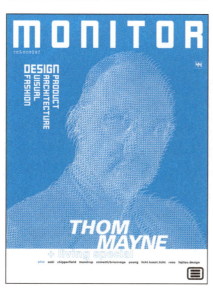

THOM MAYNE
+ living special

DESIGN INNOVATIONS FOR PROFESSIONALS

JAKOB+ MACFARLANE
+ light special

www.monitorunlimited.com

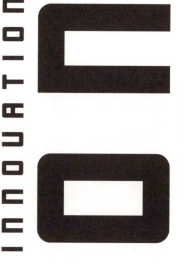

WE ARE NEXT PEOPLE

WE DO CREATIVE THINGS

WE READ NEXT EXIT

THE FIRST MAGAZINE
ON JOB OPPORTUNITIES
IN CREATIVE FIELDS

YES, WE ARE ITALIAN

FIND US IN
COLOPHON 2009

neXt
EXIT
CREATIVITÀ E LAVORO

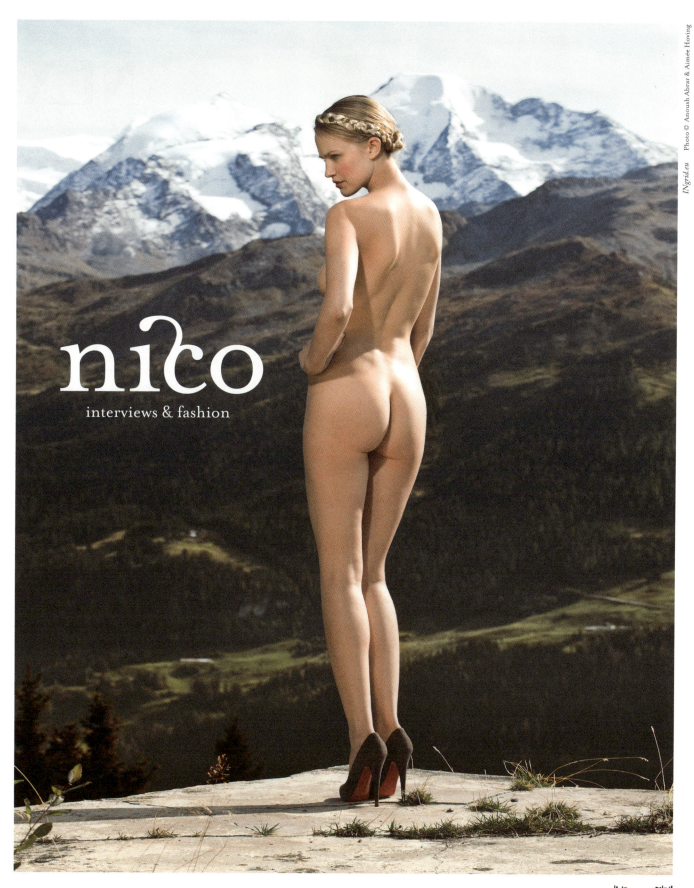

nico

interviews & fashion

Ngrid.eu   Photo © Anoush Abrar & Aimée Hoving

www.nicomagazine.com

Mike Koedinger
Independent Publisher

THE
NEXT
VOICE
OF
DESIGN

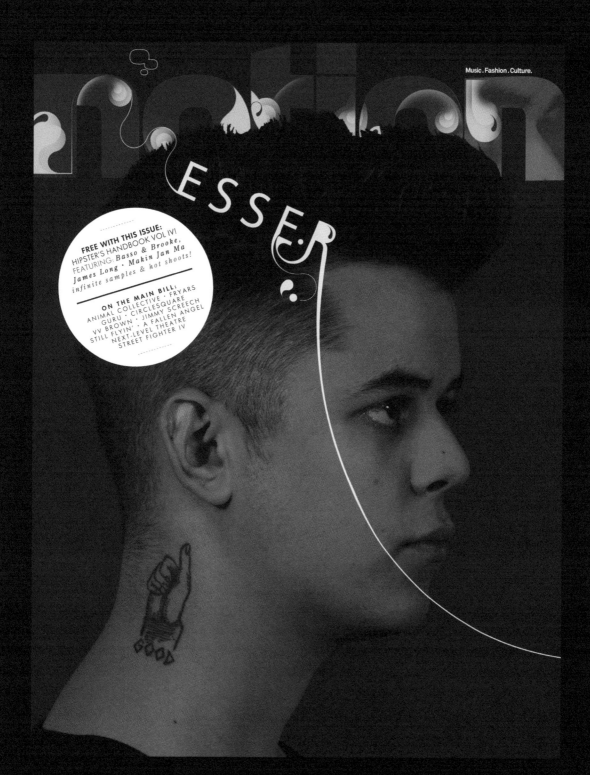

OMAGIU IS THE REMIX CULTURE MAGAZINE
*made in Romania*
www.omagiu.com

# OZON

living in a
magazine

PLAZM magazine
Documenting creative culture since 1991
www.plazm.com

Email freesticker@plazm.com to receive a free PLAZM sticker.   Foto: Joshua Berger

# PONY

HIGH VALUED SMALLNESS. SUITS YOUR POCKET.

CONCENTRATED CONTENT ON 870.240 SQ. MM.

LITTLE BIG MAG...

# Rocket

## contemporary culture magazine

www.rocketmagazine.net

info@rocketmagazine.net

RUSSIA!

Since 882 A.D.

The War/Fashion Issue

Fall/Winter 2009

RUSSIA! magazine is an English-language quarterly devoted to the most original coverage of people, trends, ideas and events taking place in or around Russia.

www.readrussia.com

# Ars HYPERMEDIA

**new media art magazine**
**info@simultaneita.net**

image: video contact, performance + live installation
by Elastic Group of Artistic Research

# sleek

*Magazine for art and fashion*

## www.sleekmag.com

*A fresh perspective on art, a deeper view on fashion – anywhere on this planet*

"It's always a pleasure shooting for S Magazine. Their unique style and originality casts a fun and playful view on photography, which allows photographers like myself to shoot more personal projects."
– *Rankin*

"I think that S Magazine has a daring and insightful view on fashion that stands at the crossroads of contemporary art and culture"
– *Jeremy Scott*

"S Magazine is visual candy. Beautiful, lush, photographic and illustrated spreads that run the full spectrum, from static to cinematic, from humorous to dark. And always sexy. But this magazine is not simply an exercise in sexuality; it's an exercise in sensuality. It has a fashion soul. Some have tried it before, but I can't think of any magazine that has succeeded. Until S Magazine. I eagerly await every issue."
– *Gene Kogan, DNA Model Management*

"S Magazine spearheads a new direction for creative photography, lending both a long-lost depth and contemporary aesthetic to an age-old theme. Having reinvented the genre with a very modern edge, all of the pale imitations and relaunched titles that have sprung up in it's wake can only envy S Magazine's tremendous reputation."
– *Ben Perdue, Worth Global Style Network*

"[S Magazine is] one of the current boutique periodicals so cutting-edge [that] they will continue to flourish in print even as their mainstream contemporaries move to digital."
– *David Renard, The Last Magazine*

S Magazine a biannual playground for photographers, artists, writers and all other contemporary creatives.

www.spublication.com, info@spublication.com
International distribution by Comag +44 (0) 1895 433600

a big magazine for small issues
afera txikiendako aldizkari handia

the balde
www.thebalde.net

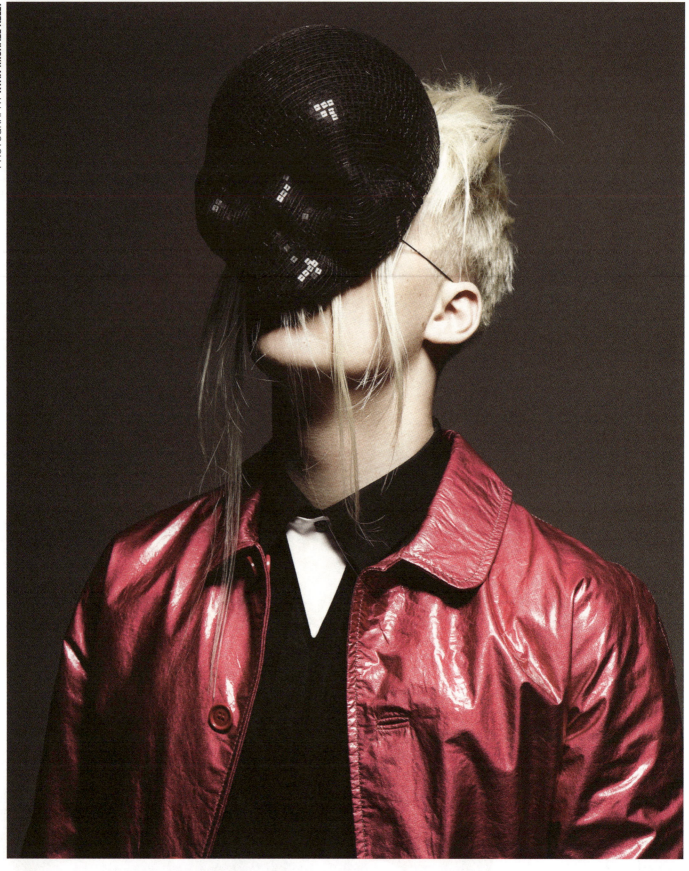

# THEBLOCKMAGAZINE.COM

# the caseroom press//

The Caseroom Press // *The Case Magazine* // Thomas Parker House // 13–14 Silver Street // Lincoln LN2 1HJ // +44 (0)1522 895 211 // www.the-case.co.uk // info@the-case.co.uk

# YET ANOTHER FUCKING WILDLIFE MAGAZINE

Magazin für Pop, Kultur und Raubtiere
**WWW.THEGAP.AT**

store.thememagazine.com
*now open*

# TOKION

Issue #01     Issue #02     Issue #03     Issue #04

## THE JOURNAL OF T-SHIRT CULTURE

Freestyle culture and skateboarding magazine. Barcelona.

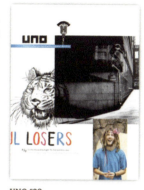

**UNO #3₅**
*DC King of Barcelona, King of Wood, Marcos Gómez, Nothing But The Truth, Zapas Tour Escandinavia…*

**UNO #36**
*Sierra Fellers, 2 weeks in L.A. Steve Harrington, Supreme special, Go in Peace, Free Pegasus, Skate Biz…*

**UNO #3₇**
*Julián Lorenzo, Zapas Tour BCN, Emil Kozak, Croco, B&B, Steve Harries, Behind the lens: 'Fully Flared'*

**UNO #38**
*Chris Pfanner, Jai Tanju, 'Lagano, Bro', Nails, Chiclana, Hong Kong, Materia Sneaker, Behind the lens: 'Beautiful Losers'*

**UNO #39**
*Adri Vilar, France melts, Travis Millard, Sangre nueva, Meriendillas, Detrás de: Foreign Family, Una parada en Copenhagen*

## THE NEW SEASON IS ON!
*check out the new issues online*

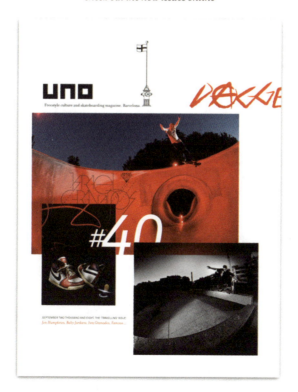

## THE NEW UNO GENERATION
*www.unopopmag.com | blog.unopopmag.com*
\*\*\*

# ART /
# CULTURE / BLUFF/
# MUSIC / STYLE
# / FILMS / PER-
# FORMANCE

SPORTS / TABLOID-SIZE / TABLOID CONTENT
GOSSIP / ARTIST-RUN / DEF-
INITELY NEWSPRINT
NOW / THEN / HERE / THERE
ALWAYS / NEVER
NEW YORK / LONDON / MONACO / PARIS /
INTERVIEWS / ESSAYS / PHOTOGRAPHY /
R E V I E W S
CONVERSATIONS / PORTRAITS / BESTIARY
ACTORS / DESIGNERS / BAKERS
COMMUNITIES / SECTS / DANCERS / THINKERS
POLITICIANS / PROSTITUTES / VICARS / ANGELS / GOBLINS
BRIDES / GROOMS / SOCIALITES / SOCIOHOLICS
DÉBUTANTES / SPECIALISTS /
RELEVANT / IRREVERENT / DICTATORIAL
STYLISED / REDUNDANT / GLOBAL / IMPROVISED
OPPORTUNISTIC / ENTHUSIASTIC / SNOBBISH / DIS-
POSABLE / INDEPENDENT / WILLING / WILLY /
OBSESSIVE / COMPULSORY / IMPULSIVE, NOW
WARM-HEARTED / IRONIC / CONFUSED, YES /
DAZZLING NOT DAZED / AT TIMES USEFUL /
G E N E R A L L Y

# USELESS

www.uselessmagazine.com

# VEᖶᑘ

## VETO MAGAZINE

*Veto Magazine is an independent publication from
Latvia covering all facets of independent culture.*

*www.vetomagazine.lv*

# *You* + Volume

*so your magazine is about architecture...*

yes something like that,
actually we go beyond architecture

*how does that work?*

well, we want to put urgencies and
opportunities on architecture's agenda

*like...?*

# WHITE

# FUNGUS

# xpublishing

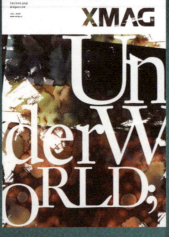

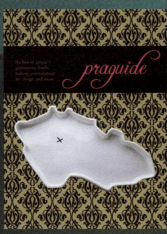

# yummy
## smartfoodesignmagazine

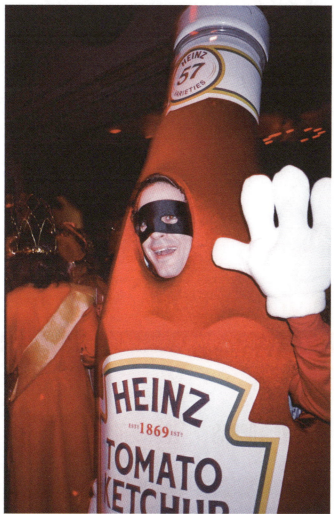

MARC JACOBS PAR KEIICHI NITTA STUDIO

WWW.EAT-FAST.NET • WWW.MYSPACE.COM/YUMMYMAGAZINE

# Zupi, world's creativity fuel.

Zupi is more then a magazine, it's a Design Studio, an
Online Portal, design conferences such as Pixel and Voxel
Show, a publishing house and much more. To sum it up in
one sentence: Zupi is art in its most varied forms.

Explore new ideas, experiments, content and services that
only the biggest Brazilian community focused on creativity
can offer.

More than a magazine, Zupi is an alternative.
Discover art and discover yourself.

www.zupidesign.com
info@zupidesign.com
+ 55 11 5084 9040

# INTERNATIONAL MAGAZINE SYMPOSIUM 13-15.03.2009

Curators: Mike Koedinger, Jeremy Leslie and Andrew Losowsky
Project Manager: Didier Damiani
Production: Colophon – International Magazine Symposium ASBL (Luxembourg)

**The curators Mike Koedinger, Jeremy Leslie, Andrew Losowsky would like to thank:**

**The patrons:** Paul Helminger, Mayor of Luxembourg City and Jean-Louis Schiltz, Minister for Communications (Luxembourg). For their very early engagement: Marie-Claude Beaud, Geraldine Knudson, Jo Kox, Enrico Lunghi, Lydie Polfer, Christiane Sietzen, Jean-Paul Zens.

**The management and teams of** Casino Luxembourg – Forum d'art contemporain and Mudam, as well as Aica Luxembourg, beaumontpublic + Königbloc, Carré Rotondes - Espace culturel, CCRN Abbaye de Neumünster, Cinémathèque de la Ville de Luxembourg, Fondation de l'Architecture et de l'Ingénierie, Extrabold, Galerie Lucien Schweitzer, Galerie Nordine Zidoun, Konschthaus Beim Engel, Musée d'Histoire de la Ville de Luxembourg, Nosbaum & Reding Art contemporain, Philharmonie for co-producing and/or hosting the symposium and the exhibitions.

**The service providers:** Imprimerie Centrale, INgrid Studio for Editorial Design, John Brown, Mike Koedinger Editions, nVision, P&T Luxembourg and also: Goeres Group Luxembourg, HotCity, LuxGSM, monopolka, ReedandSimon, Tempo, Vanksen. The institutions: City of Luxembourg, Ministry for Communications, Ministry of Tourism, Ministry of the Economy & Foreign Trade as well as: Ambassade van het Koninkrijk der Nederlanden, Café Crème Editions, Centre National de l'Audiovisuel, Design Luxembourg, IMCA 10 – International Museum Communication Awards, Luxembourg City Tourist Office, Mois Européen de la Photo, Office National du Tourisme, Université du Luxembourg.

**Our media partners:** Approx. 100 independent magazines (see ad section).

**The project manager** Didier Damiani and the production team: Aysen Calli, Irène de Muur, Melanie Diehl, Joanna Grodecki, Guido Kröger, Rudy Lafontaine, Sarah Macri, Safia Mimoun, Laurren Prieur.

**And last but not least:** Aurélio Angius, Thomas Aubinet, Jean Back, Sandra Barba, Pierre Barthelmé, François Bausch, Anne-Françoise Bechet, Mauro Bedoni, Menina Berg, Anouk Bernard, Monique Bernard, Fabienne Bernardini, Claude Bertemes, Xavier Bettel, Christelle André Bewig, Nadialine Alex Biagui, David Billion, Annick Birgen, Robert Biwer, Didier Blaise, Fernand Boden, Nicolas Bourquin, Pascale Bousquet, Anne Brasseur, Lilet Breddls, Bill Bremer, Nathalie Brocker, Maxime Buechi, Vera Capinha Heliodoro, Casey Caplowe, Carlos Carbajal, Mary Carey, Aldo Chaparro, Laurent Childz, Judith Christina, Nadine Clemens, Loïc Colas, Leonor Comin, Valérie Conrot, Marguy Conzemius, Valério D'Alimonte, Didier Damiani, Rachel David, Arnaud Decker, José de Lima, Charlotte Delwiche, Roland Dernoeden, Paul di Felice, Jaco Diederich, Saliou Dieye, Géraldine Dufournet, Lothar Eckstein, Steve Ehrnstrasser, Christian Ernster, Simon Esterson, Corinne Estrada, Nicole Federmeyer, Bobby Feingold, Annick Feipel, Hans Fellner, Vanesa Fernandez, Céline Flammang, Kirsten Foster, Zach Frechette, Claude Frisoni, Boris Fuge, Christophe Gallois, Christian Gattinoni, Martino Gamper, Robert Garcia, Edwin Gardner, Francis Gasparotto, Pit Gelz, Alain Giombetti, Cathy Giorgetti, Martine Glod, Philippe Graff, Marianne Grisse, Sarah Haggerty, Lars Harmsen, Stéphane Hartert, Marc Hauser, Bettina Heldenstein, Max Heldenstein, Christine Hengen, John Heintz, Claudine Hemmer, S.E. Eduard Hoeks, Alex Hunting, Nuredin Ismajli, Jackon, Vitor Junqueira, Mélanie Juredieu, Johannes Kadar, Pascale Kauffmann, Lucien Kayser, Anni Keller, Christoph Keller, Janine Kersten, Mark Kiessling, Jean-Claude Knebeler, Joerg Koch, Kati Krause, Jeannot Krecké, Lars Laemmerzahl, Matthieu Lambert, Deborah Lambolez, Ingrid Lamy, Angi Law, Julie Le Vacon, Andres Lejona, Sylvia Leplang, Jean-Marc Liacy, Christopher Lockwood, Tanyo Lofy, René Lönngrenn, Viviane Loschetter, Karen Lubbock, Dany Lucas, Anja Lutz, Jonathan Mander, Jenny Mannerheim, Edmond Mariany, Nathalie Matiz, Claire McLoughlin, Carlo Meyers, Judith Meyers, Steph Meyers, Claudio Minelli, Clément Minighetti, Marc Molitor, Pascal Monfort, Lyra Monteiro, Sophie Moquin, Olivier Mores, Horst Moser, Kristen Mueller, Raoul Mühleims, Kevin Muhlen, Patrick Muller, Pepe Murciego, Matthias

Naske, Tania Neyens, Chris Ng,
Faye O'Sullivan, Diego Ortiz,
Arjen Oosterman, Sanna Paananen,
Tom Pakinkis, Fani Parli, Ravi Pathare,
Nathalie Petit, Robert L. Philippart,
Roland Pinnel, Maxime Pintadu,
Damien Pochon, Stéphanie Poras,
Grégory Pouy, Jussi Puikkonen,
Angelina A. Rafii, Claire Ramos,
Susanne Raupach, Maria Rebelo,
Alex Reding, Anne Reding, David
Renard, Jessica Reitz, Duncan
Roberts, Jeanne-Salomé Rochat,
Gilles Rod, Andrea Rumpf, Paul
Scheiden, Philippe Schlesser,
Martine Schneider-Speller, Patrick
Scholtes, Françoise Schroeder,
Lucien Schweitzer, Mike Sergonne,
Christiane Sietzen, Till Schröder,
Becky Smith, Kris Sperandio, Pierre
Stiwer, Sumo, Guy Tabourin, Rolf
Tarrach, Adèle Terpstra, Pekka
Toivonen, Claire van der Ent Braat,
Thierry van Ingelgom, Marie Van
Landeghem, Sébastien Vecrin,
Matthias Ver Eecke, Chiara Veronese,
Paola Viloria, Emmanuel Vivier,
Moritz von Uslar, Danièle Wagener,
Michèle Walerich, Steven Watson,
Mady Weber, Aurore Welfringer,
Davy Welfringer, Sasha Wizansky,
Guido Wolff, Woody, Victor
Zabrockis, Alexis Zavialoff,
Nordine Zidoun, Georges Zigrand.

Mike Koedinger

**Under the patronage of**

LE GOUVERNEMENT
DU GRAND-DUCHÉ DE LUXEMBOURG
Ministère d'État

Le Ministre des Communications

**With the support of**

THE GOVERNMENT
OF THE GRAND DUCHY OF LUXEMBOURG
Ministry of the Economy and Foreign Trade

LE GOUVERNEMENT
DU GRAND-DUCHÉ DE LUXEMBOURG
Ministère des Classes moyennes,
du Tourisme et du Logement

Département du tourisme

NVISION
WEB AGENCY

IMPRIMERIE \ CENTRALE

INgrid

**The publisher** Mike Koedinger is Luxembourg's leading independent publisher, the founder and head of a media group dedicated to producing high-quality magazines, corporate publications, guides and events for Luxembourg. He currently controls seven publications, an advertising management company, a studio for editorial design, a Business Club and numerous websites. His group monitors the pulse of popular culture and society in the greater Luxembourg region. Koedinger is the initiator and co-curator of Colophon, as well as the publisher of the book 'We Love Magazines'.

**The editor** Andrew Losowsky has written about magazines and the future of print for the Wall Street Journal, The Guardian, The Times of London and Grafik among many other publications. He curated the exhibition Magazines as Objects, and his collection of short stories, 'The Doorbells of Florence', is published by Chronicle Books. He is a co-curator of Colophon, and previously edited the book 'We LoveMagazines'. He currently lives in the USA, and writes about the magazine industry at www.losowsky.com/magtastic

**The designer** Jeremy Leslie is Executive Creative Director at John Brown, the UK's leading customer publishing agency. Leslie is a passionate advocate of editorial design, regularly contributing to the creative press and design conferences on the subject. He has written two books about magazine design: 'Issues' (2000) and 'magCulture' (2003), and previously designed the book 'We Love Magazines'. He is a co-founder of Colophon, chairman of the Editorial Design Organisation in London, and a member of the executive committee of D&AD. His blog about magazine design can be read at www.magCulture.com